SERVANT
OF
GOD'S SERVANTS

The Work of a Christian Minister

By Paul M. Miller

HERALD PRESS.   SCOTTDALE, PENNSYLVANIA

1

Preface

What is the task of a Christian minister in an urbanized congregation in mid-century America? This is the question to which these Conrad Grebel Lectures are addressed. They are given with the hope that men now serving in the ministry may see the opportunities of their calling more clearly, that young men now seeking God's will for their lives may hear the call to serve as a Christian minister, and that congregations may pray more intelligently for their leaders who serve them.

I might as well admit from the outset the vantage point from which I speak about the work of a Christian minister. I speak from my own eight years of experience as pastor of an emerging congregation. These were some of the happiest and most rewarding years of my life. I speak also from the eight years of teaching future ministers in the Practical Theology Department of Goshen College Biblical Seminary. I speak also from my intimate sharing and conversations with literally scores of active ministers during the past sixteen years. I speak from an optimistic bias. I am not one of those who delight in exposing the few ministers who are breaking down. I find no satisfaction in hinting darkly that the minister's motivations might be unworthy or that maybe the churches should not ordain ministers at all.

These lectures assume that the living Lord of the church is even now present in the midst of His congregation in mid-twentieth century, and that He will guide them into a pattern of ministry and service. Certain principles which operated in the first-century congregations remain to inform present patterns, but the patterns are flexible and must be adapted to meet emerging needs.

In these lectures I have tried to picture an intelligent, prepared minister who serves in the "basin-seizing" humility of his Master. I have attempted to avoid the undue reverence for the ordained "Lord's annointed" person such as sometimes accom-

3

55959

panied ordination by lot. I have struggled even harder to avoid the clericalism, professional distance, and "hired servant" role of the minister which so frequently obtains in Protestantism.

I have tried not to merely restate the obvious, saying once more the things which are well said in so many books on the subject. Rather I have sought to lift up for attention certain aspects of the minister's work which are often omitted or treated too lightly.

These lectures everywhere assume that the minister has no other task than the church's task, and that it is his calling to serve within the congregation as she seeks to continue the preaching, healing, and teaching ministry of her Lord. The minister serves because his congregation, his Christ, and even his God take the servant posture as they confront unredeemed mankind.

I am deeply indebted to the congregations who have taught me, to my students who have helped me to learn, to my colleagues on the Associated Mennonite Biblical Seminary faculties who have given their reactions and suggestions, and to the members of the Conrad Grebel Lectureship Committee for their invaluable counsel. I am particularly indebted to the work of Howard Charles in his doctoral dissertation, *The Charismatic Life in the Apostolic Church,* for my underlying assumptions about the relationship of the service of gifted persons within the congregation to the work of the ordained leader of the congregation.

THE CONRAD GREBEL LECTURES

The Conrad Grebel Lectureship was set up for the purpose of making possible an annual study by a Mennonite scholar of some topic of interest and value to the Mennonite Church and to other Christian people. It is administered by a committee appointed by and responsible to the Mennonite Board of Education. This committee appoints the lecturers, approves their subjects, counsels them during their study, and arranges for the delivery of the lectures at one or more places.

The lectureship is financed by donors who contribute annually $500 each.

Conrad Grebel was an influential leader in the sixteenth-century Swiss Anabaptist movement and is thought of as one of the founders of the Mennonite Church. Because of the direction which he gave to the movement, this lectureship has been named for him.

Lectures thus far delivered are as follows:

1952—Foundations of Christian Education, by Paul Mininger
1953—Christian Stewardship, by Milo Kauffman
1954—The Way of the Cross in Human Relations, by Guy F. Hershberger
1955—The Alpha and the Omega—A Restatement of the Christian Hope in Christ's Coming, by Paul Erb
1956—The Nurture and Evangelism of Children, by Gideon G. Yoder
1957—The Holy Spirit and the Holy Life, by Chester K. Lehman
1959—The Church Apostolic, by J. D. Graber
1960—These Are My People, by Harold S. Bender
1963—Servant of God's Servants, by Paul M. Miller

Contents

Chapter 1

8

God Calls Ministers
To Serve His Servant People

I. God Himself Seeks to Minister in Love to Mankind

Why should the minister take the servant role? Because his God does so! God desires to minister to mankind in love until He wins man's free response. He longs to live in a relationship of covenant love with every person until each person is giving and receiving love from God's heart to his own heart. God intends that the free response to His ministering love should motivate man to glad obedience and holy living.

God ministers in love to man directly in His effort to win man's response. He sends rain upon just and unjust. He gives countless benefits, providential care, and tender wooings of His all-pervading Holy Spirit.

When man refuses to give and receive love reciprocally with God, man deifies his own finite existence. He tries to find fulfillment by enjoying God's gifts apart from fellowship with God Himself, and begins to hate the God he has wronged. The image of God within man is frustrated by this alienation from the very ground of his existence, and man suffers depth-level anxiety in his estrangement. Man invariably misuses his freedom, refuses to enter a two-way covenant of life and obedience before his God, and begins the hopeless flight of an unfulfilled life. God's gracious bending over His rebellious people comes to them altogether unmerited and unexpected. By a free deed of His sovereign grace the King offers to forgive man's debt.[1] He takes the cost of reconciliation upon Himself.

9

However, after man has often spurned God's love, God only intensifies His ministering, seeking for response and fellowship. God seeks to minister to man amidst the wreckage which man has brought upon himself. When man's sin has left him blinded, God seeks to restore sight to him. When man's pride and folly have left him brokenhearted and desolate, God seeks to heal his broken heart. When man has maneuvered himself into bondage and captivity, God ministers to man by offering a way of escape and release. God chose love-charged relationships as His favorite way to confront man. God does not seem to fear that the servant posture will lessen His sovereignty.

II. Then God Chose Israel as a Ministering People Through Whom to Work

Abraham was chosen and blessed so that he might in turn be a blessing to all the kindreds of the earth. Israel was chosen to be a kingdom of priests, ministering to all God's needy world.[2] God only urged His people to be isolated from other nations temporarily, until they might get to know Him truly so that they could represent Him adequately to all men.[3]

The intense nationalism pictured in Esther, Ezra, and Nehemiah was not God's highest intention for His people. God wanted His people to share His compassion. The Book of Jonah discloses God's struggle to break down the proud exclusiveness of His people. Isaiah matched minds with God more fully and called Israel to serve as a light to the Gentiles.[4] God wanted Israel to be His suffering servant people, and although they refused through unbelief to fulfill their high destiny, God did use them to bring to the world the divine suffering Servant.

In the midst of the God-encounter called worship, God constantly reminded His people that they were His servants or ministers to do His redeeming work in His world. The words, "all peoples," "all nations," "all the earth," often recur in the psalms of worship.[5]

Whenever Israel experienced a revival, the revivalist led her back to her task as ministers of God's redemption. Amos tried to get Israel to see that Jehovah is God of all the earth.[6] Micah envisioned many nations learning of Jehovah from Israel.[7] Jeremiah called upon Israel to serve the nations.[8] Habakkuk predicted that the earth should be filled with the knowledge of the glory of Jehovah.[9] Joel declared that even God's judgment upon Israel would be overruled by God so that the nations might learn, and that whosoever would call upon the name of the Lord might be saved.[10] Ezekiel echoed this same emphasis.[11] Daniel pictured world evangelism as the highest glory of God's ministering people: "They that turn many to righteousness [shall shine] as the stars for ever and ever."[12] Zechariah foresaw many nations coming to worship.[13] Malachi glimpsed the worship of Jehovah being carried on in every place among the Gentiles.[14]

The ministry of especially called leaders was always to help to perfect God's people for their work of ministering. All Israel was chosen to be a ministering nation in the midst of mankind, but prophets and priests were raised up by God to call His people back to their true mission and destiny.[15]

Because God Himself was the Guide and Counselor of His people none of their human leaders were ever accorded the absolute control which Hindus granted to their leaders. In the Graeco-Roman World people brought their problems to their philosophers, but these leaders did not demonstrate the same combination of compassion and faith as did the servant-leaders of God's people Israel. It is said of Moses, for instance, that he led the people out to meet God, for it was God Himself who was the real and personal leader of His people.

III. God Came to Serve Mankind in His Ministering Son

The climax of prophetic insight into the nature of the God-Man was that He would be a suffering Servant. God's Son said: "I am among you as one who serves." "[I] came not to be ministered unto, but to minister."[16] At the culmination of His whole life of ministering here on this planet, and just before He went back to God, Jesus stood before His disciples clad only in the tunic of the servant-slave and stooped to the lowly ministry of

washing their feet. Jesus demanded that they accept His servant
ministry if they were to have anything to do with Him at all.

From Christ's earliest sense of call when He was twelve years
of age, and until the day of His death, Christ identified His own
life of ministering with that of His Father's. When He ministered
to men He was about Father's business. His work was a continuation of Father's work. He did nothing of Himself, but the Father
who sent Him did His ministering work through Him. In Jesus,
God Himself invaded every part of humanity and served them in
infinite love.

Jesus felt anointed to the task of proclaiming the year or
time of God's favor. He bound up broken hearts, gave sight to
blind, preached deliverance to captives as a way of making men
feel (close-up) the redeeming love which burned in the heart of
the Godhead. D. T. Niles says it this way: "Jesus was God at work
in His world and men found themselves almost winded keeping
pace with Him."[17] Jesus did not grasp after more power or even
after full equality with the Father. His self-emptying servant-
hood was not merely a shrewd way to gain power. He served because He was and is eternally a servant at heart.

Bible students have noticed that more than half of His work
was what we call social work, caring for the physical needs and
comforts of men. But while He fed the hungry and ministered to
the blind, the same divine compassion surged through His every
touch as when He absorbed the world's hate in suffering love on
Golgotha. His ministry of loving deeds was no mere "milk of
human kindness," but was part of God the Father's own redeeming and reconciling ministry to mankind. When men challenged
His deity, He cited His loving ministries to men as proof that He
was God Himself at work. His preaching ministry was done in
the servant posture.

IV. God Continues His Ministry to Mankind
Through His Church

When Christ left the earth, He showered back gifts to men.
The gifts which the ascending Christ gave to believers were in-

tended to empower and enable the disciple group to become Christ's body. In their corporate life and ministry they were to continue to do on earth the same things which Jesus had begun to do and to teach. The church was not merely "the place where men hear God," but where the presence of the living Christ leads out a group of obedient disciples to do God's redeeming work.

The enduement of power on the day of Pentecost was to transform frightened disciples into a ministering church, ready to pour out their lives in deed and in word, so as to reconcile men back to God. In their word of witness and invitation unbelievers were to hear the very sobbing compassion of God Himself. They were to beseech as though God Himself did the calling. Not only did they tell of God's mighty deeds in the past, but they offered their lives at any cost to be the contemporary channel of God's love and power to reconcile men. Their first ministry among men was always a ministry of the Gospel.

Many signs and wonders were done by the apostles, and the first one cited in detail was the healing of a lame man. When Peter explained the meaning of this to the astounded multitude, he said that the God of Abraham . . . raised Jesus and healed this man.[18] When they talked together during their worship service about the loving ministry which God had enabled them to render, they set their ministry right in the stream of God's other mighty deeds, such as creating the worlds, stilling the raging of heathen kings, and the offering up of His holy Son Jesus.[19] The church saw itself as an embassy from heaven to earth. Because Jesus Christ carried out His errand in the form of a servant, the church too felt bound to this form.

The early church did not try to throw their Gospel at people "like a stone." They told the story of God's dying love on a cross, and they tried to be a serving community of love beneath the cross. They told that God loved men enough to climb on a cross, hanging there to accept and to absorb like a mighty blotter all the enmity and all the hate and sin of all men of all ages. They tried also to live this love in deeds. They told that God's ultimate way to make men good is to overcome evil with good by suffering love upon a cross. They tried to practice nonresistant love them-

selves. They framed words about God's love in Jesus which kept
saying, "Father, forgive," while men were crucifying Him. They
also forgave those who made martyrs of them. They sought to
enable persons to feel Calvary's love in present relationships.
They tried to follow in the steps of Him who, when He was reviled, reviled not again.

A Gospel which centers in a suffering love for enemies, even
to the point of the cross, and offers victory only through death,
simply cannot be understood by natural man, either in suburbia
or in slum. It flies in the face of all that men in their wisdom
and selfishness find acceptable. Unredeemed man can begin to
"understand" the "foolishness of the cross" only when a group of
believers will have the courage to live the way of the cross, incar-
nating cross-like love in all of their relationships with foe, friend,
or religious fanatic. The early church had not yet learned the
art of substituting learned discussions about the nature of the
church for a determined effort to actually be a faithful church in
the midst of human misery and sin.

God's limitless concern for all men finally subjugated the
apostles and made them servants to all men. The narrow nationalism of Jewish Christians was broken, and Peter learned not to
call needy man common or unclean. The church went everywhere as the obedient, serving body of the Son of God. They
ministered to men with some of the compassion which burns
eternally in the heart of the Almighty. In Iconium God granted
wonders and signs, likely of compassionate deeds.[20] Luke, medical man though he was, observed Paul's ministry of compassion
in Ephesus and declared, "God wrought special miracles by the
hands of Paul."[21] For early Christians "religion" was not merely
"one of twenty-five departments in *Time* magazine" crowded in
between advertisements of alcohol or deodorant. Religion was a
share in the here-and-now activity of God.

The New Testament writers were so busy serving that they
never tried to step outside of the church so as to observe it objec-
tively and to formulate an abstract definition of it. Their whole
existence was lived within the church, and they were overwhelmed
by the awareness that they were serving as the feet and the hands

of the living God. By a "new exodus" He had fused them into His people. Within their fellowship moved the majesty of God's inbreaking kingdom. The sovereign-bestowed gifts of God's Holy Spirit empowered them for service.

God Himself set each of them in relationship to each other so that they might move and minister together as the body of His Son. God had acted to bring them to a new aeon, and they bore the image of the heavenly. In and through their lives God was creating a new creation, a more wonderful deed than when He flung the stars into space. God Himself gave to them an armor to do warfare against demonic forces. God had prepared beforehand that they should do good works, and He now performed His workmanship in and through their lives, because they were joined in faith to His Son Jesus Christ. What was happening in their lives was part of what God had begun before the foundation of the world.

Because they sensed they were partners with God, poor earthen vessels through whom the "livingness of God" penetrated society, they cared very little about logical, abstract consistency of statement. Paul mixed in one paragraph the figures of nation, building, planting, and temple, and John visualized the bride as a city, a temple, a mother, a virgin, and a choir.[22] Jesus Christ was their Saviour and Lord and He called them to minister in His name, and that mattered more than logical consistency.

Believers fled into one another's arms for mutual support and strengthening, and then faced the hostile world together. They felt themselves to be an outpost of heaven, a little colony of God's children set in the midst of the world which God was at work to redeem. Like an early American colony on the New England coast, they felt utterly dependent upon the homeland. (In their case these were the supplies of the divine life and renewal from the throne of God.) Colonists shared their whole existence together within the colony. If one caught smallpox, all were endangered, but they still fled every evening to safety within the stockade for security from marauding beasts or hostile Indians. They retreated for renewal and safety periodically, only to advance again to their main task of subduing the wilderness and claiming the countryside for their king. Likewise, not only in early Philippi, but in all cultures until the Lord comes again the "colony of heaven" can serve as a valuable metaphor to describe the stance of the Christian church in the midst of sub-Christian, unredeemed society.

V. God Gave Gifts to His Church
To Continue His Ministry

The ascending Christ showered gifts upon the church to enable them to carry forward His messianic ministry to man. In addition to fruits of the Spirit, that is, the Spirit working within the believer to make him Christlike in character, Christ also gave abilities to serve, or charismata.

Christ, through the Holy Spirit, distributed (and still distributes) these special enablings or service abilities throughout His group of disciples, so that together they might complement one another, minister to one another, and together minister to mankind. When a group of believers detected the presence among their membership of a liberal supply of charismata, or enablements for service, they faced their task with assurance of triumph.

These lists of special enablings or concrete gifts of God's grace are not rigidly outlined or limited. The lists in Rom. 12:6-8; I Cor. 12:4-11; and Eph. 4:11 are not coextensive. God intended to furnish each group of believers with "all it needs for the prosecution of its divinely given mission."[23] There should be no "vacancies" within a faithful church, since the Holy Spirit will grant new charisma to match new needs.

God gave some charisma of feeling, that is, the ability to express, control, or interpret deep feelings. Paul called his ability to forego feeling a charisma.[24] He was enabled to deny himself the rich joys of marriage and family for the fulfilling of the unique ministry which was his. He also valued the gift of glossolalia, that is, the ability to feel deeply and to worship with ecstatic cries. These unintelligible cries, even when decoded, or interpreted, were not very profound ideas. They were likely somewhat comparable to an abstract painting which communicates a mood rather than rational ideas. Paul cherished his own periods of ecstasy as he attempted to bless God in song, prayer, or thanksgiving.[25]

However, Paul re-emphasized forcibly that the church is primarily called to minister to lost men, and so he urged that glossolalia be limited to private devotions rather than to be displayed in public worship. Paul noted that the unbeliever who came into a worship service where Christians were speaking in tongues would not be helped by what he saw or heard, but would simply conclude that the Christians were mad! Personal enjoyment dared not be the first concern of the church in her worship, but evangelism and ministry to lost men, and the ability to speak the truth in love.[26]

God through Christ gave "word and deed gifts" to His church to equip her for her ministry. To some were given the gift of prophecy, that is, the ability to speak with divinely given insight as the church was seeking Christ's mind about a given matter.[27] This prophetic word might have been a new revelation, or a fresh application of a previously given word of God to a new situation. Men like Agabus, Judas, and Silas served as prophets and helped the church to see what she might expect next in either leading or blessing from her ascended Lord. While "inspired speech" in the church should be tested for validity against the inspired Scriptures left by the "foundation layers," the apostles and prophets, yet the serving church should expect the Holy Spirit to grant inspired insight to members of the church today as Christ makes known His leading to His people. Gifts of wisdom, knowledge, and prophecy should not be expected in the church primarily at the level of theory formulation or committee study, detached from the real situation, but where the living church is face to face with a real problem and desires to obey Christ. The gift of prophecy should help to exegete the lessons and leading which God has hidden within the present problem.

A prophet has always been one who was so impressed with the reality and claim of an infinitely holy God that he could not remain silent in the face of human injustice, cruelty, need, and sin. The Holy Spirit does make God so real that sons and daugh-

ters may be expected to prophesy, that is, to speak out to edify or
exhort the church. The charisma of prophecy should enable the
gifted member of the congregation to help the brotherhood to
grasp the meaning of the present moment of holy history.

"Deed gifts" given by the ascending Christ included enablement for service in such areas as helps, hospitality, and healing.
The gift for healing, later lodged in the entire praying congregation, was designed to complete the church's ministry to the whole
man.[28] While final redemption of the body must wait for the
resurrection and consummation, yet God does sometimes grant,
when it is His will, a proleptic inbreak or foretaste of the final
redemption of the body. The church should humbly claim and
assert this to be her sacred birthright. She should pray in faith
for sick members in her midst. She should not deify finite existence or suggest that it is always a sin for a saint to be sick. The
church should glorify God for healings as additional manifesta-
tions of His grace and power which He sometimes grants to His
praying people.[29] The medical man, such as Luke the beloved
physician, should leave the corporate worship service with his
"additional" charisma of healing renewed and revitalized.

The church should not covet earnestly the more spectacular
gifts (which are played down in the listings in the later epistles)
but should seek only for those which edify the church. Likely
the lowly gifts of helps and hospitality[30] are the most needed and
should be the most honored by the church. As saints employ
their gifts in the service of the ministering church, their life
together should impress the watching world that God is at work.
There are many forms of work, but all of them, in all men, are
the work of the same God.[31] No list of ordained or elected church
officers or teachers should ever be equated with the extent of the
gifted ones of the congregation.

Last, but not least, among the gifts which the ascending
Christ gave to the church to equip her for her serving ministry
are these. He gave persons, or leaders, as gifts.[32] God wanted
things done decently and in order in His ministering church.
Likely some persons who had service charisma were the first to be
formally appointed as officers of the church. The fact that leaders

were called primarily as servants is illustrated by the fact that the general word *diakonoi,* meaning simply, servant, was used for a number of different officers. While there is little data and the terminology was popular and fluid, yet it appeared that Christ gave to the church persons who were charged to lead her in specific tasks, and as particular needs arose.[33]

Since the gift or charisma of tongues did not edify, it did not shape up into an office in the church. It may be that a brother who combined several gifts in himself was chosen for an office. It is clear that office and charisma were neither mutually exclusive nor always parallel. Not all of those who had service abilities were given an official office, and not all officerholders were persons who possessed outstanding gifts. There is nothing within the New Testament evidence to suggest that every believer who possessed a discernible charisma was therefore ordained.

In the church today, even as in the church of the first century, the Spirit-given gifts are not to be regarded as the property of the individual; they belong to the entire serving congregation. Service abilities or enablements should not be employed so as to call attention to the Christian who possesses the gift. All Christians are slaves *(douloi)* and Christ is Lord. If the Holy Spirit gives a believer a gift for administration, this gift may not be used so as to lord it over God's heritage.[34] Because each Christian is a slave to Christ, they are then servants to one another.[35] When the divine Spirit works within the heart, He makes the believer to grow more like his Master, who chose to be servant of all. After the phrase in Luke 22:27 (RSV), "I am among you as one who serves," the Western text adds the beautiful words, "And you have grown, while I waited upon you, to be like the servant."[36]

VI. God Calls Servant-Leaders to Perfect His Ministering People

God has always desired that all of His people should be totally involved in His work of world redemption. Moses caught Jehovah's intention when he cried, "Would God that all the Lord's people were prophets." The prophet preached, and the priest taught, and the king gave pastoral care, but all of this was designed to help all Israel to be God's redeeming community in the midst of God's unredeemed world.[37] God gave leaders to His church, but only to perfect the church for her work of ministering.[38] The leader called to serve God's people was not necessarily to be more fully consecrated than was every other mature believer.

God's pople were never to be her leaders' "field" but His "force." God's call to an individual leader was to be but a miniature of God's call to His servant people. God called men to serve His servant people so that they might rise up and perform their servant ministries to God's needy and lost world. "What is everybody's business is nobody's business" was recognized by God before modern apostles of "diffused leadership" learned it the hard way. God wanted central leaders to serve His people. He was careful to give His leaders instructions just how their successors in leadership should be selected. God seldom, if ever, advocated a leaderless situation among His people.

God still intends that special servants should be set apart to lead and serve His servant people. These "servants of servants" are set apart merely so that things may be done decently and in order. Leaders are necessary for a group to function effectively and so God calls special leaders to assist the group in doing its work and achieving its objectives. Groups have to make decisions, and a leader is needed to co-ordinate the decision-making process. Groups need to make progress toward goals, and a leader is necessary to guide the co-operative effort. God chose leaders simply because a leaderless group usually does not get its job done very well. James Smart summarizes it well when he says: "The more truly the whole Israel of God knows and claims its ministry, the more will special ministries within the Israel of God be held in honor and fulfill their destined function."[39] The minister as servant of God's servants helps God's people to get their work done.

Leadership among God's people is not free to copy any pattern which happens to be current in contemporary culture. Church leaders have sinned against God whenever they tried to "lord it over God's heritage" the way secular leaders did in their society. The church erred when she copied the hierarchical system of Roman government, and she may be sinning again if she merely borrows uncritically the patterns of American political democracy or American big-business efficiency. Certain realities are inherent in the relationship which God sustains with His people and in the relationship which they have to one another, and these realities must forever mold the patterns of leadership which obtain among God's people. Leading by serving is one of these realities. Leading by enlisting the charisma of every member is another of these realities.

Paul saw this relationship when he told the Corinthian believers, "I am simply a servant of yours for Jesus' sake. He who is my Lord and whose servant I am, made me your servant. I became a servant through Him. He subjugated me and, therefore, just as your controversy is not with me, neither can my controversy be with you. In all my dealings with you, whatever you do to me or say to me, I have still to remain your servant. Jesus made me that, and that I must continue to be."[40] One cannot honestly say, "Jesus is Lord," without completing the sentence by saying to every needy neighbor, "Ourselves your servants for Jesus' sake."

Under Christ's lordship, all calling is equal in status, whether one serves with one talent or with five. In Christ's service the risk is His, and risk dare not be evaded by burying talent in a napkin. The Lord's property cannot be confiscated by the servant, but remains the Lord's own through all loan and stewardship. The servant may not even judge his own work in finality, but must wait until the judgment when the Master reaps both wheat and tares. The best service which any man can render does not succeed in putting the Lord into the servant's debt, but those who bear the burden and heat of the day and those who serve only one hour receive equal pay, and that pay is pure grace. When one servant forgives a fellow servant his debt, he is only sharing part of the vastly greater forgiveness which he has received.[41] A leader who serves under Christ is one who must give account again at the judgment seat of Christ, and so he seeks the mind of Christ in every decision, moment by moment.

VII. God's Charge to Leaders to Serve His People
Has Varied Somewhat According to the People's Needs

What pattern or polity shall the leadership of the congregation assume? God's people in succeeding eras tend to look back to the Biblical patterns to mold or to justify a contemporary pattern of leadership in the church. The Reformed tradition favors the term "minister" and finds Biblical support in the concept that Christ Himself came not to be ministered unto but to minister. The Lutheran, Baptist, and many other traditions favor the word "pastor" and find support for their term in the shepherding role of Christ.[42]

There is no one clearly outlined image of the leader of God's people which emerges from the Biblical materials. Some advocates of prophetic and sermon-centered worship have leaned heavily upon portions of Amos and Jeremiah, which criticize the corrupt priests, and so have uttered wholesale denunciation of the priest and of the whole priestly system. Some Bible scholars feel that the leader of God's people should be the lonely prophet, or at least a team of prophets.

Other scholars have favored the priestly office and have drawn analogies for the pastoral ministry from the services of the priest. According to this view, leaders are called upon to follow the priest's example of compassion for the people, his concern for teaching, and for demonstrating holiness and obedience.[43]

Jesus Himself gave no directions for any formal induction of officials into office in the church. He concentrated rather upon the lowly servant character of the person who would lead others. A Christian minister as well as any other Christian servant fulfills both his prophetic and his priestly ministry the best when he presents his whole body and personality as a living sacrifice to God, but poured out in service for others.

Adaptability and variety are rather the abiding mandate from the Biblical materials to guide God's people in choosing their servants. Great variety has always existed among the types of persons and the duties performed by those who have led and served God's people. At one time God needed and used a patriarchal Samuel, at another a fiery Elisha, at another a wise Solomon, at another a stern Amos or John the Baptist, at another a weeping Jeremiah, at another a timid Timothy, a loving John, or passionate Paul. The need of the hour dictated both the type of person which God selected to lead His people and the list of duties which He performed in serving them.

In the New Testament only the office of apostle was unique and nontransmissable. The prophet served as an "insight man," giving truth for the new age and revelation to the church. The evangelist preached the Gospel on the expanding frontiers. The pastor's function was "to help individual members who needed spiritual food, counsel, comfort, reproof, and cleansing by confession and forgiveness."[44] The pastor or shepherd also led a congregation in its work.[45] The elders ruled a congregation, and were "over you in the Lord."[46] Some elders specialized in teaching and others in more of a leading and pastoral ministry. The teacher exposited and applied the Scriptures to the lives of members, giving guidance for the Christian obedience of the church.

Still other terms were used to describe the servant of God's servants as the church moved out in her world mission. The term presbyter or bishop came into use primarily among Greek-speaking communities. This term emphasized administration. Deacons, probably emerging from the seven servants set apart to administer mutual aid in the Jerusalem church,[47] emerged in the church as assistants to the bishops. The fluidity of the leadership roles is evidenced by the fact that the men chosen to serve tables seemed to turn rather quickly to preaching and evangelism.

No one term or clearly defined pattern of leadership can be said to be normative in the New Testament. In the Jerusalem church there are elders. In Antioch we hear of prophets and teachers, in Philippi of bishops and deacons. In the Corinthian church there is no clear indication of any appointed ministry. In Hebrews we read of elders. In Thessalonica there were elders. In the pastorals we learn of deacons and elders. In I Peter only elders are mentioned.[48] When the Spirit-filled church decided to terminate their communal sharing and ordained seven servants to regularize distribution to the poor, the inspired writer

did not think it important to mention how their office compared
to the ordained diaconate. The threefold order of ordained office,
bishop, presbyter, and deacon, did not come into usage until
Ignatius, about A.D. 115. By that time a drastic change from
New Testament thought had occurred so that Ignatius could decree that only a bishop could solemnize a marriage. However, if
the one-level and lowly servant character of the ordained ministry is carefully preserved, the New Testament evidence would
not prevent a brotherhood from ordaining a bishop, a minister,
and a deacon, with specific duties assigned to each.

Only the Roman Catholic Church takes the position that
their own pattern of leadership is the only possible one and that
all other leadership is invalid. Loyal Catholics are taught to look
forward to a time when all heretics will be convicted and no other
pattern of leadership than their own will be known in all of
Christendom.[49] Many Episcopal scholars have attempted to trace
a line of succession of bishops from earliest times so as to justify
a theory of episcopal succession. But as one of their bishops
frankly admits, "This succession is as muddy as the Tiber
itself."[50]

James Smart is correct when he says that acceptance of the
responsibilities of membership is "the primary ordination to the
ministry of Jesus Christ to which all else is secondary." One
cannot be a Christian without receiving the Spirit of God, which
is always an empowerment for a ministry. Only when this
primary ordination has its true meaning restored to it do special
ordinations find their proper context. A brotherhood which ob-
serves believers' baptism may well consider baptism as the
preliminary ordination of all the laity.

VIII. God's People Set Some of Their Leaders Apart
By a Sacred Service (Ordination)

Why should there be so much confusion and uncertainty
abroad concerning the meaning of ordination? A number of factors have combined to produce this. The most "clericalized"
portions of Christendom have done the least to alleviate human

squalor. In South America, Spain, and other cultures dominated by Roman Catholic religious power there has been a massive revolt against clericalism. Then, too, the resurgence of Biblical study and Biblical theology have revealed how far clericalism has departed from the entire Biblical concept of the church and her leadership. A new awareness has come of the importance of the laity, even a rediscovery that the laity are the essence of the church, and not the clergy, as clerically dominated churches have assumed.

Furthermore, the Christian conscience has been partially awakened to its "salt and light" function in society, and the church has become aware that clericalism has helped to produce "the secluded 'world of the church' with its separate introvert sacral sphere, estranged from the true realities of the day-to-day world." The church, as an organization, has allowed itself to be relegated to the backwater. Almost no one looks to the church for moral leadership on issues of race, war, crime, capital punishment, strife between capital and labor, depersonalization, population explosions, or atomic warfare.

Because many Christians have felt that the church as an institution is irrelevant to world need, they do not want to spend much time in "church work." They desire to enter the arteries of a sick society as individuals. Lay vocation has come to be honored as the most strategic way to serve mankind. In an effort to become really relevant to the social sores and needs of society a great many concerned Christians have sought for a specialized "lay vocation" as their way to serve. Service in social work, medicine, psychiatry, or education have seemed the most challenging. Too often the honoring of lay vocations has brought a parallel depreciating of service within the ordained ministry. Others suggest that we entertain without despair the idea that we now may be among the last generation of those serving the present structures of church life.

It may be also that some of the criticism of the ordained ministry as a specialized service within the serving church has come as a rationalization on the part of persons who are trying to evade a call to this specific service with all of its heartbreak and high demands. Some of the talk against the need for an ordained ministry in the church seems like a smoke screen to cover the retreat of young men running away from their call. A need so deep and basic as the contemporary refusal of the entire church to function responsibly as the church cannot be remedied by any mere repudiation of ordination.

Another result of the uncertainty about the meaning of ordination within the church has been that some have sought to tinker with ordination itself and to seek certainty in sacramental ordination. Some have tried to establish a "higher conception" of ordination by bolstering it with the theory of episcopal succession. Books like those by K. E. Kirk and A. Ehrhardt are examples of this effort. That this effort has met with some "success" is evidenced by the fact that the Episcopal Church in America now recruits a disproportionately large share of its ordained ministers from among those who have joined the church as adults, leaving a low-church denomination to do so.[51]

Those who have sought for the meaning of ordination by a study of the Biblical references have also been perplexed. The term "ordination," used with the precise connotation which it has since acquired, never occurs in either the Old or New Testaments. The early church borrowed some of her worship forms from the synagogue and it is likely that the synagogue patterns of ordination were adapted also.

But some aspects of the Jewish *semikha* or ordination practices were borrowed by the early church, while others were not. Christians never borrowed the notion, held by some Jews, that ordination must be performed in the Holy Land, Palestine. (The Roman Church brings prospective cardinals to the Vatican for their investiture. This may or may not link back to rabbinic precedent.) Jews traced an unbroken line of ordainers and ordained, teacher ordaining pupil, from Moses on down to the second temple.[52] This attempt seems to be revived by the Roman Church in its effort to trace an apostolic succession from Peter to present pope, and in the Anglican church to trace an episcopal succession. Some brotherhoods perpetuate the rabbinic precedent in that the newly ordained person delivers a discourse immediately following the ceremony. No one copied the Jewish precedent of addressing the newly ordained person by the honorary title "rabbi." The Jews had a *saliah* commissioning ceremony for a one-time service assignment as contrasted to their *semikha* ordination which was for life. Christian groups also separated specific, short-term commissionings from ordination.

The Jews seemed to resent Christian borrowings, and one of the reasons that the Jews discontinued the laying on of hands in their ordinations may have been because Christians used the custom too. The act lost its significance after the teacher stopped ordaining his pupil directly, and it was dropped altogether by the fifth century A.D.[53]

More than eleven different words in the original Hebrew and thirteen in the Greek language are translated in the King James Version by the one word "ordain." When Christ said, "I have ordained you . . . ," He used the word derived from *tithame,* meaning simply "to set" or "to place."[54] Other words which are translated "ordain" signify "to arrange in order," "to appoint," "to mark out," "to separate," "to constitute," and "to hold out the hand as a voting." The lack of precise descriptions of the ordination ceremony or its meaning can only mean that the inspired writers did not consider precision here to be crucial for the life of the church. Christ intended to continue to meet with His church throughout her history. He wanted the church to find her patterns of leadership, not by a slavish copying of a polity which He prescribed in the first century, but by the guidance which He would give in the midst of the church at any given time and place.

Ordination obviously did not need to follow one rigidly prescribed order. Paul never cited his ordination as ground for his authority. Apparently laymen and not elders did the laying on of hands as Paul and Silas were set apart for their missionary ministry.[55] When New Testament writers gave tests whereby to detect false preachers, they never suggested inquiring into the validity of the ordination of the unworthy preacher. Charismatic men and prophets served widely in the early church and apparently the New Testament writers did not urge Christians to inquire whether these men were properly ordained. There is no evidence in the New Testament that ordination conferred a spiritual or official gift upon some believers which was not attainable by all. The first-century church evidently extended ordination to other elders of the congregation in addition to the teaching-preaching elders, but neither Christ nor the apostles urged this as a precedent.

When a person was elected to lead the congregation in its ministry, he was "set before" the church. By this act the congregation declared their confidence in the man's integrity and character and asked the person to be their representative, or their "extended self."[56] The early church ordained certain believers to lead out in specific functions, simply because "the church could not fulfill the purpose for which she existed without teachers and rulers."[57] But, among all the ways of calling leaders and among all the tasks being assigned to them, the charge to minister God's Word emerged central among the tasks for which the church ordained men.

IX. Ordination Should Be a Charge to Minister God's Word

Christ Himself placed His preaching-teaching ministry above His healing or baptizing ministries. Likewise, the apostles realized the centrality and supremacy of the ministry of God's Word in the life of the church. They refused to allow their time and energies to be diverted to other ministries, regardless how good or how necessary. They insisted that other leaders be appointed "to serve tables." If this seemed to depreciate the administrative tasks of leadership it was only to accent the centrality of the Word of God in the life of God's gathered people.[58]

No other task of early church leaders other than preaching was regarded with such reverent respect, such seriousness, and such humility. Peter expected the very Word of the living God to come to Christians during the preaching of the Word.[59] Paul compared Christ's reconciling ministry to a "preaching" of peace.[60] Absolutely central in Paul's calling by God was his call to preach.[61] The exposition of the meaning of the inspired Scriptures should forever remain as the central source of renewal of the life of the church and the way by which God addresses men. Because the church follows the apostolic precedent, preaching of God's Word which succeeds in "transfiguring the cross and the resurrection from ancient facts to living realities of the present" should be the central task for which the church ordains men.[62] "Ordination should be a charge to preach and to teach from the Scriptures the relevance and meaning of the Word of God for the birth, life, death, and eternal existence of every living soul." The exposition of God's Word in a preaching-teaching ministry is so important, so all-pervading, and so sacred an assignment that ordination is certainly appropriate.

The church should be reluctant to extend ordination to other types of ministries, such as administration of church institutions or editing of church papers. If a brother who was ordained to minister God's Word to a congregation should leave this ministry, he should likely surrender his ordination. If later he should again be led into the central ministry of the Word of God to a congregation, his ordination charge could be renewed in a special service. While installation services, commissionings, and other similar procedures may well be held for Sunday-school teachers, or other servants of the church, the church will be wise to limit ordination to the charging of persons set apart for a ministry of the Word of God to the whole congregation, in a charge which is seriously intended to be for life. Licensing may be used when a brother is charged to preach in a temporary assignment, or when the lifelong call is not reasonably certain.

The ordination service itself should be primarily a "strong prayer for blessing" upon the person being ordained to minister God's Word to the congregation. The "laying on of hands" should be regarded as a "gesture of intense intercession." It should symbolize the focusing of the prayers of the church upon the life of the person who is charged with the awesome responsibility of giving his life to the ministry of the Word. It should be regarded as an expression of earnestness somewhat akin to fasting, which often accompanies prayer.[63]

Because the ministry of the Word of the living God is so central in the life and obedience of the church, the brother who is set apart for this ministry becomes servant to the whole team of congregational servants. From his continuous immersion in the Word of God he must come to serve as a guide and counselor to the group of leaders who "serve tables" and serve in other ways. The ordained minister is a "chaplain to God's ministers," a "head oarsman," an "other laity," a servant of God's servants, a "first among equals," or a person who perfects God's people for their work of ministering. Because he devotes himself so continually to the Word, he becomes something of a "steward of the mysteries" of its sublime truths to all of his co-workers. A church council, or board of elected elders, should carry heavy responsibility in guiding the congregational program.

The ordained minister is also charged by the congregation (assisted by the larger brotherhood of which the congregation is a part) to represent the congregation. Paul did not call the entire congregation to meet him at Troas, but only the elders. The ordained minister should be one of the elders who represents the church in conferences, anointing services for the sick, and other such occasions. The ordained minister in today's congregation may compare very well to the "teaching elder" who labored in preaching and teaching in the first-century congregations.[64]

The state prefers that the ordained representative of the congregation, and he alone, shall solemnize marriages. The church co-operates with the state in this regard, but not because anything intrinsic in her doctrine of the church or of ordination requires it.

Just as the minister represents the united voice and faith of the church when he exposits and proclaims her faith in preaching, so he also represents the congregation when he leads the congregation in applying her faith in appropriate ministries to members at times of birth and death. He leads in these ministries, not because he has been mysteriously qualified to do them through a sacramental ordination rite, but because God is a God of order and desires that leaders be set apart to perform necessary ministries in a reverent and ordered way. Because the ordained minister is giving himself almost constantly to the study and exposition of Scriptures, he is also charged with the responsibility of leading the corporate worship of the congregation. These added duties, beyond the exposition of the living truth of Holy Scriptures, come to the ordained leader because it is the truth of the Scriptures which must forever judge the changes which constantly come into the life of the church. The person who gives his life to the ministry of the Word should be the best qualified person to help to lead the congregational life in faithfulness to that Word.

The congregation (through recognized leaders) lays its hands upon the head of the brother being ordained, thus placing upon him the charge to give himself to the ministry of the Word and to lead the team of congregational leaders in faithfulness to the principles of the Word. The brother being ordained kneels, submitting to the act of the congregation, believing that the call of God to this sacred ministry has come to him through God's people. Kneeling indicates that the ordained person is not a law unto himself, but is bound in servitude to God, to His Word, and to His church. The ordination vows add definiteness and solemnity to the sacred occasion.

Other duties, all well and good in themselves, and urgently demanding to be done, will press in to claim the central attention of the man who has been ordained to preach and to teach. He must gently refuse them, help other members of the church to learn to do them, and in every way possible keep himself to his central task of the preaching and teaching of God's Word. When Paul charged Timothy he listed duties such as administration and working with other leaders,[65] but predominant in the charge was the command to teach, to proclaim the truth, to attend to the reading of Scripture, and to do the work of an evangelist. A present-day congregation would be most faithful to the New Testament assumptions if a layman with gifts of administration would serve as moderator of the congregation's business meetings.

Nothing about either the ordination charge or ceremony should allow people to infer that it is necessary so as to validate the sacraments of the church. No one should get the notion that the ceremony is itself a sacrament, raising the ordained person to a new order of Christians, or conferring a special dispensation of the Holy Spirit. A higher level of righteousness should not be expected of the ordained than of other mature believers who are also called to live exemplary lives. Ordination does not give the congregation the right to regard their minister as a "glorified errand boy," a person to be hired or fired much as a country club might treat their manager. Ordination should not be regarded as a charge to do the work of the church by proxy in behalf of passive members who do the preacher a favor by coming to hear him preach.

Ordination is important and necessary so that the ministry of the Word might be kept central and regulative in the life of the church. In both Old and New Testaments God made clear His will that the teacher-preacher should be set apart in a sacred service of prayer and commissioning. Just because the exact meaning of ordination is not precisely set forth, there is no excuse for an iconoclastic attack upon the system of ordination and church leadership. The leaderless congregation at Corinth should not be idealized for its polity any more than for its carnality. There might be some connection between the fact that no official leaders were mentioned in the church and the pettiness and rivalry of power-hungry people in the congregation. The Corinthian congregation discovered to their sorrow what group dynamics researchers have corroborated since then: that, when duly appointed and authorized leaders are not set apart and given responsibility, emergent leaders will inevitably appear. These emergent leaders tend to be more power hungry and to dominate the group in more subtle ways than officially appointed leaders would do.

The living Christ did not prescribe the pattern of organization and leadership which His disciples should follow until the end of time because He intended to be with them by His Spirit to give guidance as new situations would arise. He gave His followers just such guidance when He led His church to close the canon of Holy Scriptures.

The living Christ superintended the process as literally hundreds of worshiping congregations sorted out those prophetic and apostolic writings which were proving most profitable in "sparking" and guiding their charismatic life together. He guided them further as they set the canon of inspired writings over their charismatic life. Thus the record of previous encounters of God with man was used to "spark" the present encounter, and awaken charismatic gifts.

Although the charismatic gifts are distributed and redistributed within the contemporary congregation by the sovereign working of the Holy Spirit to meet new needs as they emerge, and so seem to ebb and flow within the life of the congregation, the Scriptures are given as a constant element which does not change.

Furthermore, the Scriptures constitute one of the most normative, energizing, and stabilizing elements in the midst of the congregation. In fact, the charisma of prophecy will have nothing "to work with" and may become either sterile or susceptible to error unless there is a continuing input of the whole counsel of God as this is expounded by the teaching-preaching of the message of Holy Scriptures. The church is certainly wise to make of ordination a charge to preach and to teach the abiding message of the Scriptures to the church.

But in the years ahead one of the central challenges which will confront the "man of the Word," who is ordained to preach-teach its message in the midst of the charismatic congregation, will be to help congregations to identify and to release the charismatic gifts which the Holy Spirit bestows in their midst. As the Holy Spirit sovereignly distributes and redistributes gifts, the congregation will not dare to identify charisma and office, insinuating that only office bearers have received gifts. Neither will the congregation want to cease electing and appointing office bearers, so that only the fluid, unpredictable, emergent, leadership is relied upon.

X. God's People Must Resist Perversions in the Pattern Which Leadership Assumes

(Here see Appendix 2, "The Historic Episcopate and Apostolic Succession Theories of the Ministry.")

The church must resist the notion that ordination creates a

separate class of Christians, or confers special status. Clericalism, which carries the implicit assumption that ordination has conferred indelible grace upon the soul and has lifted the ordained person to a separate order of believers, is a tacit denial of the Protestant doctrine of the priesthood of all believers. As a corollary of this serious error there has arisen the conception that some believers are merely "laymen" which in American semantics has come to mean one who is incompetent. In contrast with this distorted notion, the whole people of God were called the *laos,* and to be one of the laity was (and is) an honored position.

Along with the acceptance of the "holy man" conception of the ordained ministry has often gone the notion within Protestantism that the minister is something like a celestial druggist, dispensing heavenly vitamins and medicines in the form of sacraments. Furthermore, he is expected to grace sundry secular occasions by his presense and "drop a little holy water" upon it all by saying grace at the Rotary Club or intoning an invocation at a completely secular convention.

Illion T. Jones reports that some ministers are reacting against the "holy man" role in a tragic and pathetic way. "From many sources we hear that pastors and their wives are making declarations of independence . . . against the puritanic, narrow-minded prejudices of church people toward so-called worldly pleasures. . . . They are engaging in such practices as smoking, drinking, dancing, attending night clubs, using profanity, and reading sophisticated sex literature. . . ."[66] The cure which these ministers are attempting to use is indeed worse than the disease of clericalism itself.

Mennonite life and thought has not remained immune to certain inroads of clericalism. Ordained ministers have been described as the new "sacred office" which Christ established after He had abolished the Old Testament priesthood.[67] The ordained office was described as "the most exalted calling within the province of humanity." Some ministers have often been heard reminding the laity that they were to be careful not to touch the Lord's anointed!

While Mennonite life and thought has resisted many applications of clericalism, it has succumbed somewhat to it at still other points. In some areas of the church it has been decreed that only the highest level of the hierarchy, the bishop, may perform a marriage ceremony or administer the ordinances. In view of the fact that an influential source of Mennonite theology had suggested that the ordinances were the new "law of the Gospel" to replace the ceremonial and Levitical law, it is small wonder that in some areas of the church the unspoken assumption prevailed that the ordained leader performed holy rites which an unordained Christian simply should not perform.[68] Mennonites have ordained some Christian men a second and a third time (as deacon, minister, and bishop) without even attempting to give Scriptural justification for repeated ordinations.

An additional overtone of clericalism could be noted in the Mennonite Church in the fact that a two-level ethic was accepted. A higher level of nonconformity was required of the ordained Christian than of the lay Christian. In some areas a lay Christian could own a radio or wear a business suit, whereas the ordained Christian was forbidden to do so. Many Mennonite ministers continued to advocate the wearing of a religious garb by ordained men, even after laymen had ceased wearing it, and its meaning had shifted almost entirely from a symbol of a Christian's nonconformity to that of a clerical garb to set apart the clergy from the laity.

Then, too, clericalism often implied that the ordained Christian was to some degree infallible. It was assumed in some areas that ordination conferred "rightness." Unordained Christians tended to expect the ordained Christian to be an authority on many matters, and the "man of the cloth" was tempted to admonish and pronounce judgments upon issues in which he had little information or competence. An officially approved source of Mennonite theology suggested that ordination automatically qualified the recipient, and many Mennonites have assumed this to be true.[69]

Mennonites have accepted a number of by-products of clericalism within the culture, such as clergy permits from railroads, clergy signs for their cars, and honored seats on civic occasions, but have resisted others, the title of "reverend," for instance.

In much of Protestantism today the success standards and promotional methods of big business have been brought over into the church and a pastor has been hired as a professional expert to promote the program. The congregation no longer looks to individual members for a charismatic service gift which can help the group to function as Christ's body in the community. The hired, ordained expert attempts to perform the congregation's ministry in its stead. He preaches for it, visits for it, advertises for it, raises money to improve its real estate, and administers its office affairs, much as if he were the manager of a middle-class country club. The pitfalls which accompany this perversion will be discussed in chapter 5 on "Church Administration."

Some Protestant ordained persons, in attempting to break away from the "business executive image," have attempted to pattern their role after that of the physician or therapist. Some research indicates that ordained Christians like to think of themselves as religious counselors and therapists, working in a one-to-one relationship with disturbed members, and that ordained leaders resent the way in which administrative detail absorbs their time. In his pulpit ministry the ordained leader who conceives of himself as a therapist will likely dispense "psychologized Bible stories." The distortions which may follow this pattern of ministerial leadership will be discussed in the chapter on counseling (chapter 3).

Partly as a reaction against the "holy man" or the "business executive" image of the ordained leader, a number of Christians have attempted to belittle ordination. Some have insisted that because every believer possesses a spiritual gift, it is inconsistent to have one person contribute a disproportionate share of the service and admonition in a brotherhood. Group-centered and diffused leadership has been held up as the way in which to involve every member, and it has been feared that if one leader's special gift is recognized and central leadership assigned to him, then the universal gift diffused throughout the brotherhood will go unenlisted. Others have insisted that leadership must pass from one to another as the inner light flashes, and that the "gospel order" for the ministry is no order at all.[70] Still others have suggested that every member of the congregation who possess a discernible Spirit-given charisma should also be ordained.

Elton Trueblood has noted that this overemphasis upon the universal ministry of every believer "tends to lead to no ministry at all, or a ministry so fragmentary and so secularized that the meeting for worship begins to have the mood of a political forum . . . messages given tend to be trivial or merely anecdotal." Trueblood goes on to point out that the nourishment of the universal or lay ministry is the chief reason for the development of a special or partially separated ministry.[71] The Jehovah's Witnesses attempt to solve the problem by asserting that every member is an ordained minister.

Many argue that for God and His ministering people to become contemporary the church must needs match step with the world in its efficiency expert leaders, advertising technique, statistical data, promotional methods, and emphasis upon bigness and success. But in subtle ways the church leaders may find themselves relying upon gimmicks more than upon godliness. Calculated expediency and compromise may creep into the decision-making of the congregation. The leader may be tempted to rely upon church politics rather than upon prevailing prayer and repentance. The church at best may become one countervailing power amidst the others—big church alongside of big business, big government, and big labor, and the ordained leader may become an executive oiling the clanking ecclesiastical machinery. When the institution must be served, and its vested interests preserved, then the leader is tempted to shift from loving people and using the church machinery to loving the church machinery and using people. The congregation in the twentieth century must choose and charge her ministers with one eye upon the contemporary scene, but her other eye must be firmly upon the New Testament precedents.

An atrocious piece of doggerel helps to illustrate the caricature with which too many persons view the minister's role:

    Like a corporation works the church of God;

    Brothers, we are treading where Henry Ford has trod.

    We are all mass-minded, one huge body we,

    Planning world salvation, through the hierarchy.[72]

The attempt of tormentors within the church to scapegoat all of the ills of the church upon the minister, or worse yet upon the system of having one trained person to lead a congregation, is unfair, unrealistic, and not helpful. Scoffers refer to the pastor as a bewildered person, standing helplessly alongside of a social order which has its inner fortresses bombed out. The minister is sure that there is a place in civilization's present crisis for the social worker, the engineer, the teacher, and the doctor, but he can find no significant task for himself. "What he has the world does not want, and what the world wants he does not have."[73]

The real culprit, however, is a church which has refused and is refusing to be the church. Average members do not want their congregation to be led in a program which has any recognizable similarity to the early apostolic church. Members refuse unlimited liability for one another and for world evangelism. The much vaunted "church program" is too often an ingrown thing, spending nearly all of the congregation's time and money for itself. Committee is built upon committee and a feverish round of busywork is perpetuated, little of which goes beyond keeping the members comfortable, amused, and feeling respectable. The call of God to any man to minister His prophetic, life-giving, reformation-arousing Word amidst the Laodicean deadness of such a congregation requires more humility, courage, patience, and consecration than many men can muster.

XI. God Calls to the Ordained Ministry of the Word With Both an Outer and an Inner Call

Roman Catholics have invited "those who would be perfect" to come out from the laity and to take an additional step of consecration and self-surrender which is not required of fully consecrated laity. Some Protestant groups have unwittingly joined the Catholics in this error by presenting service within the ordained ministry as something one may "surrender to" which is above and beyond that full commitment to Christ's service which may be actualized in any other vocation. To be faithful to its New Testament doctrine of brotherhood and total discipleship for every believer the Protestant congregation can not elevate service within the ordained ministry above the service possible within any other honorable vocation. The ordained servant has a specific ministry with unique responsibilities and rewards, but is not called to greater consecration or honor.

The call to accept service within the ordained leadership usually has come as two "calls." First, there came the private inner sense of calling by God to serve His serving church in a special role of servant-leader. Secondly, there came the call of the church to validate and corroborate the personal inner call. Thus the call came immediate from Christ, and then was mediated through Christ's church.[74] A more healthy pattern and more consistent with the brotherhood church and the priesthood of all believers might be to have the call come first as a tap on the shoulder by the church. This could then be God's agent to arouse the slumbering inner call.

Mennonites have in the past tended to give the call by the congregation more weight than the private inner call. In some areas the male candidates for baptism were required to promise that they would submit to ordination if the church should call them. It was more acceptable to Mennonite opinion to refuse to function after ordination than to refuse to accept ordination. It was considered a mark of pride and presumption for a man to step forward and offer himself for service in the ordained ministry.[75] Thus the person who was called by lot did not need to worry about aptitudes, but could be assured that God had seized him for the work by an act of divine and even miraculous working. This system unfortunately has resulted in the ordination of some men for the ministry who were not at all "apt to teach."

How shall a fully consecrated brother detect whether he is being called to serve the serving church within the role of an

ordained leader? How shall he know whether he is called to minister as one of the whole ministering congregation, or to be ordained to minister God's Word to his brethren? What kind
of leading or call shall he expect?

Some sections of the Mennonite Church have used "the lot"
to call ministers, patterning their practice after the example of
the eleven apostles in their choice of a successor for Judas. But
Biblical studies have caused Mennonites to raise increasing questions about the use of "the lot." Clayton Beyler notes that the
lot continued in use only as long as the church sought to maintain
her identity with the twelve tribes of Israel, and so insisted that
there must be twelve apostles. After Pentecost and after the
church unhooked fully from Judaism, the lot is never again mentioned. Rather, the congregation looked for her Lord's leading
through the vote and censensus of a Spirit-filled congregation.[76]

Some continue to rely upon "special leading." Those who
rely primarily upon special leading tend to regard the ministry
as a sacred, special vocation among all the vocations of earth.
They expect God to give to them a crisis call, an overpowering
awareness in their inner conscience, and they feel that the
decision is primarily between God and their own heart and
will. If they waver in responding, God will cause things to
happen to further clarify and intensify His call. They believe
that God who is calling will qualify and enable, and so they do
not need nor dare to examine their aptitudes. Private prayer
is the way to become willing to surrender, and surrender brings
a flood of peace, and assurance that all is well.

Some rely upon "natural leading." Those who rely primarily
upon natural leading tend to feel that the ordained ministry is
only one among many roles in which a fully consecrated Christian
can implement his complete dedication to Christ and His church.
However, they notice that the deepest needs of mankind are their
uniquely spiritual ones, and that the ordained role calls the
person to minister in a specific and a unique way to these spiritual
needs. They find out just what is involved in the task and role
of an ordained minister. Then they weigh their own gifts,
aptitudes, and qualifications prayerfully to see whether their

own God-given gifts seem to coincide with this specific type of ministry. They continue to try to "fit together the pieces" of inner leading and advice from the brotherhood. They finally decide to prepare for service as an ordained minister if they are convinced, after much prayerful consultation and seeking of God's will, that God has entrusted to them the gifts which are most needed in this unique ministry to men, and that it is in this form of service that they can make their best contribution to God's kingdom. The voice of the brotherhood should always be weighed most heavily in detecting the call of God. Even the eleven apostles did not merely appoint a successor to Judas, but called the church together and expected God to choose a leader through the voice of the church.

Leading to accept the service within the role of an ordained minister needs to be a combination of both natural leading and special leading. The inner call and providential leading to the individual needs to be tested by, and corroborated by, the judgment of the brotherhood. Whenever possible, this should begin with the local congregation in which the brother has been serving. While the ministry is regarded as only one among many noble vocations, yet it should be recognized as one which is unique in its demands and opportunities. The individual should feel that he has been seized by God for a lifetime of unique service, and yet he should feel that he has made a rational decision, too. He should be tremblingly aware that he is an unworthy instrument in God's hands, and yet he should be assured that he has been given the stewardship of some of the gifts and aptitudes which are essential to the task.[77] A young man who is hearing and testing what he feels may be a call to the Christian ministry should counsel with his pastor and other church leaders, and should prayerfully study the qualifications listed in the pastoral epistles.

XII. God Sets Forth Qualifications
Which Servant-Leaders Should Possess

The New Testament does not merely copy Judaism when qualifications of leaders are set forth. The Jews insisted that the leader who was to be ordained must be a married man, that he must be forty years of age or over, and that he be without bodily defects. Some traditions even suggested that he should be a tall man.

The supreme requirement for any and every leader, as Christ pictures him, is that he should genuinely seek to be servant of all. He must see Christ in his neighbor's need, and do his serving unto any one of the least of these just as he would do it to Christ Himself. But he must do his service in the power and compassion which Christ gives so that the neighbor being served sees Christ in the minister as he does the service. As D. T. Niles puts it, "I must serve my neighbor as if he were Christ; I must also serve him as if I were Jesus Christ."[78] The ordained minister must also be convinced that ministering the message of the Scriptures to persons is one of the highest services which anyone can render.

The qualifications cited in the pastoral epistles and elsewhere in the New Testament seem to focus upon two requirements: (1) personal spiritual maturity and (2) ability to relate helpfully to other people. The lists in the pastorals, I Tim. 3:1-13 and Titus 1:6-9, re-echo the emphasis that the minister should be of such integrity that he is above reproach from the watching world, hospitable, temperate, sober, gentle, not contentious, not soon angry, trustworthy, and free from avarice. He should not be a novice, but should have served the Lord with all humility,[79] should have an exemplary home life, and should have proved his spiritual maturity before both the congregation and the watching world. Certainly a brother's ministry as a layman should have been characterized by the demonstration of the Spirit and of power before he may be considered for ordination.

Biblical qualifications for leaders seem to concentrate upon personality factors which affect the person's ability to get along with people. Little is said about intellectual competence except that he should be "apt to teach" and able to exhort in doctrine and confute the gainsayers.

There was a time when the minister could speak out on nearly any subject without fear of rebuttal. But in the modern congregation experts in many fields of study listen to the sermon.

Every casual allusion is heard by someone who subconsciously checks it for accuracy in a field in which he is proficient. Honest worshipers soon lose respect for a minister who reveals his ignorance by making sweeping generalizations which are contrary to facts. The minister should have a broad background education, in addition to theological training, so that he can be a more understanding "chaplain" to the laity as they serve in their on-the-job ministries.

Three great leaders seem to strike out the pattern for leaders of God's people. There were three leaders who cared for their people until they actually felt—"Blot me out if that will help to save them." Moses, Paul, and Jesus thus stand as towering examples of redemptive concern for their group. Furthermore, they kept in moment-by-moment contact with the living God for guidance for their work. Finally, they brooded with God over His people and world until their inner experience became a mold used by God to present His revelation to men. Many secondary qualifications could be listed, but if a leader has these three, he will be a usable man.

XIII. The Minister Should Be More Than A "Professional" Person

If the church is to serve responsibly in the midst of society, she may not ignore entirely what society expects an ordained minister to be. Most persons, unfortunately, expect a minister to be a "professional" person, in much the same way as a doctor or lawyer is regarded.

In so far as being a professional person in a community provides prestige, social status, and automatic deference, the minister should not want to be a "professional." He is the servant of all and should avoid being a "great one" on the world's totem pole. He does not want to hold out his hand for tax exemptions, clergy discounts, favored positions, thus helping to "scramble the dollar sign and the cross." He wants no "cloying deference," no imputed goodness, no awkward silence when he appears, no vestments of the "holy man."

He does not want to be thought of primarily as one who has mastered an "educably communicable technique." His ministry is not essentially a set of techniques which he employs. Rather he gives himself to the ministry of God's Word so that its truths shared in the midst of the congregation may guide them in their ministry. He does not seek, as do most professions, "to be free from lay evaluation and control."[80]

But the minister should be willing to submit to "a form of licensure approved by society." He should be willing to pursue a level of excellence and mastery in his field of service even higher than the minimum which society would demand. He should "dedicate his understandings of a body of knowledge" to the service of persons, not from a profit motive but from a desire to serve.

The minister is professional in the best sense in that he does not work in order to be paid, but he is paid so that he may be free to work at the task which is his to do. A vigorous and competent trained minister of the Word is the only right counterpart of an awakened, spiritually gifted, ministering laity. After a penetrating probing of the problems which accompany a professionalized ministry, Walter Wagoner says, "A professional ministry raises the level and the effectiveness of the church, as the Society of Friends is just now finding out in the United States. . . . There is no surer way of nurturing heresy and obscurantism within Christianity than to abolish a paid specially educated professional leadership."[81]

But the minister of the Word is a different kind of a professional from any servant of the community. Whereas other professional persons may introduce themselves as "your servants," the minister must always add, "your servant for Jesus' sake," for he serves and is a part of the whole serving body of Christ, the church.

XIV. The Minister of the Gospel Should Live of the Gospel

Why should an ordained minister of the Word be supported, if the other members must pay their own way? How does the ministry of the ordained servant of the church compare with that of other fully consecrated but self-supported members? The ordained brother is called and charged to give his time and energies to the ministry of God's Word to persons as his first assignment, and not incidentally or in connection with some other service which he is rendering to them. The minister of God's Word serves the church when it is gathered so that the church when it is scattered may serve with greater power.

As an illustration, the fully consecrated Christian doctor focuses his attention first upon the bodily health of persons who come to him, and discusses the person's spiritual condition only if and when a given patient may indicate readiness for such discussion. The Christian teacher gives first attention to teaching arithmetic or whatever his given assignment might be, and only discusses salvation history or the pupil's spiritual need if and when an occasion may require or permit. The Christian carpenter devotes most of his attention and energy to his work of framing materials of wood or stone. Only rarely and as opportunity affords does he focus upon God's work of building from redeemed men His holy temple in the Lord.

Even the Christian social worker concentrates primarily upon the horizontal human relationships of the counselee. Only on rare occasions and when a particular client's interests will permit it does the social worker mention a client's vertical relationship with the God of all the earth. The Christian worker in a factory can speak to his fellow workmen about their need of Christ, but the punch press operator simply must keep his mind and attention upon his punch press as he works. His time is not his own to study his Bible just as he chooses, or to take time off for deliberate counseling.

In spite of the fact that it is a marginal time ministry, these on-the-job relationships of Christian with non-Christian constitute one of the most crucial missionary frontiers which the church faces. Even though actual conversation about spiritual things can only go on on marginal time, yet on the job the life and love of Christ can be lived into the warp and woof of human relationships. The church needs to have all of its members constantly engaging in such a ministry. It is likely that as the church pioneers into unchurched areas and primitive cultures, much of the evangelism will need to be done by ministers who combine a tentmaking ministry with their ministry of God's Word.

However, in twentieth-century industrialized, urbanized America, whenever a congregation of 100 to 150 believers has gathered so that it is possible to do so, the ordained minister of God's Word should be supported at least part time by the congregation so that he can be available, on call, to minister God's Word to men. Although every Christian seeks to "catch men" all of the time, many of the most crucial "men catching" opportunities come at crises of birth, marriage, tragedy, sickness, and death. Moreover, the most profound and depth-level ministry of God's Word is required to minister to persons during just these times of crisis. The modern carpenter, factory worker, truck driver, and teacher simply cannot be free and available on call to minister in the name of God and the congregation in times of crisis. Furthermore, the person who does not give himself to the ministry of God's Word cannot bring out from its treasures things new and old as well as can the person whose time is freed to mine in the treasures of the Word of God in depth.

No lethargy on the part of the ordained minister, desire to be free to go to Florida for the winter, dislike for the strenuous work of mastering the message of the Scriptures, or desire to be independent and enjoy a higher standard of living may be allowed to contradict the clear mandate of the Apostle Paul that they who "preach the gospel should live of the gospel." The example of the carnal congregation at Corinth should not be lifted up as an ideal. The more active and faithful the congregation is in fulfilling its every-member ministry, the more a fully supported minister will be needed to lead the ministering congregation.[82]

Chapter 2

The Minister Preaches God's Living Word

I. Preaching the Word Is the Central Task Of the Minister

Preaching is the setting forth of God's living Word from Scripture so that God Himself confronts men here and now. In the first chapter the affirmation was made that all of the members of the congregation are the Lord's ministers. The ordained minister, set apart to serve God's ministering people, has no other task than to seek to perfect God's people for their work of ministering. In this lecture the assertion will be made that the ordained minister perfects God's people for their work of ministering primarily by preaching and teaching God's Word in their midst.

In the preaching of the Word the ordained brother ministers *to* the ministering church directly. Why should this task of preaching be so special and so sacred that the one who serves in this ministry should be ordained, set apart, charged to the work, and supported financially so that he can give this time to it? Why is preaching so great a part of "perfecting the church for their work of ministering"?

One reason for this emphasis upon preaching is that God has set preaching, the exposition of God's deeds and words in holy history, central in the very formation and life of His new people, the church. God's Son, the Founder and Head of the church, declared that He was anointed to preach. Christ's apostles placed the ministry of the Word in first priority and insisted that other leaders be chosen to serve tables. Paul relegated even the sacred rite of baptism to a secondary place when he insisted, "Christ sent me not to baptize, but to preach."[1] Until Paul's dying day in faraway Rome he devoted himself above all else to "preaching the kingdom of God, and teaching those things which concern the Lord Jesus Christ."[2] Paul first heralded God's gracious mercy and forgiveness which came in Christ, and then taught those who wished to respond to this grace how they might do God's will.

The great prophets, apostles, and leaders of Christian history all placed preaching very high, if not supremely central in their ministry to men. God's mighty men all believed that when they preached, they were introducing men to God so that God and men had dealings with one another in an encounter of eternal consequences. Whenever a period of decline in Christian preaching occurred, a period of moral and spiritual decay was sure to follow.

The Bible writers dared to believe that God chose preaching as His way to speak to men. Peter declared that God Himself came "preaching peace by Jesus Christ," and Peter meant that God did it partly through sermons.[3] Paul commended the Thessalonian believers because they received his preaching, not merely as the words of men, but as the very words of God.[4] Evidently, the greatest service an ordained minister can render to people is to preach God's Word to them.

II. Preaching Must Not Be Replaced by Every-Member Testimony

Even though God has set preaching central in the life and worship of the church, cannot every member take his turn in preaching, giving his testimony and witness? Has not Pentecost given to every Spirit-indwelt believer the "passion of utterance"? Can not every worshiper tell "the wonderful works of God" with holy joy and convicting power? Why need one of God's servants be ordained and supported to give his time to the ministry of preaching God's Word? Should not many laymen in the congregation have the prophetic gift? Why not merely rely upon "every member prophesying," speaking under the "immediate inspiration of the Spirit"? Would not this eliminate the need to support one minister, and avoid all of the possibilities of hierarchy, professionalism, and lay passivity which the church must avoid at every cost?

There should, indeed, be many occasions in the life of the congregation when the spontaneous prophetic testimony and insight of members may be exercised. In times of doubt and difficulty some modern Agabus should speak out and help God's people to discern His will. God can, indeed, come to any member of the congregation with fresh illumination and insight. If every member is prophesying in a members' meeting or testimony session, the sense of newness and Holy Spirit power may well convict the visiting believer.[5] Present-day congregations need to see their life together as a continuation of holy history, and to live in holy expectancy of the present action and word and leading of the living Christ in their midst.

III. But the Message of Scripture Must Judge And Correct Spontaneous Testimony

But God has set the apostolic writings over the later prophetic utterances in the church. Endless prophesyings tend to cause confusion which leads to Montanism. God guided the worshiping church to set the apostolic and canonical writings over the life of the church as the norm and judge of all subsequent "revelations" and prophetic insights. When prophets continue to arise (even though they insist that they are receiving revelations equal to those which came to Peter, John, or Paul), the church is not to despise these prophesyings, but is to prove all things and only to hold fast to that which is good.[6] God gave to the church the canonical Scriptures by which to test the good, and to prove any prophesyings which continue in the church.

The Roman Catholic Church insists that the canon is not really closed, but that statements of the present Peter (the pope) are of equal weight with the apostolic writings. Some Quakers imply that the living Lord still acts and speaks in and through

His church, and that the revelation which comes through the inner light now is on a par with Scripture.[7] But this is not the faith of evangelical Protestantism. Prophetism was not universal, nor primary, nor intended to be permanent as the normative, controlling, authoritative word within the life of the church. "The absolute character of the revelation of Jesus Christ stands or falls with the primacy of the apostolate over prophecy."[8] All later insights or revelations in the church must be tested by the truth and revelation given by the inspired apostles, and at the apex of their revelation stands the ineffable Christ. Because of the closeness of the apostles to Christ God has set their writings as the permanent norm of truth and the test of all later self-disclosures. One of the most important functions of the Holy Spirit in the present era is to help the student of the Scriptures to bring out from its treasures things new and old.

IV. Preaching the Message of Scripture Requires Intensive Study

Let it be granted, then, that all preaching worthy of the name must be the exposition and application of the message of the inspired Scriptures. But why ordain and support one minister, from among all of God's ministering people, to preach the message of the Scriptures to the church and to the world? Does not every layman have the Holy Spirit? If he has the Scriptures in his own language, can he not understand them in depth and so be ready to expound their message? Are not the Scriptures so simple, so perspicuous, and their meaning so clear and readily apparent that any sincere believer can grasp their message?

Fortunately, the truths of the Gospel message which are minimum essentials for salvation are thus easily grasped. But a mastery of "the whole counsel of God" from the total message of Scripture, so as to be able to relate God's Word to the emerging problems of men, is a study so vast and so difficult that it demands broad preparation and training coupled with sustained exegetical study.

The problem is made acute because the words of men, in which the Word of God originally came, have changed their meaning so often and so radically throughout history. The words of men gained their original freight of meaning out of a total cultural womb and milieu. But the winds of circumstance blow over the words that men use to communicate meaning, and words change their freight of meaning even within one generation. When the same words are expected to convey their meaning across many generations, the risk of missing the original writers' intent is great indeed. God's Word must come in the words of men, but men's words change meaning constantly.

As cultures have risen and passed away and the world views have succeeded one another, new words have been needed and have been coined to serve as a communication bridge to help the original writer to be heard accurately by contemporary man. The Scriptures cannot be exposited in depth and accuracy unless the minister knows the freight of meaning which the original words of Scripture carried in the mind of the original writer. It is not enough to know what the English words used in a certain version of the Scriptures may mean to one's neighbor now. The minister should not be completely at the mercy of version writers, interpreters, and commentators, but should be able himself to understand the languages in which the inspired writings were originally given.

In order to really match minds with inspired writers, the expositor of their writings must be able to enter into their whole world view, and look out at their world through their eyes. Thus, Paul and the apostles could interpret the thought of the prophets' message into Koine Greek because they understood Hebrew so well. But when later leaders at the ecumenical councils tried to interpret the prophets' ideas to the Greek world they often failed. They understood Greek thought forms well enough, but did not understand either the world view or the semantics of the Hebrews.

The Hebrew thought of man in the group as part of a covenant community or a corporate personality, whereas the Greek thought of him only in separate individualistic terms. Greeks thought of immortality of the soul, but Hebrews of either sheol or bodily resurrection. Hebrews thought of time as linear, mov-

ing toward an end, but existing only so as to enable response to
Jehovah. Greeks thought of the eternal as a supermundane order
existing parallel to and above the temporal.[9]

Any preacher who is inclined to underrate the magnitude of
the task of translating meanings from one world view to another
should ponder the experience of Paul on Mars' Hill when he
attempted to borrow and use the thought forms of the Stoics. The
preacher should try to understand the host of problems which
John encountered when he borrowed the Greek concept of logos
to try to explain the incarnation. Some preachers in the United
States have been quite willing to admit the vastness of the task
which was faced by the missionary as he sought to translate the
message of the Scriptures for the person in the Congo. But it is
only slowly dawning upon the Western preachers that tribal
peoples may be able to hear the deeper meanings of the Scriptures
with more ease than can the scientifically oriented person from
the concrete jungle city of America.

The task of translating the transcultural meaning of the
Scriptural message into the thought forms of an alien culture is
extremely difficult. The minister who is ordained to preach to the
congregation her essential faith must really give himself to the
ministry of the Word. This requires intensive study and mastery
of many fields of inquiry. No accumulations of versions can
ever make the task easy.

The man who prepares a sermon from the Scriptures should
know who the adversary was then, and who the adversary is now.
He must know the literary forms of poetry, allegory, and simile
which were used then, and the thought forms which serve as
vehicles for similar meaning now. He must know the urgency of
the hour in which the original message was written and the
urgency of the situation to which God wants His living Word to
be addressed now.

The expositor of the Scriptures should learn the favorite
phrases of each Bible writer, his unique ways of using language,
and the amount of poetic license the writer uses in his communication. He must also keep in mind the message of the whole
book within which a specific paragraph or verse is found. He

must remember also where a given writer stood in the whole development of salvation history. (Thus an expositor of the meaning of an imprecatory psalm may not use its emphasis to supersede the emphasis of the Sermon on the Mount.) He must understand salvation history thoroughly enough so that he can detect which predictions have already found either partial or full fulfillment.

V. Preaching the Message of Scripture Requires A Committed Preacher

Christian preaching begins only when faith in the message has reached such a pitch that the experience of the man proclaiming it becomes part of the message preached. Even the preacher who has taken time to master the original languages of Scripture, and has learned to understand the Bible's world view, history, geography, and backgrounds, may still not be ready to expound the Bible's message in depth and faithfulness to the original writer's intent. The expositor of the Scriptures dare not simply ask what the inspired writer was saying then, 1900 or 2700 years ago. He must be asking earnestly what God's living Word to his own heart is saying from the passage right here and right now. Only when the Bible student has surrendered any pretense of neutrality, and is ready to hear from the text a word that as yet has no place in his understanding, but that will demand of him a decision which will involve his whole being— only then can he fully hear and relay God's living Word from Scripture.[10] Truth is for obedience, and God does not promise to give it to detached speculation.

The minister of the Word of God must study in awe before the "unfathomable mystery of God's mercy and judgment," trusting the same Holy Spirit which inspired the original writer to help the preacher to grasp the writer's intent, and then to translate this and re-mint it into current coin. "If any man will do his will, he shall know." The preacher dare not seek "it-truth," but should be praying all the while he studies and preaches, "Lord, what wilt thou have me to do?"

VI. Preaching Must Be Informed by a Biblical Theology

Furthermore, faithful interpretation of the transcultural message of the Scriptures must be done within an adequate Biblical theology. Every expositor has some theology which decides the framework he uses to present the fruits of his exegesis and interpretation of the Bible. For instance, a preacher's Biblical theology will determine what application he makes now of the instructions regarding the Levitical sacrificial system. All Scripture remains profitable, even after the crisis issue to which certain passages were originally addressed has passed. But, the preacher's own theological position will decide how he seeks to derive the contemporary profit from culturally dated teachings, such as land tenure laws, meat offered to idols, women keeping silent in churches, apocalyptic imagery, three-decker universe, imprecatory psalms, or "drink a little wine for thy stomach's sake." One of the most severe temptations which Christ ever faced came exactly at this point—how could He detect which strand of Scriptural teaching was the Father's will for His obedience in the present situation?

VII. A Proof-Texting Use of Scripture Must Be Avoided

Ministers are constantly tempted to use texts of Scripture in violation of their true meaning in context. The minister and the congregation should both know that a proof-texting use of the Scriptures is dangerous, irreverent, and inadequate. The congregation should believe with deep conviction that God has made the exposition of the truth of Scripture to be the central sacrament of their worship. They should charge and support their minister, so that he can give himself to the careful ministry of all of God's Word. They should insist that his sermons should actually be a declaration of the whole counsel of God, and should rise up in protest if their minister serves to them a spiritual diet of unrelated ideas based upon a proof-texting use or abuse of the Scriptures.

The minister himself should refuse to stoop to carelessness in his use of Scriptures as a base for his sermons. It is an irreverent use of the Scriptures to seize a verse and to use it for one's own purposes, assigning a meaning to the verse other than and in opposition to the meaning intended by the inspired writer. Such a proof-text abuse of Scripture is the favorite method employed by the religious cults. Any error can be "proven" from the Scriptures by the use of this method. This use of Scripture creates the impression that Bible verses are merely a row of isolated magical pills, with power in and of themselves, regardless of their real meaning in their context.

VIII. Preaching and Teaching Should Be Blended in the Sermon

The preacher should consciously seek to join preaching and teaching in his ministry of God's Word in sermons. For some years a too-sharp dichotomy between preaching and teaching was in vogue. Fortunately, later scholarship has been correcting the notion that preaching was pure *kerygma,* that is, announcing the facts about what God has done, and teaching pure *didache,* that is, explaining the way a disciple ought to walk. There is no longer any ground for the notion that any sincere laymen can do the preaching, that is, testify and recite the facts of the *kerygma,* but that theological training is necessary for the teacher who interprets the *didache* and draws out implications for present-day obedience.

Preaching and teaching should be joined in the sermon because they were already interwoven in first-century preaching. Mounce and others have demonstrated that apostolic preaching was no stereotyed six-point recital. Rather, some *didache* was always included; the implications of the lordship of Christ were interpreted also.[11] In both Gospels and epistles *kerygma* and *didache* are joined. They should not be separated in Christian preaching. Paul, Stephen, and Peter risked their lives because they insisted upon going beyond mere recital and testimony to interpretation and ethical appeal.

Furthermore, the teaching-preaching sermon is needed by all of the hearers. The believer needs to hear the "facts" of the Gospel story repeated over and over so as to conquer his own temptations to unbelief. The unbeliever needs to hear a penetrating interpretation of the ethical implications of the Christian faith. The men who actually observed the "facts" of the *kerygma,* that is, the incarnation, Calvary, resurrection, and Pentecost, were not convinced by the "facts." Rather, they missed the meaning of the facts until there was Spirit-guided teaching and interpretation.[12] No simple testimony of "facts alone" may ever be substituted for the teaching-preaching sermon at the center of the worship and life of the church.

IX. The Message of Scripture Must Be Addressed To the Life Situations of Men

It is true that present-day affairs and happenings in political, interpersonal, economic, and international life call aloud for Christian interpretation by the preacher. But when the church is at worship, receiving from her God the sacrament of His living Word which is coming to her by Spirit-guided exposition of the meaning of the inspired Scriptures—then human reflections about contemporary problems dare not be made central. The sermon needs always to be anchored in the Biblically disclosed realities. While exploring God's will for men, God's ways with man, and man's life with his fellow men as this stands revealed in Scriptures, then and only then can applications be made to the contemporary scene.

The minister is not being most relevant to the anxieties of his age if he keeps lecturing his own brilliant reflections about them. He is most relevant when he sets forth in true Biblical content and perspective the transculturally relevant realities about human need and God's redeeming deeds. He helps worshipers to find their way, amidst the ambiguities of human existence, if he expounds with Biblically based authority the things eternal.[13] As the worshiper learns to love more deeply the God whom he has not seen, he is prepared again to love the "ornery" brother whom he has seen so often.

The deep inner anxieties which rage beneath the brave fronts which worshipers wear were also present in Bible times.

The minister who expounds the message of the Scriptures will find there souls wrestling with the futility of life, the agony of loneliness, the struggle to control the sex drives, the feelings of inferiority, or feelings of guilt and frustration. Sibling rivalries, marriage infidelity, adolescent rebellion, and parental partiality for one child above another are clearly portrayed in the Bible narratives, but they lose their power to panic the soul because in spite of them all God is seizing men in love, and those who respond are being changed into saints.

The minister who expounds the message of the Scriptures in depth will examine the life problems of aggressive behavior, immaturity, inner conflict, and the ability to get along with other people, but he will examine all problems in the context within which they should be examined, that is, the redemptive activities of the living God. Thus, the sibling rivalries of Joseph and the partiality of his parents can only be transcended when both Joseph and his brothers are caught up within the larger purposes of God to preserve mankind from starvation. Joseph can forgive and his brothers can be reconciled because they awaken to the amazing discovery that God is using them all in His grand design. After the deep lessons from salvation history have been set forth in the teaching-preaching sermon, then the charismatic gift of prophecy can apply God's Word to specifics in a discussion situation.

X. Only the Message of Scripture Should Be Called Either "Preaching" or "Sermon"

The minister should seek to prepare and to preach a sermon which sets forth and makes clear a portion of the total message of Scripture. Unless he is seeking to do this he should not use the word "preaching" or "sermon," and it should not be set central as the primary sacrament of worship. Other words such as talk, lecture, testimony, or address should be used for the minister or layman's remarks about life in general, reflections drawn from experience, and observations drawn from other literature. But the terms "preaching" and "sermon" should be reserved for that address which exposits or makes clear what God has said and done to redeem men and to guide men's lives, as this is recorded in Scripture. A topical essay which is not molded, informed, and corrected at every point by the Scriptural message should not be called a sermon or preaching. Even when dealing with Biblical themes such as God's sovereignty and love, man's need and predicament, God's deed of redemption, man's response and how God's grace transforms him, and God's continuing work through His ministering people—even the treatment of these themes which dominate the Bible itself should not be called "preaching" or a "sermon" unless what the Bible as a whole says on these themes also dominates the discussion.

XI. The Sermon May Be Structured in Any One Of a Number of Ways

The setting forth or exposition of the meaning and message of Scripture is indeed the only religious address which deserves the title of "preaching" or "sermon." But this does not mean that only an exposition of a certain passage of Scripture, and limited to it, can really be a sermon. A topical, textual, biographical, or other type may be a Scriptural sermon also.

In preparing to preach God's living Word through a topical, doctrinal, or thematic sermon, the minister first seeks God's guidance as to the choice of a topic, subject, or theme. The sermon need not bear an analytical relationship to any one passage of Scripture. The sermon may attempt a comprehensive coverage of a subject which is treated at many places throughout the Scriptures. The total Biblical theology of the minister must guide him as he assembles his materials and ideas. It is not enough to merely use a concordance and to string together all the verses which mention the subject, much as a child puts beads upon a string. All of the hermeneutical principles cited earlier in this chapter must be applied as the minister prepares a topical or a subject sermon.

Although the topical or subject sermon is especially adapted for the presentation of a doctrine or truth in its wholeness, it is one of the most difficult of sermons to prepare and to preach rightly. Preachers are tempted to take a vast theme and then to say a few smattering and obvious things about the theme. Few preachers have the theological profundity and the gift of brevity and clarity so as to be able to adequately cover in thirty minutes of preaching a subject like justification by faith, divine providence, the atonement of Christ, or the work of the Holy Spirit.

Superficiality becomes the bane and even the curse upon much topical preaching. The preacher begins by admitting, "A whole book could be written on this theme, but I will preach one sermon about it." If the average minister chooses one of the majestic themes or doctrines of the faith, he can not even "break it open" in twenty or thirty minutes. A series of sermons would be the solution, but too few preachers or congregations have the seriousness and determination required for the sustained interest and study which this demands.

The other blight which so often affects topical preaching is "itsy-bitsy" preaching. The preacher is tempted to look around for little subjects which he can "cover" in one sermon. Fads, fancies, items of interest from the headlines flit through the pulpit and reduce the sermon to irrelevance. Much topical preaching fails to reach either the height or the depth of the Christian message. It fails to present truth in its wholeness. Sincere people can listen to it for a lifetime and remain Biblically and theologically illiterate.

Textual sermons may also set forth and exposit an undistorted portion of the total Biblical message and so merit the name of preaching or sermon. In a purely textual sermon the main ideas of the sermon are drawn only from the text itself. Jones is certainly correct when he asserts that it is difficult to find in the entire Bible 100 texts suitable for the textual development as a sermon.[14] There are some "epitome texts," which gather up the Scriptural message within a very brief compass, but not nearly as many as some preachers seem to assume.

Often the main ideas are drawn from the text itself, but then each idea is developed in subject fashion. Too often, however, a preacher prepares a topical sermon and hurries around seeking for a text to fit it. Texts may be used as "launching pads" for topical sermons, but the preacher should not pretend that he has found all of the ideas within the text. Hearers are apt to develop a false idea of the Scriptures if ministers merely "jack up a text and run a topical sermon under it." The only honest way to use a text as the basis of a sermon is to first honor the writer's original intent and meaning in its original context. Then, when truths and applications drawn from other Scriptures or from life are gathered around it, these truths must be consistent with and controlled by the truth set forth in the text itself.

It is "wresting the Scriptures," it is "exegetical sleight of hand," it is irreverent "touching of one's hat" to the Bible to use texts as pretexts in violation of their contexts. The preachers who disgrace the Bible by treating it thus would become very angry if someone would take portions of a letter which they had written and would misquote, use out of context, and tamper with the meaning which they had intended to convey.

In the expository sermon the minister seeks to explain the inspired writer's intention and meaning from a more extended passage in which the writer has treated a subject with some completeness. The minister interprets the Bible writer's ideas and does not merely assemble some of his own. By careful exegesis the minister recaptures the original, vivid feeling and meaning of the writer, and relays this to the worshiping congregation.

In "pure" expository preaching the minister only analyzes, and then passes on to his hearers the actual content of the passage. In "expository sermonizing" the minister draws out the main thoughts from the passage, but arranges them in sermon style. He prepares a suitable introduction, sharpens the inspired writer's own outline, if it seems desirable, so as to gain attention, adds illustrations which help relate the truths to life today, and even adds arguments and exhortation from his own convictions.

Some expositors take still more liberties, rearranging the material from within the passage, and even omitting entirely some portions which had relevance primarily to a situation which obtained in Bible times. Such tampering with a passage needs to be done with respect for the inspired writer's intention, and with a justifiable reason for doing so. Since no one passage of Scripture includes a total Biblical theology, the minister's theology must guide him in the interpretation he gives to a passage, even in expository preaching. The task of the expositor is to apply to the issues of life today the real and essential meaning of Scripture as it existed in the mind of the writer and as it stands in relation to the total message of salvation history.

Expository preaching gives the nearest to a "thus saith the Lord" authority in preaching. The preacher is demonstrating that the Word he preaches is not really his, but God's. Expository preaching interprets the Bible directly more than any other method does. It forces the minister to break new ground and to quit dodging difficult or "dangerous" truths. It can help discourage a minister from riding his hobby. It can teach the members of the congregation, by example, how to study the Scriptures and to find there the truths for themselves. It can help to show that the minister and congregation really believe that the Bible is central in the life of the church, the source of divine authority, the central sacrament in worship, and the guide which the Holy Spirit uses to direct the consciences of God's people. Too many worshipers think that Philippians is a book of four chapters with a lot of good texts in it, but after a minister has preached a series of consecutive expository sermons through the book, their concept of the Bible may improve radically.

Expository preaching has been discredited too often because ministers have been too lazy to wrestle with a passage until they discovered the author's outline. The preacher merely "made a few remarks" upon the passage. When he was "persecuted in one verse he fled to another." But, when ideas are grouped around appropriate headings, well-selected illustrations show their relevance to the contemporary scene, and a conclusion gives the call to a verdict—then expository preaching can be one of the most interesting, effective, and genuinely instructive types of preaching.

XII. An Introduction Can Prepare Worshipers to Hear God's Word

Some ministers feel they should begin abruptly when they preach a sermon. Why waste time; why not just plunge in? Would not a simple "hear the word of the Lord" be enough? In this fast-moving, headline age, why not dispense altogether with an introduction to the sermon? In most modern short stories does not the action begin at once, with a skeleton falling out of a closet already in the first paragraph?

Most ministers feel that an introduction is needed to prepare worshipers to hear the Word of God in depth and in context. Orientation can be provided in the introduction, so that hearers can grasp meanings and respond more profoundly. The interest of the congregation can be polarized, and worshipers can be helped to hear and think and feel together as a group. Just as great books usually have a preface and great musical compositions a prelude, so most great sermons have an introduction.

The introduction should be brief, with not one word wasted. It should fit just the particular situation. The minister should ask just what must be said to pose the problem which the sermon will seek to solve. How can a few vivid sentences sketch the setting of the situation and the context of the Bible passage? Would a brief preview of the sermon development help the hearers? The introduction should not promise too much so that it is as if a cannon exploded and then a pea rolled out of the barrel.

The minister should never apologize as part of his introduction. He should avoid calling attention to himself, but should seek to set his hearers and himself into the very presence of the living, speaking God. Humor is almost always out of place, as are statements which are too startling. The minister who introduced a sermon on God's omnipresence with the statement, "God is in the garbage can," did not really prepare worshipers to hear God.[15]

XIII. An Outline Can Help to Make the Word Clear and Coherent

Is it really possible to outline a living Word of God as it proceeds out of His mouth? Is not this like attempting to control a lightning flash, or trying to varnish the sunlight? Is there not danger that an attempt to outline a sermon may hinder the Holy Spirit who ever blows where He lists?

In spite of the minister's awe before the mystery of the Holy Spirit's working through the preached Word, he still tries to outline his sermon. God is a God of order and He desires order rather than confusion in the sermon. God wants man to remember the Word which comes to him in the sermon, and outlined material is easier to remember. Man's attention span is limited, and outlined material can regain attention when it starts to waver.

The outline should be suggested by and grow out of the body of truth to be presented. Each subpoint should be one facet or phase of the whole. The outline should have unity and simplicity. There should be logical progression, and the movement should be toward a climax and the inevitable appeal for the worshipers' response. Some research indicates that hearers will remember crucial material better if the strongest point is presented first.

The Word which God wishes to say to man may often fall naturally into a three-point outline. Often God's Word to worshipers will include a description of the way things are, set over against a picture of the way they should be, and climaxed by a presentation of what God has done in Christ to make change possible. Other variations of this three-point division may well be the problem, the principle by which to solve it, and the program of action indicated. Similar to this would be man's need, God's deed, and man's response.

Sometimes the minister will find that what the Word of God desires to say can best be relayed under a twin, or two-point outline. This may include before and after, cause and effect, either/or, positive versus negative, true versus false, diagnosis and remedy, man's need and God's action, or what God has said and how His Word applies to worshipers now.

The minister should brood with his God over the needs in God's church and world until what God wants to say becomes clear. If the minister really has a message from God, it can be presented in statements. These statements, in clear, staccato affirmations, may well form the points or outline for the sermon.

A clear outline, with its logical progression and arresting climax, is a challenge to the worshiper to think, and to love the Lord his God with all of his mind. Many influences of mass psychology and group dynamics operate when persons worship in a crowd. Emotions tend to become intensified. Rhythm and syncopation in music can lessen intellectual control. Art forms can stimulate kinesthetic responses. Suggestibility can operate at a submerged level of consciousness, and persons can become partially hypnotized until they are ready to act with almost irresistible impetuosity. While many of these effects can be all to the good, and all of God's glory, it is wise to also have the mind stimulated and led along by means of clearly outlined, thought-compelling preaching.[16] The minister does not want to manipulate worshipers, but to help them to make conscious, rational decisions in favor of God's will, which they will seriously intend to implement in their life on Monday.

XIV. Illustrations Can Help Worshipers to Apply the Word to Life

The minister who longs above all else to relay God's own Word to worshipers will copy God's own method of communication. When God spoke in His Son's preaching He used many stories, parables, and illustrations drawn from the common life. God knows that man bristles with defenses when he is approached with logical arguments, but lowers his defenses and really listens when he hears a story. Through the illustration, parable, or narrative the truth steals into the soul quietly in a kind of delayed action. When God gave the Scriptures, He did not couch His Word primarily in logical arguments, but in stories and narratives. Usually a life situation is sketched in the inspired writings in a few bold strokes, leaving the imagination of the reader or hearer to fill in the details.

The minister often uses Bible characters and their encounters with God as sermon illustrations, because man's need and God's actions are the same across the centuries. As the story is told of a man long ago who was encountered and changed by the grace of God, the similar needs of the hearer now are exposed before the same grace of God which even now presses in with readiness to invade his life to redeem it. The minister uses real-life illustrations of God's seizure of men, because what comes out of real life fits back into real life. But if the illustration is not quite in focus, suited to this truth and this congregation, the worshiper can see better without it. There is always the possibility that the minister will unwittingly distort a truth by the illustration he chooses to illuminate it.

The minister chooses illustrations which will flood light in upon truth. Illustrations can clarify meaning, arouse emotions, build atmosphere and mood, and help to make truth personal. By employing varied illustrations the minister can re-emphasize a great truth without seeming to be guilty of tiresome repetition. Well-chosen illustrations can be instructive in and of themselves and can enable hearers to remember the Word of God which has come to them. Illustrations drawn from common experiences of the worshipers can help them to move together emotionally, to yield to reciprocal influencing as a brotherhood, and to make group decisions regarding obedience almost as if they had participated in a group discussion.

XV. The Conclusion Can Suggest the Worshiper's Response to the Word

The coming of the living Word of God in the sermon should create a little preview of the judgment day. "This is the judgment, that the light has come."[17] The minister gives careful attention to the last words of the message he brings in God's name. When he brings all the thrusts of the sermon together into one powerful appeal, he needs to be very sure that the verdict and call he gives is God's Word for the hour. In brief intense sentences he summarizes what the sermon has said, relates it to life, and points to possible courses of action and obedience. The sensitive minister refuses to "push the panic button" in his conclusion merely to gain a reputation as one who can get "results."

The minister can never know all of the private business God wishes to do with each individual worshiper. God, who knows the unfinished business He has on hand with every heart, can personalize the call and claim of His Word. The minister need not try to mention all of the specific responses which might be needed. As one worshiper who is also standing under the judgment and call of the living Word of God, the minister may well conclude the sermon with the direct appeal: " 'Choose you . . . but as for me and my house, we will serve the Lord.' This is what this Word from God is saying to me."

The conclusion should suggest to worshipers that "all of history is but prelude. The future begins now." The minister should try to help worshipers to make responsible decisions in line with Holy Spirit promptings and the Scriptures' appeal. He should assure the worshipers of cosmic support and purposes which invite him onward in the paths of right action. Whoso doeth these sayings of mine builds his house upon a rock. It is an awesome responsibility to attempt to speak for God. The congregation should be undergirding the minister in intercessory prayer as he makes clear the appeal for response and the call for a verdict.

XVI. The Art of Persuasive Speech Can Be Made To Serve the Word

The minister must be supremely concerned that Holy Ghost-given discernment has guided his study and that God-given power and unction are operating while he delivers the sermon. People with itching ears may desire oratory rather than unction, and the minister himself may be tempted to rely upon cleverness and elegance, the "excellence of speech and men's wisdom." But, art and holy skill can be brought into the service of the proclamation of God's living Word in a reverent and effective way. Only spurious art calls attention to itself, and the art of persuasive speech can be employed so that men see Jesus only.

Clarity of style can avoid "darkening counsel with words." Skillful repetition can emphasize a truth. The "torrential simplicity" and earnestness of a passionate soul can make the sermon more effective. Good taste which eliminates stylistic blemishes can avoid offending unnecessarily the cultured hearers. Picture words and luminous phrases can make the truth live and linger in the memory. Sanctified imagination can recreate the drama and intensity of the original scene portrayed by a Biblical narrative.

The minister communicates with his whole person when he preaches. Bodily tonicity and gestures can help or hinder. Eye contact is important. Variations in voice volume and posing of questions can help the worshipers to keep thinking and feeling together. Although the "holy whine" is offensive, an appropriate use of sincerely reverential tone can add to the total communication process in preaching.

XVII. The Sermon Should Be Three-Way Communication

The minister is standing in an I-Thou dialogue with the living God as he preaches. The message he is preaching is laying bare the thoughts and intents of his own heart. Often he is so humbled and almost crushed with the message of judgment which comes from the Word of God upon his own life that he must forget for a moment the unclean-lipped people, and cry out to God, "Woe is me!" The offer of God's forgiveness and grace for growth in Christlikeness must be newly claimed by his own soul even as he offers it in God's name to others.

But the minister is also a "prompter" in a dialogue which is going on between God and the congregation. In Scripture reading and sermon the preacher attempts to articulate what God is wanting to say. The sermon should be saying aloud some of the very pleas which the convicting Holy Spirit is saying deep in the heart of many a worshiper. In his audible prayers the minister attempts to articulate for the worshipers their cries of response to God. As he preaches and prays he is trying to declare the common faith of the congregation, the fresh commitments of the people in this present moment, and the Word which is even now proceeding out of the mouth of God. Furthermore, the congregation which is listening intently and worshiping actively all the while is sending back to the sensitive minister its own signals of response, its wordless cries of "No, no, I don't understand," or "yes, yes, go on."

Thus the preacher participates in the alternates between three tremendous realities as he preaches. He must enter deeply into the reality of the God-man dialogue which is being described in the passage of Scripture which he is expositing. He must share totally in the new creating and redeeming deed which God is even now performing in the life of every worshiper who responds in Spirit and in truth. He must also feel keenly the two-way communication which is flashing between himself and the listening, worshiping congregation.

XVIII. The Minister Should Plan His Year's Preaching

It is a great responsibility to be God's servant, charged to give to God's family "their meat in due season." How shall the minister decide, amidst the almost overwhelming mass of Christian truth, which themes he shall preach? He might decide to preach through the Bible, taking six years to get from Genesis to Revelation, as some preachers have attempted. Would this be a good way to plan a preaching diet for a congregation and to be sure that the whole counsel of God has been preached? Obviously this method is faulty. Once in six years might be too often to preach upon certain passages in Chronicles, and not often enough to preach on the ascension of Christ or the coming of the Holy Spirit. Any plan should be flexible enough to provide opportunity for the minister to preach sermons addressed to crisis situations in the lives of members of his congregation, in the community, or in the world at large.

Preaching is worthy of a plan. Only trivial things dare to be haphazard. The preacher who serves for years, choosing themes by impulse from week to week, will not likely present the whole counsel of God in fair proportion. His ideas may fail to agree with one another in a total whole. Anyone who floats like a sea gull over the whole sea of Christian truth, and merely dips here and there without a plan, cannot imagine that his ministry of God's Word is giving a coherent and comprehensive presentation of Christian truth.

The minister who has a plan for his preaching can avoid the temptation to ride his pet hobby and overuse the easy texts. He can avoid wasting time and energy in the week-by-week uncertainty regarding what he should preach next. He can use his wider reading and study to better advantage if he has file folders waiting in which to place materials relevant to sermons which are in the slowly ripening stage. He can make better use of small units of time if his preaching is following a plan. His sermons will be more mature, showing the benefit of ripe reflection, if they are not always wrought out in the few days before a given Sunday.

Some ministers have tried to guarantee variety and coverage in their preaching by deliberately varying their objectives throughout the year. Thus, New Year to Easter might be given to evangelistic preaching, Easter to summer to devotional, summertime to doctrinal, and fall months to ethical sermons. Other ministers outline the great doctrines, and "things most surely believed," or the "fundamental facts of the faith," and preach through the list so that every few years the people have had a good coverage of Bible doctrine.

Some ministers suggest "The Church and the World" as an overarching framework within which to plan a year's preaching. Before Christmas the ministers would preach sermons relating to the world's need of a Saviour and around Christmas time, the coming of the world's Saviour. Before Easter he would preach about man's repentance and clinging to the world's Saviour, and at Easter time about the way the Saviour gives eternal life to men. Until Pentecost the preacher would select themes which set forth the way in which men fellowship in the life eternal in the Christian church. Then through the summer he might preach about the privileges and duties of individual discipleship.

XIX. Salvation History Provides a Good Plan for a Year's Preaching

"Salvation history" offers many advantages as a suitable framework for a year's preaching. Just as God's people Israel refused to make the recurring seasons (winter, spring, summer, fall), or a fertility cycle, the framework of their yearly worship, so the church may well refuse semi-pagan suggestions. The calendar of preaching emphases or the Christian year of worship should not be cluttered with Insurance Sunday, Be Kind to Dumb Animals Sunday, Memorial Sunday, Independence Sunday, and other special days. The church should be exceedingly reluctant to seize upon certain Sundays to promote denominational programs, such as Church Camps Day.

A "salvation history" pattern of yearly preaching would insure that the great trunk-line themes of the Christian faith would be reaffirmed again and again. A faith which is completely rooted in the actual redeeming deeds of God in history might well pace its very worship life by a recurrent remembering of God's mighty acts. Evidently the early church followed some such pattern since the Gospel of Mark's arrangement of materials fits the early Christian-Jewish festivals, and John's discourses seem to fit the sequence of Passover, Pentecost, Tabernacles, and round to Passover once more.[18]

In the months before Christmas (September, October, and November, and including what the Christian calendar calls Advent) the preaching themes might well deal with God's deeds in creation, His providential leading of His people, and His redeeming deeds at the Red Sea, Mt. Sinai, and Canaan by which He called His people into covenant. The period which the Christian calendar calls Advent is entirely too brief to lift out representative truths from this vast portion of salvation history.

The Christmas season calls for preaching on the incarnation. The launching of the God-Man into history fulfills the hopes and fears of all of the years. Sermons should ponder and probe as deeply as possible into the unfathomable mystery and glory of Emmanuel, God with us.

The manifestation of the God-Man to earth's wise men

(called Epiphany) shows God coming to the Gentiles, even as Christmas shows Him coming to expectant Jews such as Simeon and Anna. When God finally rent the veil of the temple and came out of the Jewish holy place, the Gentile centurion believed. Jesus Christ is indeed the true God whom pagans ignorantly are seeking in their worship. He is the "unrecognized depths of all pagan expectation." As pagan religions become resurgent in the world, the Christian preacher will want to include the Epiphany theme in his preaching.

In the weeks before Easter the minister may well picture the temptations which seduce a man to deny his God and his Christ. Like Israel's forty years being tempted with daily bread anxiety, and Christ's forty days being tempted with hunger, questions about divine providence and protection, and the glitter of the world's glory—so the church moves through the forty days preceding Easter. Man cannot meet the tempter's power in his own strength and must have resurrection life and power.

Because this portion of the Christian calendar—Lent—has been deformed by Roman Catholic misuse, there is no reason why the evangelical minister should ignore the season between the commemoration of Christ's birth and season when His death and resurrection are celebrated. Worship leaders, by making much of the preparation for Easter, help to symbolize the truth that the hope of man lies not in a return to Garden of Eden innocence, but through the resurrection and its new release of power toward final consummation and full Christlikeness in an aeon beyond history.

Easter time deserves centrality in the life and worship of the church and in any calendar of Christian preaching. Just as the early apostles could not grasp the real meaning of Christ's life, miracles, teachings, or death until after the resurrection, so the church of all ages must look through the open tomb to understand all of her faith. No misuse by materialistic merchants or anyone else should muffle the church's message at Easter time. In the resurrection, God acted supremely and led out His new people in the new exodus. The resurrection should be a central "watershed" and emphasis in preaching to believers who are called to "walk in the resurrection." The awful height and depth of the Christian faith are set side by side in Passion Week, as the church commemorates again the horrible hour when the world's sin descended like an avalanche upon the Son of God, and when God's love triumphed over sin and death, and raised Christ from the grave.

The ascension of Christ to His present place of mediatorial power and glory and the coming of the Holy Spirit to endue His church with power—these form another mighty mountaintop in salvation history. Once a year is infrequent enough to preach on these tremendous themes, and at what more appropriate time could this be done than when these miracles are commemorated in the Christian calendar? The minister who chooses to ignore the Christian year, and who selects his themes by his private personal leadings or impulses, may well find himself passing by, without notice, these crucial and momentous occasions in the life of the people of God. Every minister intends to preach on the work of the Holy Spirit at least once each year. Why should he not do so on Whitsunday?

Those who choose to pace their preaching each year alongside of a commemoration of the redeeming deeds of God will find that for the one half of the year, from October through April, they are preaching about the divine activity. Sermons deal with incarnation, passion, death, resurrection, ascension, and coming of the Holy Spirit. During the other one half of the year, May through September, the sermons may well deal with the human response. The first part of the year's preaching will accent the *kerygma,* God's saving deeds; and the last half of the Christian calendar will accent the *didache.* But just as October through April traces the ways in which God broke in in redeeming power long ago, so in May through September the sermons should trace the ways in which God waits to break into human awareness and confusion now.

The period from Pentecost until Advent season begins may well be filled with Bible book studies. A series of expository sermons from prophets or epistles may be used in which God's will for His people's obedience is set forth. When sentimental worldlings celebrate Mother's Day, the minister may preach upon God's plan for the home. Near to the Fourth of July the minister may preach on Christ's lordship over history and human governments, or upon the social responsibility of the salt and light church. The second half of the Christian year is sometimes referred to as "kingdomtide" or "Trinity season," and is a good time to observe the present situations in which God's kingdom is waiting to break through in power.

The use of salvation history as a framework within which to plan a year's preaching provides a compass whose needle always points to Christ. It offers a large and adequate design within which individual sermons or brief sermon series can be set. It attempts to balance *kerygma*—the acts of God, and *didache*, the believer's obedient response, in Christian preaching. It ties the worship of the church to those actual redeeming deeds in history which are the factual basis of the faith of the church. It offers a uniting tie to bind believers of all brotherhoods, if they are all commemorating the saving acts of God at nearly the same time. Salvation history, surveyed each year as a framework for preaching, can help to make the Bible come alive and Biblical theology to penetrate the pulpit and Christian preaching.

Chapter 3

The Minister Serves as a Counselor

I. The Minister Sometimes Leaves the Ninety and Nine and Counsels with the One

The minister of the Word soon learns that he must do more than preach God's Word to the congregation. He cannot lead the congregation to become good counselors to one another unless he takes time to counsel too. Always the Christian minister seeks to pattern his ministry after that of his Master, Jesus Christ. Christ often left His preaching ministry to the crowds and gave His undivided attention to the one. In fact, the inspired prophet had foreseen that one aspect of Christ's redeeming ministry would be that of "Counselor." If detailed verbatims had been preserved from His interviews, we can be certain they would reveal His usual suffering love.

Many requests for undivided and sustained attention will come to the minister as he moves among persons ministering God's Word during their happy and solemn crises such as sickness, birth of a child, tragedy, vocational choice, marriage, or bereavement. During crucial choices and crises along life's pilgrimage the average Christian comes to his best understanding of himself and of his faith.

Each of these happy or solemn crises of life will polarize the counseling situation in a slightly different way. During premarital counseling the person's understanding of what true love is will come into focus. His understanding of the place of sex within a mature person's personality will be scrutinized. His ability to give and to receive love within a covenant of growing oneness will be noted. His awareness of the unique roles of male and female will be probed.

During vocational counseling the counselee will need to examine his own charismatic gifts, his selfhood, his unique potential, and sense of purpose in his existence. His ability to relate his own life to Christ's call to discipleship and the world's need for help will be searched out. The counselee will need to clarify his basic self-image, his sense of destiny, his deepest convictions as to the meaning of life itself, and his belief about the way in which a man's daily work should be related to the redeeming work which God is doing in His world. Temptations of materialism or social snobbery will abound during the crisis of vocational choice.

A grief situation again calls for counseling, but the inner integrity and values of the person are searched out by the grief process in still other ways. The person's tendencies to deify finite existence, to make a god out of a loved one, or to doubt immortality are likely to come into focus during grief. The person's ability to deal with guilt feelings, to endure a meaningful loss, or to cope with loneliness are laid bare during the counseling situation in the midst of acute grief. The resurrection may become a personal reality for the first time, rather than a remote date on a cosmic calendar. The grieving person needs a counselor whose faith is grounded in eternity, but who knows how a grieving person feels.

Members of a congregation may really learn the length and breadth and depth and height of the love of Christ in which they live their lives when they attempt seriously to rejoice with them who rejoice and to weep with them who weep. The minister learns what themes should recur in his preaching as he listens to the deep longings of the human spirit which are expressed during counseling.

Each of the specific types of counseling situations cannot be explored in this one brief lecture, but rather basic principles will be set forth which should guide the pastoral counselor and the members of the congregation in their counseling, whether the situation be sickness, guilt, marriage problem, grief, or incipient mental illness. The goals of the minister's counseling are always to lead the person to autonomous insight, so that personal faith may be brought to bear upon the underlying causes of the problem.

II. The Minister's Role as Servant of God's Servants Can Add Strength to the Minister's Counseling

As servant to the members of the congregation the minister may take the initiative and start the counseling relationship with a troubled person. Other counselors must wait until the person seeks them out. By then the trouble ofttimes has progressed almost beyond redemption point. Furthermore, the minister usually knows the case history of the person, the interpersonal relationships of which he is a part, and the person's past performance in social functioning. The minister is one of the leaders of an entire congregation of caring, sharing, burden-bearing believers. He is the pastor of the priesthood of believers.

The minister of God's Word usually enjoys the confidence of his counselees. He does not need to risk driving them away with a charge which they cannot pay. Because his time is paid by the church, he represents the good will and concern of a great number of persons. He also represents moral order, righteousness, and God's Word and will in the minds of most persons who come to him for help. With some extremely neurotic persons this may be a hindrance to good relationships, but with many troubled persons it is a distinct asset.

The minister fits into the "brother role" rather than the "father role" as a priest would do. People come to him for help, tacitly admitting that their trouble lies in the spiritual side of their existence. When they go to a medical doctor they stubbornly hope that he will find some physical maladjustment upon which they can "blame" their trouble.

When a church member comes to the minister for counsel, he is asking that the Christian faith be made relevant in a specific situation. This is exactly the attitude which is necessary and most favorable for God to work His deeds of deliverance. Whereas neurotic guilt can be removed by removing illusions, fantasies, phobias, resentments, and repressions on the purely human level, real guilt is removed only when the guilty person deals with specific sin, claims God's forgiveness in an act of faith, and becomes willing to disown it by making restitution. The minister has, in the Christian Gospel which he preaches and teaches, the only adequate cure for the real guilt of man. Because the minister consciously seeks to embody the full power of agape, divine love in his relationship with the counselee, this love-charged relationship becomes a great source of strength in his counseling.

Because the minister can proclaim God's forgiving grace, the counselee can dare to become honest and to admit his weaknesses, fears, and sins. The minister himself stands in constant need of and must constantly claim Christ's grace and forgiveness. He is always aware as he counsels that Christ's convicting Spirit reveals sin and need only that He might offer to take it away. Because the minister knows that he himself is living before God only by God's gracious acceptance, therefore he can offer that same accepting love to a counselee whose unworthiness may be of a different kind than his own.

The minister preaches a Word of God which asserts the tremendous worth and redeemability of every man. The Word points the way to the power available for man's depth-level renewal and transformation. The Word of God points toward man's final redemption and perfection in Christlikeness. The minister listens and suffers with the seeking counselee so that he may help the living God to say His Word of judgment and forgiveness. The minister helps the counselee to bring the problem out into ultimate reality before the face of God. Then the minister attempts to translate God's offer of forgiveness into the terms which the counselee must hear spoken now and must feel in relationships.

Persons sometimes impute wrong roles to the pastoral counselor. The minister must refuse to pose as "the protector from the wrath of God." He must not allow persons to regard him as a "celestial druggist," dispensing heavenly antibiotics and vitamins. He is not the "magical medicine man" or the "special priestly intermediary" between God and man. The minister has been charged and ordained primarily to preach God's Word. God's Word does give understandings of man which are crucial in counseling, and these insights do enrich his counseling ministry. But the minister does not seek a special relatedness because he is ordained.

The minister of the Word is convinced that the living Lord has promised to reveal Himself uniquely in the "two-situation," where two (or three) are met in Christ's name, seeking to find Christ's will in a matter and to bind themselves to it in fuller obedience. The minister of God's Word should remain primarily the brother, the servant, the preacher, the teacher, even while he serves as counselor.

Because the minister counsels as a "brother" and not as a "father," he is in a better position than is the Roman Catholic "father-priest." Transferences of hostility toward a father figure are not so likely to confuse the situation. The minister is in a better position to point away to the heavenly Father who alone has love and grace enough to absorb all the hostilities of all men.

III. The Minister Needs Self-Awareness as a Counselor

One who would serve as a psychoanalyst must first submit to psychoanalysis. This is so that he may discover the beams in his own eyes before he sets out to remove motes from the eyes of other persons. The sincere minister will also seek self-awareness. Christ cried, "For their sakes I sanctify myself," and the minister will want to be as free as possible from inner contradictions, inhibitions, compulsions, and personality quirks. In every person whom the minister counsels he will find some aspect of his own unmet needs mirrored. If the minister has not achieved some self-awareness, he will not be able to really help the other person, but will unwittingly use the other person, projecting his own unmet needs upon him and the situation.

Some ministers are threatened by this fact. Cannot God transcend His servant's weaknesses and mistakes? Did not God overrule so that Wesley's inability to get along with his wife at home helped to set him upon the open road in effective evangelism? Cannot God use the weak things of the world? After all, the excellency of the power is of God and not of man, so why be concerned about the emotional maturity of the minister who counsels? It is gloriously true that God can pour His clean Gospel and grace through slightly warped and soiled channels, but why tempt the Almighty and make His work still more difficult and ineffective?

The minister needs to seek (and almost to agonize) to achieve self-awareness because a number of factors conspire against his really knowing himself. Some persons impute to him a "prima-donna," "holy man" role and expect him to be one who lives above the temptations to which human flesh is heir. He must struggle to free himself from this imprisoning stereotype and to be really honest.

Furthermore, his theological and Biblical education may have been too much a "farsighted" thing, focused only upon persons long ago and far away. The struggles and reality which Jeremiah or Paul knew twenty or more centuries ago may have been safely "embalmed" in verbal categories. The student may have become an expert in playing intellectual "ping-pong" with theological propositions without ever facing his own unmet needs. In recent years field work and the study of the dynamics which operate in Christian groups have helped to make God-man relationships become contemporary for some students, but the danger of verbalism and unreality still persists.

If the minister hears only the clamor of the inner warring in his own members, he may not be able to hear the half-articulated groanings of spirit hidden in the conversation of the counselee. If the minister is an insecure person, he may not be able to endure to have the counselee to disagree with him. If the minister has suppressed guilt fermenting in the deep places of his own stored memories, he may need to expose and to judge harshly the guilt of another. If the minister does not have a feeling of genuine core worth and self-respect, he may need to dominate others and to show his authority so as to reassure himself. All the while the counselee is not really being helped, but is being used and abused by the counselor.

If the minister is troubled with inferiority feelings, he may compensate by displaying his erudition and learning. He may not be able to listen quietly until the counselee achieves insight but may "tell him off" too soon. If the minister has a neurotic need for love, he may seek admiration or pity as a substitute for it. He may tell stories of his own sufferings, similar to those being recounted by the counselee, merely to satisfy his own insatiable need for love and attention.

The minister who would counsel others should understand what scars (or festering wounds yet unhealed) may remain within him from his own interpersonal and spiritual pilgrimage through childhood and adolescence. He should be secure enough in his own understanding of reality as it is between God and man so that he is unthreatened by deviations or persons who act out before him their need to rebel. He should be able to "catch himself at it" when he himself engages in security operations or attempts detour routes around reality. Even though he is aware of the way both heredity and environment have molded his life, yet he should examine carefully what he is doing now with the free space he still has in every moment as he decides either in line with God's will or against it.

The minister may achieve some self-awareness by keeping verbatim records of his own counseling interviews and then re-reading them in soul-searching reflection. If the minister can secure some "clinical training" by sharing in a group of counselors (who are also re-appraising their behavior as counselors) this will be an invaluable learning experience. If this sharing can be guided by someone with experience in clinical training, the maximum benefit will be secured.

The minister who goes often into the very presence of God in worship, Bible exposition, and prayer should expect some self-awareness to come to him while in the midst of the most intense and transparent God-encounter. The most intense revelation of God is at one and the same time the most humbling revelation of man. When Isaiah saw God he discovered the uncleanness on his own lips. The minister should cherish, and even write down for later reflection, the selfhood which he discerns during his most exalted moments of worship. After times of failure, if the minister will go before God in desperation crying, "Lord, why could not we . . . ?" God may often grant new insights into areas of his life in which divine grace needs to penetrate.

The minister should seek self-understanding also by periodically practicing confessional meditation in the prayer closet. He should avoid the pretty phrases, pious clichés, and strive to relive his shameful and "doghouse" experiences in transparent honesty there alone before God. What he "there remembereth" about his relationship to his brother may be an insight more penetrating than any psychoanalyst's couch could afford. While in confessional meditation the minister should let one incident "hook" on to another by free association. As new incidents come to awareness they should be "dredged" up into the healing, forgiving presence of God Himself and there be disowned. Sins which are discovered should be named for what they are without evasion. Much help can come from such honesty in prayer. The person who has fallen on his face before God, overwhelmed by a feeling of his own unworthiness will soon find, as did Ezekiel, that God sets him on his own feet again and invites him to go on serving.[1]

The minister who would counsel others must be willing to receive counsel from others as well. He should cultivate relationships of openness and transparent honesty with a brother or brethren who are known to possess the gift of Holy Spirit wisdom and discernment. The minister should periodically go to trusted and qualified counselors both within and beyond the local congregation who may help him see himself as he is. Ofttimes the minister's wife can speak the critical truth in love. In some cases a fellow minister or bishop may be able to bring understanding and help as a minister seeks to identify the areas of growth in his own inner life. As the Word of God is mediated to the minister through the lips of a Spirit-indwelt brother, the Word may again lay bare the very thoughts and intents of the minister's heart.

The reflected appraisals of others in face-to-face group interaction may also help the minister to know himself as he really is. When members of a searching, witnessing group will speak out honestly, the very secrets of a person's heart may be laid bare by the experience.[2] If sometimes a trained observer will "hold the mirror" for the minister, and will report back to him just how he operates in a group process, the findings may be extremely helpful.

In all of the minister's search to "know himself as he is known" it is important that self-awareness should not lead to dull despair. The minister needs to know where his growth areas are so that he may open them consciously to the creative and redeeming activity of God's grace. If he is doing this, he can still preach, "Follow me as I follow Christ," even though in some areas of his personality spiritual maturity is not fully realized. He can help a counselee search for God's intent for his life, taking the form of a servant as he listens in love, even though the counselee may have gone on beyond the minister himself in some aspects of Christian maturity. The minister who lives honestly before God and man need not retreat behind shibboleths, but can minister the truth of the Gospel even in the counseling situation.

IV. In Many Situations One Interview Is Adequate

The minister should not be so eager to counsel persons that he seeks to establish a long-term counseling relationship every time a member comes to him for help with a problem. Part of his "holy skill" is to discern when one interview will do and then to let it go at that. There are some earmarks to suggest when this is the case.

If the person is stable emotionally, has reasonable intelligence, can talk about the problem without emotional blocking, and if there is good rapport between the minister and the member, then many problems can be dealt with in one interview. The minister's task then is to "walk along side of" the person as he moves through a complete act of thought. Many persons have never learned a technique of problem solving and the minister can be a friend to help them to learn it.

First, the minister should help the person to identify the problem, to localize it, and if necessary to separate it from other problems. Often a problem is so related to other areas of confusion that this is difficult. As the problem is lifted up for a detailed analysis, other problems cling to it like spaghetti being forked from a dish.

Only a quack will prescribe without first having a diagnosis. A wise minister will "hear the person out" as the person analyzes the problem in his presence and will be slow to begin suggesting solutions. He may ask questions to fill in missing gaps of information. He may ask what solutions the person has already tried, to whom he has talked about the problem, and what solutions he sees as most promising at the moment.

The minister may help the person to "count the cost" of each projected solution which is being contemplated. He may attempt a summary of all that the person has said so far, and even suggest other solutions or offer other facts which have not been a part of the person's problem-solving data. The minister may lift up for attention the person's long-range goals which may help to guide the person in making the present decision. The minister should support the person in prayer as he decides and may loan him reading material which will help him.

The minister should refuse to "play God" and to decide for the person. If the person can plan a realistic solution and plan of action the interview may be considered as complete. If the person's decision-making powers are deadlocked in filibuster, this may be a sign that longer counseling is needed.

V. Some Cases Need a Deeper, Sustained Relatedness

Some of the happy crises, such as premarital counseling or vocational choice, usually call for more than one interview. The interviews lengthen out into a counseling relationship, simply because of the complexity of the problem, or because the problem comes to focus only gradually in the person's experience.

Grief, which is a solemn crisis, always calls for a counseling relationship, because of the "stages" of grief through which the person moves. Grief's work simply cannot be hurried or telescoped so that it can all be dealt with in one interview.

Problems of doubt, guilt feelings, broken interpersonal relations, unreality in Christian experience, and marital problems are the kind with which the minister has to deal most frequently. In the description of the counseling process which follows, these more "negative types of problem" will be assumed rather than the happy crisis-type problem such as vocational choice or premartial counseling.

A long-term counseling relatedness is called for if and when the counselee is too emotionally involved to come to a sane decision. If there is fantasy or unrealistic wishful thinking, the minister should labor to restore the person's capacity for autonomous decision rather than to "save time" by deciding for him. If the person's will power is too feeble to act, the minister should try to put the person "on his own before God" again. The minister should help the person to trace his emotional problems upstream to the spring or dam which affects them. Time, privacy, and a relationship of trust and love are needed for catharsis and emotional re-education.

Many problems which persons have are not completely rational. They forget in selective fashion, repressing some of the things which are too painful to contemplate. They "scapegoat" the blame upon someone else. They find an acceptable "reason" for their unacceptable behavior. They build a "detour route" around the center of the problem or "talk it to death" by attacking a secondary aspect of the problem. Even sincere Christian people can fall into such evasion patterns. The minister offers to enter a responsive relationship with the person as he seeks to work his way through to insight and a realistic solution.

VI. The Minister Should Invite the Counselee to Share In a Covenant of Trust and Mutual Search

Before deeper anxieties and fears can be safely shared, it is essential that mutual trust exists. The counselee must be confident that the minister will not betray him, use his case for a sermon illustration, or allow it to become neighborhood gossip. The minister can propose a mutual understanding that both the counselor and the counselee will consult with each other before either of them discusses their interview with anyone else.

After insight has come and God's grace has begun to work and to heal in the troubled spirit of the counselee, then the counselee himself will most likely want to share his new-found insights and release with other concerned friends. But in the early stages of counseling the "covenant of confidence" may provide needed structure and be of real support and help to the counselee.

The minister and the member who are seeking together for a solution to a deeply rooted problem should plan for a series of interviews, preferably of one hour each, and at the same hour each week. They agree to "march around the wall seven times" before they expect to claim the victory. They agree to move forward toward solutions only as the counselee gains the needed insight, strength, and confidence to act decisively in line with what has been discerned to be God's will in the matter.

Within the covenant of trust and confidence the minister and the counselee explore the problem together. Even though the minister says very little, he should listen deeply, asking himself just how he would feel if he had experienced exactly what the counselee has gone through. Together they explore the deeper meanings and motivations which underlie the counselee's conduct. They relive the "burning bush" experiences of the past, the times when the counselee has said either "yes" or "no" to the living God. They explore the counselee's basic way of existing before God and with the brother. They talk together about the "durably meaningful" things which have been found in life. They look for the satisfactions which outlast life itself which the counselee has been finding in his life so far. They notice patterns of aversion or dependency in the relationship of the counselee with those persons who matter most in his life.

Physical or functional symptoms which may appear in the counselee's person during times of deep anxiety also deserve attention. Sometimes symptoms are "the amplified voice of conscience." A person's body often reveals what his voice will not reveal. Thus ulcers may reveal the presence of suppressed tension. Sleeplessness may disclose the presence of a massive frustration. Asthma may be the body's way of calling out for love and attention.

VII. The Minister and Counselee Count upon the Holy Spirit

If the person who has come for counsel is one in whom Christ's life dwells and moves, then the Holy Spirit is already a participant in the counseling situation at a very deep level. The Holy Spirit can help to decode the unutterable groanings of the distressed person. The Holy Spirit can work beneath the level of conscious awareness, convicting of sin, and bringing the words of Christ to remembrance at the appropriate time. The minister need not judge, since it is the Holy Spirit's task to bring conviction if that is needed. When feelings surge which are too deep for utterance the Holy Spirit can help the minister to "hear," even when no words are spoken.

The time may come during the surfacing of guilty secrets that the counselee will "scapegoat" the minister, heaping hostility upon him. If the Holy Spirit power is at work within the minister so that "rivers of living water" well up from his inner being, then he will have the grace and strength to absorb the hostility and to overcome evil with good in nonresistant, suffering love. If the minister can allow death to work in him, then life can work in the groping soul to whom he is ministering in a counseling relatedness.

There will be many times throughout the agonizing search for understanding in which the minister and the troubled counselee share when neither one will know what to say. The Holy Spirit can help both together to interpret their groanings before God in prayer. If in penitence and confession the counselee has poured it all out before God, the Holy Spirit can enable the minister to say the absolving, forgiving word with assurance and reality. The minister should claim the Spirit's enabling for this so that he may loose only that sin which has already been loosed in heaven. The minister should claim in simple faith the promise of Christ: "He breathed on them, and saith unto them, Receive ye the Holy Ghost; whose soever sins ye remit, they are remitted unto them, and whose soever sins ye retain, they are retained."[3] Christians are more likely to claim the Holy Spirit's help when counseling with their minister than if they are counseling with someone in a secular agency.

If the minister is a "growing saint" himself, he will remember occasions in his own life when a brother helped him to achieve forgiveness or clarity in a situation of his own need. The minister will be touched with the feelings of the counselee's infirmities. He will constantly admit by his attitudes that he is a man of like passions with the counselee.

VIII. The Minister Suffers with the Counselee In Their Search

The minister should not announce to the counselee that he is going to give him accepting, nonjudgmental, listening love. He should concentrate upon actually giving such love, and the person will sense and feel it like a subterranean flow of reality between them. The counselee, because of his anxious and burdened condition, may resent little things, such as pictures on the wall, something about the minister's desk, his clothes, or his opening remarks. The minister should be sensitive and responsive to all of such cues.

The minister should respect silences. Many a sufferer would cry as did Job to his too-talkative counselors, "Hold your peace . . . that I may speak." The minister seeks to enter deeply within the counselee's own private world of experience until he can look out upon life through his glasses. Silences, tears, bodily tonicity, gestures, twitchings can all be an eloquent language to the counselor who has trained his heart to understand and to care. The feelings of the counselee are often more important than the bare facts which he may be recounting. The minister should be there, living with the person's search, and not merely observing alongside.

Listening will come hard for the minister who is constantly being invited to "say a few words." He has outlines of speeches ready on many subjects. Something the counselee says will seem to call for some nuggets of wisdom from a favorite sermon. The minister needs to discipline himself sternly to remain silent and to listen deeply. He remembers that often love and truth can only come to persons through meaningful suffering.

If the minister has succeeded in becoming a "participant observer" of the counselee's sufferings, then his own feelings can be a clue as to the way the counselee is feeling. The minister may well ask himself: How would I feel if all of this had happened to me and if I were sitting over there where the counselee is? There are no "data" which a minister dares to evaluate in a completely detached and objective way. The listening love of the minister, while it should be fair and impartial, dare not be felt by the counselee to be indifference. In his deep desire to understand, the minister will often record the basic interchange of the interview, and study and restudy a series of these records carefully.

As he listens the minister must resist the tendency to classify and to pigeonhole the person's problem. If the minister has been counseling for many years he may conclude too quickly, "Oh, I know this type." The counselee's uniqueness must be respected, his core worth appreciated, and he must be allowed to come to insight and to self-awareness at his own pace. The minister should "join God" as a watcher and a participant, believing that because of the universal priesthood of all believers the counselee has direct access to the mind of God and can be hearing God speak to him in precious immediacy.

IX. By "Reflecting Back" the Minister Can Help The Counselee to Gain Insight

The questions which the minister does ask should not be of a cross-examining, "third-degree" type. Often the minister's questions will be "calls in the dark." He may ask, "Did I understand you to say? . . ." or "Am I hearing you correctly?" and then proceed to rephrase and reflect back the counselee's thoughts as he himself heard them. This also reassures the counselee that the minister understands and cares. When puzzled, the minister can honestly remark, "I wonder why you said that." Often the minister's questions, grunts, and nods will be merely encouragements to the counselee to keep talking.

As the counselee verbalizes his problem he gets it "on the outside of himself" where he can look at it better. Because he himself says a certain thing about himself, he can accept it. The minister can encourage the counselee to go on with more revelations of his inner self if the minister uses understatement when he rephrases. If the minister can really give unconditional love, the counselee may feel secure to admit the unpleasant parts of his problem more quickly. Most of the problems of persons reside in their emotions rather than their intellect.

The counselee selects, session by session, often unconsciously, just what he will reveal about his inner life and feelings. The minister responds to the most dynamic factors and those in which traumatic or repressed feelings are most likely to be found. These areas include early relationship to parents, early sex experiences, excessive rivalry with siblings, early sickness or deformity, traumatic failures, crucial choices along life's way, present relationships to persons who are important to him, and the loss of a sense of direction for the future.

As insight dawns, the counselee begins to see new depths in old facts and relationships. He starts to understand his own contribution to the pattern of relationships of his life. He can explain why all of his "tracks are defaced," like a bear which was once caught in a trap. His patterns of reaction and evasion may come clear to him as an almost overpowering revelation. If, however, the counselee begins to "spout psychiatric banalities," talking about his "electra complexes," this is a bad sign. This is almost always an evasion device.

The minister knows that the counselee's characteristic way of evading or confronting reality in his life will likely indicate his way of relating to his God. If the person constantly offers alibis, he is not yet ready for constructive help. If the counselee consistently deposits the "blame for what's wrong" at the door of other people in his life, then he is not yet able to hear God's Word of forgiveness for his own very real sins. If the counselee can dare to look at his whole self, just as he is, and can accept himself because God and at least one person, his minister, also accept him, then he can begin to claim God's grace to change and to grow.

The minister should not work either ahead of or behind the counselee as he moves through his problem-solving process. If the person's "decision-making powers are deadlocked in fili-buster," the minister should labor to free them, and not decide for him. The counselee will usually reject a solution which is sprung upon him too soon.

X. The Minister May Use the Scriptures As an Interpreter's Guidebook

The Scriptures are filled with "case histories," actual records of the anxieties of persons, clashes in relationships, and of God's working to free and redeem man. The minister should not "seek the parallel case" within the Bible, however. There are too many variables which are unknown, so that the minister cannot know when he has before him a person whose need "just exactly fits" the case of the rich young ruler or the maniac from Gadara.

If the person is seriously neurotic or disturbed, the minister may need to be slow to turn to the words of Scripture for help. A sick person will often "ink-blot" the Scriptures much as a neurotic imputes weird meaning to the blots in a Rorschach test. The neurotic person will often distort the meaning of a Scripture so as to retread his own disturbed pattern of thinking and so miss the Bible's real message. Thus, a neurotic legalist may seize tenaciously upon the phrase, "Work out your own salvation with fear and trembling."

The minister can call attention to the great, recurring theological themes of the Bible and point to specific illustrations of the way in which God accepts and forgives, even while His absolute holiness judges. The God who loves more than His prophet Jonah can understand, who absorbs hostility on Calvary so as to forgive, and who tirelessly invites persons into covenant—this is the God whom the troubled counselee needs to meet anew.

The psalms contain many portions which record the desperate search of a concerned person for God's answer to a problem. Many of the psalms begin in the minor key of complaint and end upon the note of release and praise. The New Testament is filled with "omnibus words of blessing" and pictures the "neither do I condemn thee" spirit of God's Son. If the counselor has been able to embody the love of the Gospel in his relationship with the counselee, then passages of Scripture which relate to the counselee's need may be assigned as "homework reading," to be reread and meditated upon until the next interview.[4] Thus personal discipline and discovery may dovetail with redemptive counseling.

XI. The Minister Encourages the Counselee To Face Reality and to Choose

The minister watches for the "teachable moment" when he can give a gentle encouragement to act in line with the clearest understanding of God's will. Even as Christ did with the rich young ruler, the minister respects the counselee's right to choose the wrong. Yet the minister should encourage the counselee to courageously forsake his fantasy world, to refuse former evasion patterns, and to choose what he believes to be right. The minister may help the counselee to probe to his inner motivation as God did with Cain. "Just why is your countenance fallen?" "Do you well to be angry?" Within the atmosphere of redemptive love the counselee may be able again to contemplate unpleasant truths about himself and gain the courage to attempt to change.

By a careful summary of the issues which have come to light the minister can help the counselee to choose wisely. Although the minister does "walk a little way" with the deciding person, he should encourage the counselee to look full upon the face of the forgiving God and then to make his own decision in faith.

There will always be some element of going "out, not knowing whither" to the life of faith. Counseling should not be prolonged until all questions are answered and perfect security assured. The "creative insecurity" of the walk of faith is the door out of the problem-solving counseling situation.

Even though the minister feels fairly confident that he knows the way of obedience and release which the counselee should take, he should not presume to know absolutely what God's will is for the other person. "You will be like God, knowing good and evil" (RSV) is a very subtle temptation for a minister. The counselee should stand alone before God when he chooses and when he takes a fresh position toward his destiny.

XII. The Counselee May Need to Confess His Sins in Prayer

The minister should not unconsciously elevate his pastoral counseling to a new "trafficking in forgiveness." God acted rather drastically when the Jews did this with their money changers in the temple, and again when the Roman Catholic Church huckstered her indulgences. The minister should not gauge the success of his counseling by how many members confess during interviews in his study.

Any confession which occurs in pastoral counseling should be seen as part of the brother-to-brother "confess your faults one to another, and pray one for another" which the Apostle James urges upon the entire congregation. It cannot replace the general confession of sins which the worshiping congregation makes during their corporate worship. Neither can private confession in the pastor's study replace the confession and restitution which may need to be made to someone who has been wronged.

However, just because the minister regularly expounds God's living Word with all of its power to convict of sin, he should expect that some confession will be a part of the counseling which he does in private.[5] Counseling itself may be the "cock crowing which awakens a new awareness of guilt."

But why suggest that confession be made to God in prayer? Why not just draw out the person's confession much as a priest does in a confessional or a psychoanalyst does in analysis? Because the counselee, if a Christian, is also a part of the entire priesthood of believers. He can go before the face of God directly. Furthermore, his sin is ultimately against God, as David realized, "against thee, thee only, have I sinned." If the counselee begins to sort out his feelings and deeds before God in prayer, he has already begun to step out into the light of eternity. Here his unclean lips show up. Here he can lay his sins down before God who alone can absolve, cleanse, and forgive. Sin is much more than merely "cheating on one's group," as O. Hobart Mowrer seems to suggest, and demands much more than mere restitution on the human plane.[6] There is only one fountain in all of the universe from which flows forgiveness for all the guilty secrets and sins of man, and that fountain is the heart of the eternal God as revealed in Jesus Christ. The pastor counsels so as to lead persons to the "higher Counselor," God Himself.

Only the light and love of God's judging and forgiving presence can stop the evasions by which a guilty person seeks to avoid admitting his guilt. Persons become self-righteous as a way to justify themselves. They may judge other persons harshly as a way to reassure themselves that they are "no worse than the rest of the swine." They may try by volubility to talk the issue to death. They may try by self-imposed sickness and suffering to atone for their guilt. They may resort to certain magical-religious rituals in efforts to appease their own conscience and their God. If they have refused to admit and to accept their whole selves before God, and have denied their unacceptable feelings and deeds long enough, they may have developed a split personality, a "me and a not-me," a "Dr. Jekyll and Mr. Hyde" duality. It is in face-to-face encounter with Christ that many a disciple learns that he is partly "pebbles and partly rock-man," partly Simon and partly Peter, living partly in Romans 7 and partly in Romans 8.

But the minister should also encourage the counselee who needs to confess guilt to confess it audibly in his prayer, so that the minister can hear it and really be a brother to him and help him. Only as a sin is confessed to a brother does it lose its power to terrorize and to condemn. Confession to a brother seems to be a little preview of the openness of the judgment day. The minister, as a brother in the church, represents the congregation which lives together by the grace of God.[7] Jesus gave to every Spirit-filled disciple the authority to declare absolution for a repentant brother's sin, and the minister is merely fulfilling his brotherly function when he hears the counselee's confession and declares to him, in God's name, God's forgiveness. (Whose soever sins ye remit, they are remitted unto them, and whose soever sins ye retain, they are retained. John 20:23.)

The minister often asks himself whether he should also confess his own similar need and sin to his counselee. The minister needs and wants no inscrutability such as some counselors seek to maintain. He wants no "professional distance" and anonymity behind which to operate unscathed. If he has been properly horrified at his own sin, he will not be horrified at anything the counselee divulges. If he is really living his own life in dependence upon God's unmerited forgiving grace, then he will feel no compulsive need either to hide or to divulge his own failures. He need not pretend that he is immune to the failures which human flesh is heir to.

The minister should confess or not confess his own needs to the counselee only if it might really help the counselee for him to do so. It might help the counselee for the minister to admit in a few simple sentences that he too knows the attacks of guilt feelings and failures, and that he too needs to cling hour by hour to the grace of God. But in the counseling situation the counselee already has about all he can carry of mental anguish. The attention of both minister and counselee should be totally given to the counselee's problem, and so any confessions by the minister should be kept to a minimum.

Karl Menninger hopes when therapy is completed, that then "objectivity toward the analyst increases and the magic omnipotence of the great man begins to diminish."[8] But the minister always resists any conception of himself as the "magic omnipotent great man." He serves all the while he counsels as an heir together of the grace of God. He wants Christ to increase in the counselee's life, and he is willing as a counselor to decrease.

As the minister helps the counselee to separate his real guilt from his neurotic guilt, he can reassure the counselee that God's grace has preceded them into the very depths of the counselee's spirit, and no new disclosures need frighten. Many psychoanalysts try to transfer their client's guilt from being ashamed that they have sex impulses and hostilities over to being ashamed that they were ashamed to use these urges. The minister helps the counselee to sort out his real guilt from his guilt feelings by quite a different criteria.

The minister tries to relieve the counselee's "quantitative" guilt, from "how many man-made taboos did I violate?" to a "qualitative" guilt, "I am a sinful man, O Lord." The minister tries to relieve the guilt feelings which come from admitting that one is still human, and to transfer them over to the failure to live humbly by the forgiving and enabling grace of God. The minister tries to shift the guilt away from the futile "comparing ourselves among ourselves," over to the basic sin of elevating "some other God before me" (that is, God). Many a person has not been able to stop feeling guilty for disappointing the expectancy of parents, ("thy father and I have sought thee sorrowing"), because they have not learned to assert, "I must be about Father's business."[9]

XIII. The Minister Helps the Counselee to "Plan His Homework" Between Sessions

In some cases acts of restitution may be called for, and the minister should encourage the counselee to carry through with this extremely important homework. Persons who have genuinely repented and turned from sin do desire to go and show their deeds to the involved persons. Alcoholics Anonymous urges that the repentant alcoholic make restitution "except where to do so would cause more harm." The minister's counsel can be very helpful as a counselee honestly tries to disown his past and to symbolize the reality of restored fellowship with God, with himself, and with his neighbor.

The minister should be careful not to "prescribe acts of penance," however, because this is one of the fatal practices which shifts counseling over toward the Roman Catholic confessional with its false system of earning merit by penance. Rather, the minister commends the counselee to God and the Word of His grace, reassuring him of his own and of God's sustaining concern. The counseling has not been done in the spirit of the Catholic confessional with its legalistic cataloging of mortal and venial sins. The road ahead is not charted by acts of penance and good works. Rather, the minister believes that God's grace teaches us to deny "ungodliness and worldly lusts . . . [and to] live soberly, righteously, and godly," and he merely helps the counselee to consider how his future conduct might best respond to God's grace.

XIV. The Minister May Sometimes Refer a Counselee To Other Counselors

The minister should not be in too great a hurry to refer counselees on to others. Research by Hiltner and Colston indicates that a minister's counseling tends to be more effective partly because he is doing it in the context of the life of the church. The minister "has double-barreled resources for those who have been willing to consult him."[10]

However, even though the minister is not a coward and even though he is backed by a congregation which is willing to be a redeeming fellowship of love and concern, yet he should refer some types of need on to other specialists. For example, when there are undiagnosed and untreated physical symptoms and complaints, he should insist that the counselee should see a competent physician. When the counselee has lost touch with reality at many points, is hallucinating, or is threatening violence to himself or others, the help of a competent psychiatrist should be sought. In some cases the minister himself should seek advice from a specialist in order to better serve the counselee. A book like *Where to Go for Help*[11] can be a great help to both the minister and counselee when referral is needed.

The minister should refer counselees to other counselors both within and beyond the local congregation because of the specialized services and information which they may have. Problems involving business judgment may be referred to the Christian banker. Problems involving adoption should be referred to a social worker.

The minister should encourage the member of his congregation to avoid quacks and to go only to counselors who have merited the respect of both the medical profession and Christian thinkers in general. While a few psychoanalysts may be too slavishly devoted to pure Freudian assumptions to be able to grasp the spiritual dimensions of a client's problems, yet most psychiatrists are glad to leave the client's religious faith unchallenged.

If the psychiatrist is himself a dedicated Christian, he can obviously understand better the inner spiritual experience of a Christian client. Even though the psychiatrist may be friendly toward Christian faith, if he has not known personally what it means to have the Holy Spirit at work regenerating his personality in the depth, he will be somewhat like a "blind art critic" or a "deaf music critic" as he listens to the inner thoughts of a Christian. Even so, he may be able to help correct a morbid mental state so that another person who is a Christian can lead the sufferer on to a fuller appropriation of God's grace and power. The psychiatrist who is living as a humble believer in and receiver of the grace of God should be regarded by the congregation as one of God's gifts to the community and to the church. The minister of God's Word should keep in constant dialogue with dedicated Christians who are trained in the life or behavioral sciences.

XV. The Minister Dismisses the Counselee into the Loving Care of a Church Group

The minister does not encourage the counselee to return to him again and again in an endless repetition of confession. He does not encourage the person to become completely dependent, returning for several hundred recountings of piddling bits of odds and ends from consciousness as do some of the Freudian psychoanalysts. The average length of pastoral counselings should likely not exceed four to eight interviews. If the minister's congregation is fulfilling its mandate from Christ to be the realm of redemption, the fellowship in which the forgiving love of Christ is mediated back and forth between members, then a subgroup of the church can be the perfect therapy group in which the counselee can "work out his own salvation with fear and trembling." No other counselors have a ready-made therapy group to which they can refer counselees as does the Christian minister.

Edward Thurneysen expresses it well when he says, "The advice above all other advice to come from pastoral care is: Seek the brethren! Submit to the Word! Partake of the sacrament! If it does not lead to active membership in a congregation, pastoral care is done in a void. There is no isolated forgiveness and no isolated sanctification; forgiveness and sanctification exist only in the context of the Christian community, in whose center grace and obedience continually flow from the Word."[12]

The minister does not want the counselee to feel chained to him, partly because he does not want to "play God" before people, and partly because his time must be free for his central ministry of preaching and teaching God's Word. But he calls upon the Sunday-school class or the fellowship group of the church to receive his counselee into their healing fellowship also because the church needs to be thus challenged to really be the church. The life of the congregation will be enriched and deepened if groups meet consciously and deliberately as agents of God's redeeming and reconciling love to one another and to anyone who can be drawn into their circle.

Persons who have learned, through their own experience in counseling with the minister, how to listen deeply in Christlike concern, can engage in a "group counseling" type of life together. In a Christian group of accepting love, when all admit they are in the same boat, defenses go down, the mechanisms of projection and identification lose their mystery and power, and each one finds the father, or mother, or sister, or brother which he or she may need. The atmosphere of mutual respect helps the individual to respect his own self. The positive environment of understanding love makes the false front, the guilty secret, or the neurotic bid for attention unnecessary. The group is more apt to be "right" than is one isolated counselor. Group pressures come upon the deviant in many subtle but powerful ways: by facial expressions, tonicity, and a subverbal feeling of approval or disapproval.

Within the Christian group, where Christ is present and the Holy Spirit is a participant, persons should be able to trust one another and to abandon their defense mechanisms. Infantile behavior and negative responses should be absorbed by the suffering love of Christ who dwells within and in the midst of His people. If "Mr. Bull Dozer" tries to dominate the group, or "Mr. Hiram I. Que" tries to display his learning, or "Mrs. Para Noya" feels persecuted, or "Miss Minnie Payne" needs to tell of her aches, the Christian group should have the combination of realism and love that will help the neurotic person to see himself as he is and to gain the needed power and support to change.[13] The church group should gently help neurotic people to unlearn their wrong ways of thinking, feeling, and behaving which have been causing trouble, and help them to explore and find better ways of coping with life.

XVI. But the Minister Counsels So That All May Learn To Be Better Counselors

The minister attempts to mediate God's help, guidance, and comfort to a member by counseling, so that the member in turn may comfort others with that same comfort.[14] The minister sees himself as a "servant of the Word" to all of God's serving people. He does not want to become primarily a specialist counselor who relates perpetually to each member in a one-to-one counseling relationship. The minister counsels to help to prepare a congregation of persons who can tactfully talk to one another about those things that matter most. The minister should encourage elders and other leaders of the congregation to seize opportunities for clinical experience, reading, sharing, and any other training which will improve their service as counselors. The minister should disclaim any occult power as a counselor because he has been ordained.

Jesus Himself promised to be present in a unique reality and power when two believers are talking together about a serious choice, a problem, a fault, or a growth area in the life of one of them. By thus drawing the issue out into the open in the healing atmosphere of genuine care and concern, a member receives new self-awareness and support for needed choice and change. Counseling is merely a good Christian relationship of intelligent concern lengthened and deepened and focused upon a specific problem of one person. Few problems which any one person faces are completely novel or unique. Countless others within the community of faith have already met and conquered a problem which was very similar. Within the fellowship of divine love, people seek to bear one another's burdens and so fulfill the law of Christ.

Thurneysen aptly describes the new quality which pervades the conversation of a person who lives his life before the gaze of God. "When a man makes room in himself for the Word and Spirit of God, there is something of the joy in the presence of God about him even when he does not sing. It echoes even in his common speech and lights up even in the midst of everyday conversation in a word that he says, perhaps unintended and unsought, perhaps in table conversation or in a discussion of secular matters from the newspaper."[15]

XVII. The Congregation Needs to Be Challenged To Take up Its Counseling Ministry

Christians are entirely too ready and too quick to turn their burdened or distressed loved ones over to a psychiatrist. During a meeting of the Academy of Religion and Mental Health, at the close of a day of discussion, a psychiatrist of long experience declared that 90 per cent of the persons who came to him for help did not really need the specialized care which he was trained to give. They merely needed someone with common sense and genuine concern to give them love and undivided attention. A second and then a third psychiatrist arose to say that in their experiences the same thing was true, but that they would estimate the percentage of such persons to be even higher than 90 per cent.[16]

The congregation needs to be reminded that the members, in their Spirit-infused fellowship, are the real bearers of pastoral care. Through their fellowship, mutual rebuke, and loving acceptance, God's forgiveness is to be mediated. Christ has promised His presence when two or three gather to help an erring brother. The congregation is to be a priesthood of believers, mediating God's help and forgiveness.

Members of the congregation need to be challenged by the fact that God's people have helped one another to solve problems and to find release from anxieties for centuries before Freud and before the modern counseling movement was begun. The fact that human stresses and anxieties are increasing now is no reason why the congregation's members should shy away from one another. Congregations should be called to repentance if "the less respectable sinners" and "the disturbed people" have to go outside of the bosom of the congregation to get help, to Alcoholics Anonymous, to Rescue Missions, or such other "fellowships of the disinherited." Furthermore, many a young woman, trying to fulfill her task as a mother in a home, but who cannot do so because she never really knew a mother's love herself, could be helped if a motherly woman in the congregation would take time to love her and to instruct her in the ways of rearing children in love.

The real growth of a congregation should be measured, not in numerical statistics, real-estate holdings, or social status, but in the extent to which the brotherhood has been able to bind up the brokenhearted and to bring release to captive personalities. God has committed the word of absolution to the Spirit-indwelt brother, and members of Christian congregations must be reminded of their responsibility to one another under God.

Jackson says, "It may be helpful to know that, in all probability, twenty out of every hundred of our people have been so recently bereaved in family or close circle of friends that they are seriously concerned about their personal loss and the whole matter of life, death, and immortality. Of each hundred, there are thirty-three who have problems of adjustment in marriage and home life serious enough to make deep inroads on their happiness. Probably one half have problems of emotional adjustment at home, in school, at work, or in the community that seriously impair their efficiency and affect their happiness. Twenty in the hundred are contending with neuroses that may range all the way from alcohol addiction to obsessive behavior and neurotic anxiety. From three to eight are struggling against a sense of guilt and social ostracism that comes with homosexual impulses."[17] But, a feeling of unworthiness resulting from experiences in sorrow-bearing and suffering may help to prepare some of these humble, suffering Christians to perform a helpful ministry of counseling for another sufferer. All that is required is that the first sufferer can be sufficiently healed himself and can learn some of the methods of listening, caring love which all good counselors use.

XVIII. Christians Should Know Something About the Areas in Which Human Frustrations Tend to Focus

The master urge or need which may be frustrated varies with the person and at various stages of a particular person's pilgrimage. During childhood the person seeks purely self-satisfactions and pleasures. The Freudian theory of personality dynamics offers a partial explanation of some frustrations which may happen in childhood. The adult world with its curbing of instinctual urges does frustrate the pleasure-seeking little person. Sex and aggression do remain as powerful forces within the personality and need to be reckoned with. During childhood the child struggles to individuate, to become a person, a self.

During early and later adolescence the person is attempting to wean psychologically, to become an independent, autonomous person. But remnants of helplessness and awkwardness create inferiority feelings, alternating with rebellion against any or all authority figures. Lack of parental tenderness, or neglect and ridicule, can cause traumatic hurt during these years. The Adlerian theory of personality offers some understanding of the way in which the frustrated power drives of the growing persons may be compensated for in ways which may cause the person to become neurotic. Persons do have a basic desire for significance, a "will to prestige," a "style of life" which can merit their own self-respect and the respect of others. The minister should keep alert to this powerful drive within human nature as he counsels with a person who seems to be overcompensating for inferiority feelings.

Harry Stack Sullivan stresses strongly the effect of real love and acceptance in interpersonal relationships. Christians also believe that this is important, and that believers need to be one in Christ, with a mystical union of Spirit between them. The deepest frustrations of the human person are likely to be those which occur when meaningful interpersonal relationships are distorted or cut off.

The counselor will be wise to remember also the theories of Karen Horney and to observe carefully the "present life situation" of the counselee. If the person cannot love his brother whom he has seen, he will likewise not be able to give and receive love from his God whom he has not seen. The counselor will notice whether the counselee habitually moves toward people, away from people, or against people.

Some insights offered by Eric Fromm can be helpful to the Christian counselor as he refocuses them through a Christian perspective. The counselee needs to discover what his own uniqueness is as a person and then to learn how to live in fidelity to that uniqueness. After the person outgrows his infantile distortions and learns to "think truth" about himself and the world, he may learn to accept himself, both strengths and weaknesses, as he has been created and endowed by God. Then only is he able to "live love," giving and receiving love with other persons who are also using their unique abilities in a creative way. After a person begins to be able to live love, he can also begin to be able to think truth.

The Christian counselor will sometimes find persons who have been blessed by God with unique native endowments and gifts, who are frustrated because they feel doomed to an antlike existence in a monotonous factory or kitchen routine. The minister will also find frustrated persons who have discovered their own uniqueness and a creative outlet for their gifts, who have made a success of life according to the world's standards, and who are ready to "live off of the coupons," but who are deeply discontented and neurotic. These gifted persons may have yielded to the temptation to commit the crowning sin of idolatry by giving primary devotion to something less than to God Himself. They are crusaders without a cause.

The Christian counselor may find most help of all from the ideas of psychiatrists like Vicktor Frankl, Paul Tournier, and Fritz Kunkel. These psychiatrists do not approach man at all as a veterinarian approaches an animal. They frankly accept the spiritual dimension of man's existence, his search for ultimate meaning in his day-by-day living, his need to take a courageous position toward his destiny, and his need to find fellowship in a life which is eternal.

The Christian counselor will find some persons in his counseling who have a permanent "Sunday neurosis." Their spirit is "idling at full throttle." They need a fixed point in the future, a cause big enough so that they can gladly invest their life in it with abandon, and a fellowship within which they can meet the living God.

The counselor will examine the meaningful human relationships of his counselee. He will notice whether his conscience is free of guilty secrets and whether he has learned to live with his sex drives and to keep his id-bits under control. But the counselor will notice most of all whether the person is living in a reality each moment before the face of God so that all of the past is flooded with peace and all of the future is diffused with hope. This is the life which the prophet called "walking humbly with God," and Christ called "the life more abundant." When faith in Christ enables the person to face the sins of his own past, and when trust in God's grace and promises enables him to face his future with hope, then he can accept God's love in the present moment.

XIX. Counselors from Outside the Congregation Also Serve Some of the Members

Many of the specialized ministries to human need and suffering which the modern community provides were once provided by the church. But while the church (like the priest and the Levite in the Bible narrative) passed by on the other side, secularly oriented agencies arose to serve the needs of persons. Guidance services in the public schools, clinics, social workers, counseling bureaus, and family guidance centers often serve members of the modern urban congregation. The minister should be aware of the assumptions and methods which these other counselors employ.

Marriage and family counselors are quite eclectic in their approach and workers come together from many disciplines. They often presuppose simple ignorance on the part of their counselees. They try to impart helpful information, and try to re-integrate the family situation and the personality of a troubled family member all in one counseling process.

Social casework counselors make extensive use of community resources in their efforts to help persons. They visit the home, carefully evaluate the total environmental situation, and attempt to reconstruct the social milieu of the counselee. They give attention to delinquency, economic assistance, adoptions, and emotional therapy. A number of workers may co-operate as a "health team." They also emphasize the helping, healing quality of the present relationship with the counselor.

Psychoanalytic counselors, in the strictest sense of the term, are those psychiatrists who follow Freudian theories and techniques. These psychiatrists have been psychoanalyzed themselves, are medical doctors, and hold to a "depth" view of personality dynamics. They subscribe to some doctrine of the unconscious, and seek to surface material from the unconscious, bringing it up into conscious awareness. They use relaxation, dream recall, and free association, and aim at a total reorganization of the personality. They require long periods of time for their therapy and expect regression, hostility, transference, resistance, and even "acting out" before the patient comes through to insight and reorientation of life. While "pure Freudian" psychoanalysis is still prevalent in America, it is coming under increasing attack as a too partial understanding of the human person.

Non-Freudian psychiatrists and psychologists are also serving persons in clinics, mental hospitals, private hospitals, or in their own private offices. Some rely heavily upon the testing apparatus of clinical psychology. Others use what is called "creative questioning." Some combine their counseling with shock therapy, hydrotherapy, drug therapy, fever therapy, or other forms of psychotherapy. By combining direct medical examination and treatment with their counseling they seek to help the whole person.

An increasing number of counselors, who might be described as "relationship therapists," are serving in many agencies. For a "relationship therapist" the quality of the relationship is the healing element. The counselor seeks to achieve a mystical union of spirit with the counselee. The flow of feeling, the non-verbal communication, the clarification of selfhood, and the feeling of the counselor himself disclose how much progress is being made toward self-awareness, self-acceptance, and responsible decision. The counselor becomes a "participant observer," suffering with the counselee through the birth pangs of autonomous insights and the emergence of a new and changed self.

Few good counselors wish to limit the goals of their counseling to the emphases or insights of any one particular theory or "school" of personality dynamics. If the counselor relies most heavily upon the theories of Carl Jung, he will say that the goal of his counseling is the integration of the counselee's personality. If he is informed primarily by Freudian concepts, he will likely say that his goal is to enable the counselee to control his "life stream" within him so that he is free to love and to work creatively. If influenced greatly by Adler's ideas the counselor will hope for a changed style of life through better understanding of self and others. If influenced by Sullivan's ideas the counselor will seek for genuineness and immediacy of experience in the present interpersonal relationship, as a preparation for satisfying relationships with others. If the counselor is guided by the assumptions of the Horney group, he will seek to help the counselee to accept and to realize his own true self while interacting constructively with other persons.

Obviously these goals are all variations on the same theme. All good counselors are attempting to lead the person to self-awareness, to self-acceptance, to a program for constructive growth, and to the capacity to enjoy and contribute to community.

Some clinics to which members of the congregation may be going for help operate in an "assembly line" manner, with each specialist giving attention to one facet of the human situation. Thus the psychologist administers the battery of tests to detect the level of adjustment and social functioning, the general physician prescribes any medical care which may be needed, the social worker contacts relatives and seeks to enlist the co-operation of the family group, and the psychiatrist treats the anxieties and psychosomatic symptoms of neuroses or psychosis.

If a member of the congregation has been served by such an "assembly line" of specialists, the members will most likely come to the minister as one more specialist, not on the staff, but able to give help in one narrowly conceived area. While other counselors may have helped the person to deal with neurotic guilt, the minister is expected to help him to find forgiveness and absolution from real guilt. While other counselors have helped him to understand conflicts he has been having with persons on the horizontal, human plane, the minister is expected to help him to clarify his relationship with his God. Other counselors may help him to resolve the anxieties of the day, but the minister helps him to find meaning for time and all eternity.

XX. The Minister May Ask Specialists in Counseling Who Are Members of the Congregation to Serve as a "Consulting Advisory Committee"

The minister who has within the congregation which he serves professional persons who are trained as counselors may well invite them to serve as a "Consulting Advisory Committee." Each one could be called upon as his special skill had prepared him to advise.[18] As each professional person sought thus to help serve the needy member within the church fellowship, he would add to the effectiveness of the total pastoral care.

Most professional persons who are Christians regard their service within a secular agency as part of God's good gifts to men, partaking of the same order as God's gifts in creation. But when such persons join with others in the church fellowship, in the atmosphere of worship and prayer, and when they consciously seek to function together as God's holy people, a new blessing and power can be expected. If they seek to sense the mind of their living Lord, sharing His resurrection life and power together, a new dimension of reality is added. The charisma of wisdom does not automatically answer all questions. But if counselors gather and share their impressions in a prayerful spirit, in conscious reliance upon the Holy Spirit, and while they themselves are feeding together upon the life-giving power of God's Word, they may become and experience together the fullest and richest type of therapeutic community.[19]

The minister should be grateful for any and all of the help which specially trained counselors can bring to the well-nigh impossible task of understanding man. Man is fearfully and wonderfully made. His personality, like a diamond, has "64 facets" to it. The minister, even when supported by a team of experts, may need to sit humbly before the troubled person whom all of them together understand so poorly.

Doubtless many experts who are themselves Christians and who counsel in secular agencies would be glad to share in a serious consultation within the setting of the congregation. Counselors all know the tragic superficiality of the polite society, with its forced gaity, too hearty back-slapping, and wide, toothpaste smiles. This leaves the spirit of man empty. Too often correct conversation consists of "sweet nothings," polite lies, courteous pretense, and appears like a verbal dual between two people wearing masks. Serious issues are studiously avoided. Counselors know that such interaction only increases the basic estrangement of persons from one another. Within the fellowship around God's Word, counselors could discuss the issues of ultimate concern, of both time and eternity, of temporary disorder and final destiny.

Christian counselors find much satisfaction in serving mankind through a secular agency, no doubt, but they would find a new depth of meaning in their life vocation if they could bring some of their efforts more directly into the community of divine love, in the midst of the worshiping, praying church. By utilizing the counsel of many experts who serve on a professional advisory committee, a better total congregational ministry might be achieved than if the congregation merely employed one social worker on its staff.

Chapter 4

The Minister Leads God's People
In Their Worship

I. The Worship of God's People in the Past
Offers Guidance for Worship Today

The minister cannot merely copy from neighboring brother-hoods as he seeks guidance for his leading of worship. His Quaker friends would suggest that silence best conveys a sense of God's immanence. They believe that when the mind waits in live silence, in complete attentiveness, and in holy dependence upon God, then God can speak in fresh revelation, immediate and direct. Quakers urge that every worshiper prepare his spirit to be addressed by God directly, rather than that the minister should prepare a sermon through which a large part of God's speaking is to be expected. Quakers who hold to their early tradition insist that no person should go to the meeting presuming that he will be inspired to speak more often than any other person, unless Christ the "inward Teacher" inspires him at any given moment.[1] Worship may be vital and valid even though no one speaks.

Christians who worship in the holiness tradition insist that ecstasy is the mark of reality in worship. Joyous abandon, floods of feeling, exultant praise, spontaneous testimonies, and even healings of bodily illnesses are considered desirable in Christian worship. Worship is to be punctuated by happy crises, either of sinners being converted or of believers receiving a second work of grace or complete sanctification. Biblical support for these patterns of worship are found in the worship services alluded to in I Cor. 12 to 14 and in isolated passages in the Book of Acts.

From the churches which practice sacramentally centered worship comes the insistence that the Lord's Supper is the central bearer of reality and blessing in Christian worship. Christians who advocate sacramental worship declare that God in His sovereignty has chosen to come to His people in the material elements of the bread and the wine of the Lord's Supper. These Christians emphasize the need for a deepened sense of the holy, a more profound respect for God's transcendence, and for the mystery which surrounds His self-disclosures. The spoken Word from Scripture is expected to move alongside of and to corroborate the reality, the grace, and the truth which are symbolized and conveyed in the sacraments.

Along with sacramentally centered worship there is usually included the use of prayers drawn from earlier periods in church history. There is a rich use of symbolism and a reliance upon the aesthetic and the art form to deepen and enrich the experience of worship. Those who favor sacramental worship find Biblical support in the Old Testament temple patterns and in the worship forms prevalent in the third and fourth centuries.

One danger common to all of the contemporary patterns of worship cited above is that they tend to give inadequate recognition to salvation history. Too much attention seems to be focused upon the action of God and the experiences of the worshiper in the present moment without seeing the present experience alongside of and in continuity with the redeeming deeds of God recorded in the Bible.

As the minister turns to the Biblical patterns of worship for his guidance, he notices that a recounting of salvation history is always prominent. Worshipers retell the redeeming deeds of their God as they gather before Him and seek His redeeming power in their present worship encounter. God has always been worshiped as the God who hath appeared, who doth appear, and who will appear. Thus Israel may have feasts in their worship somewhat like the feasts of the Canaanites, but Israel's feasts are not focused upon a year's fertility cycle. Israel's feasts of worship are to commemorate God's mighty acts at the Red Sea, at Mt. Sinai, and in deliverances in the wilderness. In New Testament worship the Lord's Supper was observed to commemorate God's mighty act at Calvary, the way in which believers now feed upon His divine life, and the way they look for Christ's return to consummate their redemption.

The Biblical patterns of worship, in both Testaments, assume that God is infinitely superior to man, not only in one area of striving, but in all. He is above manipulation by man's magic or cunning. But in infinite love He stoops to enter a two-way covenant of love with the man who will allow himself to be redeemed and transformed. God offers Himself to man in self-sacrificing love, even unto death. He invites man to reciprocate by giving himself to God in a covenant of love to the death. This covenant of reciprocal love to the death is to be refreshed and renewed in every worship encounter.

In Biblical worship human personality is valued, respected, and enriched. Canaanite worship degraded and devalued the person by its practice of human sacrifices and cultic fornication. Isaiah may feel himself undone and devalued momentarily as he cries, "Woe is me," but he soon finds himself honored by a call into divine partnership. In New Testament worship, fresh glimpses of God's glory (as He is revealed in Jesus Christ) transform the worshiper from glory to still greater glory as he is changed into Christ's image.

In both Old and New Testaments the experience of being spoken to by God lies very near to the center of the worship experience. In Old Testament worship the prophet's word became God's own Word as he called God's people to heart religion and obedience before their God in their present situation. In the New Testament Jesus declared that man is not fully human, not really living in reality until he is aware of a Word proceeding out of the mouth of God, addressed to him in his unique condition. The coming of the Word of God to man must always be considered one of the central realities of the Christian worship which the minister leads.

According to the Biblical view, worship goes on both in

heaven and on earth, whether a particular believer joins in it or not. But one of the highest privileges any man can experience is to join with the whole family of God both in heaven and on earth, in their worship.[2] Worship then becomes the chief end of man. All of his existence is drawn into orbit by this powerful gravitating center. All of service is offered up to God as an act of worship. "Ye did it unto me." All of beauty is brought under tribute to holiness and worship. All of life's experiences, both sorrow and rejoicing, fast and feast, are brought into relationship with the central outpouring of life to God. All natural abilities are brought to God to be charismatically heightened and used of God in his service and worship.[3]

Thus the minister should regard the group worship as the gravitating center of the lives of members of the congregation. Here they gather to join with the saints of all the ages in corporate praise. They assemble to receive God's Word of guidance as the Holy Scriptures are opened and expounded. Here they experience cleansing and renewal in God's grace as they prepare to scatter, again, penetrating areas of human need and sin as God's agents of redemption.

In New Testament worship patterns many precious "family-of-God" experiences are portrayed. Believers are invited to address God as Father and to claim a new intimacy and relationship. The Holy Spirit is poured out upon all sons and daughters, and the family of God is now also the prophetic circle. Emphasis upon the Sabbath and rest decreases because those who walk in the resurrection have already entered into rest of soul. Believers are so sure that the new aeon has dawned that the phrase, "thine is the kingdom," is added to the Lord's Prayer. Worshipers feel that the kingdom and rule of God has already begun in the midst of their worshiping assembly, and that the experience which they are having is a foretaste of His kingdom, power, and glory forever.[4]

In New Testament worship the prayers are lifted to a new level. Gone are the older notes of vindictiveness toward enemies, the swings from self-assertion or self-depreciation, the seeking of material good on a par with the spiritual, and the attempts to drive hard bargains with Jehovah. But the profound notes of prostration, adoration, petition, intercession, confession, and praise still continue. The minister will be wise to pattern his prayers after Biblical prayers, even more than after the prayers of leaders throughout church history.

In New Testament times the presence of the risen Christ was sought, acknowledged, and counted upon. Believers gave spontaneous testimony, not only to the remembered words of the Lord and of their certainty that He had arisen, but also to His here and now action in their own personalities. The Jesus of history was also the saving Lord of their lived experience in the present moment and the One who would complete and consummate all He had begun when He returned in glory. Worshipers cried, "Lord, come" (Maranatha), as readily as they said, "Amen."[5] The early Christians felt about each Lord's day morning of worship just like the church later felt about Easter Sunday alone. (Every minister should lead a worship service which has in it always some of the wonder and joy of Easter morning.)

The inspired writings were also an important channel of divine blessing in the midst of worship. In addition to the Old Testament writings, Paul praised the Thessalonian believers that they also received his letters as the very Word of God.[6] Paul commanded Timothy to read the Scriptures in worship,[7] and took for granted the fact that his epistles were being read in the worship gatherings at Colossae.[8]

Some scholars think that Scripture reading was so highly regarded in early Christian worship that even prayer was to be deferred until the heart had been warmed and moved by the hearing of the Word.[9] Likely it was the frequency of their use in worship services during the first and second centuries which helped to decide which epistles and memoirs of the apostles should be gathered together and passed along as the canon of Holy Scriptures. Certainly the Christian minister, as he leads the service of worship, will want to place the reading and exposition of the meaning of inspired Scripture into the very center of the God-man dialogue.

Worship as praise poured from the hearts of early Christian

worshipers like the full-throated song of a bird. They ate with
gladness as they shared their love feasts and Lord's Supper meals
together. They brought over from the synagogue worship only a
few isolated phrases. The wonder of Christ's dying love and
living presence and Holy Spirit power in their midst set the mood
of the meeting.[10] They sought to pattern their worship after
heaven's worship, even more than after either temple or synagogue. The minister will need to be yielded to the Holy Spirit's
power and leading if he is to lead a worship service which feels
like a coming to the New Jerusalem, to the spirits of just men
made perfect, and which partakes of some of the reality of both
apostolic and celestial worship.

The minister should always remember, as he leads God's
people in their worship, that the heavenly Father is actively seeking for the response of His children in worship. He seeks and
longs for the meeting with His children in worship as intensely as
He seeks and longs for the wandering prodigal to come home.
Jesus taught that the central reality of worship is that the
heavenly Father is seeking a meeting with His children, and
that His children are responding with worship.

Public worship will be more charged with reality and meaning if the private devotions of individual believers have been
real and vital. No minister can lead a worship service in which
the regenerating Spirit of God "bloweth where it listeth" in renewing power, unless the individual believers already experience
some openness toward God and some warmth and fervor in their
own private prayers.

II. Group Worship Helps to Deepen
The Private Devotion of God's Servants

The minister who leads corporate worship should understand how this experience relates to private worship. Everyone
who comments upon the question is agreed that private worship
and corporate worship mutually enrich each other, but which
contributes the most to the other? Quaker worship, as well as
Roman Catholic and Eastern Orthodox worship, seeks to inter-

twine private worship and corporate worship. The Scriptures seem to presuppose that corporate worship should be expected to feed private worship even more than the reverse.[11] The heathen convert could not experience God's full blessing until he united with God's covenant people in their worship. In the New Testament the Holy Spirit fell upon the worshipers when they were in corporate worship.

In group worship something more is added. Group worship helps to curb egocentricity and forces the worshiper to consider others. A Brahman may not need a group for his worship as he seeks to become part of "the world soul," but a Christian is taught to approach God saying, "Our Father, forgive us," not "My Father, forgive me." A Muslim is really only having his private devotions in public, but for a Christian the very life of Christ the Head of the body comes to him through the joints and bands of interaction with other members who are joined to Christ.[12] The Bible does not idealize the "flight of the alone to the alone" of the solitary mystic. Becoming a son launches one into brotherhood and family life, and something is wrong if a son seeks his richest experiences apart from his family.

The "priesthood of believers" doctrine provides that the individual priest should serve and be served by their brethren, and this includes ministering to one another in worship. Public prayer should express some of the person's private yearnings, but it should arouse and incite other and deeper yearnings too. It is true that petition in public worship cannot mention specific details of any one person's need, but Father knows already before His children tell Him.

Corporate worship should help to establish the pattern for private devotions. Group worship usually has order, movement, comprehensiveness, and climax, and private worship will be enriched also if it has order rather than confusion. When Christ gave a pattern for prayer, He suggested a movement from adoration, through intercession, submission, petition, confession, supplication, and praise.

Group worship can include rich and varied experiences which private devotions cannot quite duplicate. The heartfelt testimonies from Christians with shining faces can bring a personalness and contagion which cannot be experienced in solitary worship. There is more vocal expression, more singing, and more appeal to the eye and ear in corporate than in private worship. The giving of money and the corporate act of dedicating an offering to God is a sacred experience which is seldom known in private worship.[13]

The blessing which comes from mutual testimony, admonition, and rebuke cannot come when worship is done in isolation. The sacraments of worship cannot be shared in solitary worship. The warmth of mutual concern, wherein every member suffers when anyone does, cannot be felt by the solitary mystic. "There can be no Christian worship if each person remains an Alpine peak in the grandeur of isolation. Real worship is done with others in a genuinely corporate sense."[14]

It is true that the grandeur of corporate worship may launch the individual into a specific quest until "the worshiper goes on to still higher flight, beyond the realm of words, the soul stretched out in blank, naked intent of desire and worship toward its God."[15] Group worship can help to preserve reverence for God's transcendence and sovereignty and can help to prevent the "cozy chumminess" which creeps into the private worshiper's attitude toward God.

III. A Call to Worship Helps God's People To Prepare for Their Worship

The worship leader should see himself as a prompter in the dialogue between God and His people. It is his duty to help each articulate what each wishes to say. God is not reluctant nor unready for the worship reunion with His family. He is ever seeking, ever pressing toward them in wooing love, always ready for meeting and dialogue. The leader of Christian worship need not plead, beseech, or invoke God to give His attention, as though He were some Baal who might be gone on a journey. God is already active as worshipers gather, speaking quietly to the heart of each by His Holy Spirit, ready to teach them what to pray for as they ought, ready to make the living Christ real, and ready to reveal the deep things of God to them.

The call to worship is needed by the people who are to reply to God in worship. They need help if they are to fight off distractions. They need help to focus their full attention upon the face and voice of the living God. Christians find it extremely difficult to shut the door and to commune in the secret place with their seeking Father. The leader needs to help them to respond unitedly, in spirit and in truth. Even worth-while service can distract the soul from worship, as Martha learned.

The worship leader dare not assume that all of the worshipers have left their distractions behind when they entered the church door. The church is no longer at the center of the city with its steeple dominating all other buildings, as in the medieval city. The church no longer draws all of life into orbit around itself, but seems rather like a shrinking institution crowded out to the marginal fields of man's attention. It is extremely difficult to reverse this prevailing mind-set during an hour of worship.

All week long the average worshiper has looked with some awe toward science, expecting it to dispel the mystery of the uncharted spaces, the energies of the universe, and the origin and meaning of life. It is hard to recapture a Biblical sense of wonder for the hour of worship. Department stores have suggested all week long that gadgets and food are the real significance of Christmas and Easter, and the worshiper can scarcely shut out the din of the commercials long enough to ponder deeply the eternal significance of the incarnation and the resurrection. The rivalries of denominations seem to give the lie to any church's claim to absolute truth, and the churchgoer is tempted to wonder wistfully whether it is worthwhile to worship.

The best call to worship is a reminder of previous occasions in history when God accomplished a redeeming invasion of man's isolation and estrangement. "To induce worship now, take a running start in redemption history." As Israelites came to their cultic centers for worship, they heard narrators telling of God's saving acts in their past. The people were chanting psalms which gloried in God's redeeming power and deeds. The prophet was speaking of God's readiness to visit and redeem His people in the present moment if they will come with a true heart.[61] God always seeks to gather His people, like a hen gathers her chicks to shelter, and a reminder of God's gracious invitation is a good way to begin a meeting.

The leader of Christian worship may well open the service with a call to worship recorded in the psalms. The psalms of approach, 120-134, used by devout Jews as they approached their temple, might be used of God to call His people to present encounter. No call to worship, intoned invocations, church bells, mood music, candles, incense, or pageantry of processionals can mediate immediacy or guarantee that supernatural and divine presence and power will confront persons. Worshipers must believe that God has pierced the crust of everyday life in visitations in the midst of His people in days gone by and that He is eagerly waiting to do it again where there is expectant faith.[17]

IV. A Spirit of Reverent Dignity Should Prevail

The worship should be led with reverent dignity "according to thought-out procedure." The worship leader should be worshiping in deep reality while he leads others. Some worship leaders march in in a processional, to symbolize that worship is a pause to rear an altar of praise in the midst of life's pilgrimage. However, all pageantry is difficult to execute reverently and hard to justify. The worship leader should avoid everything of fanfare or which calls attention to himself. Neither he nor any of the leaders of worship should regard what they do as a performance. Details of the order of service should be carefully reviewed together beforehand so that no whispered consultations are necessary during the period of group worship. Whenever possible the persons who lead the worship should meet together for prayer before the service begins. In this time of prayer leaders should pray for one another and seek to open their lives to be unctionized and controlled by the Holy Spirit. Leaders should feel some of the same reverent awe and smittenness which Moses felt at Mt. Sinai, or Aaron felt as he entered the holy place, even though now God's presence is expected in the indwelt brother, among the two or three met in Christ's name, and in the Scriptures which testify of Christ.

Some worship leaders prefer to start the worship service with their own words of welcome and greeting, but this seems to encourage the all-too-common heresy that people should come to church primarily to hear the preacher, to do him a favor, and to watch him perform. An adoring hymn of praise and invocation may sometimes be used as the first act of corporate worship. It should be the type of hymn which symbolizes that God has the right to speak first in the meeting, and that worship begins with God, or it does not begin at all. The same God who once said, "I will be sanctified in them that come nigh me," still expects worshipers to act in seriousness and earnestness.

One way to secure involvement and participation of every member right from the start is to read "call to worship" Scripture portions responsively. Thus the minister might read such a portion as, "God is a Spirit: and they that worship him must worship him in spirit and in truth," while the congregation replies with, "O come, let us worship and bow down: let us kneel before the Lord our maker." If it is desirable to continue for a second couplet the minister might read, "God [is the] Father of lights, with whom is no variableness, neither shadow of turning," and the congregation reply, "O send out thy light and thy truth: let them bring me unto thy holy hill."[18] There are a great many such appropriate passages in the Scriptures.

V. The Acts and Responses of Worship Tend to Fall into a Pattern

While the movements of the soul which is engaging in dialogue with God in worship cannot be fixed to a set cadence, yet a worship service must have "order as well as ardor." God gave a pattern in the holy mount for the tabernacle worship of His people, and Christ taught a pattern of prayer which had distinct liturgical progression within it. Heimsath suggests that the Isaiah 6 pattern is a good order to follow: vision of God, confession of sin, cleansing and renewal, and dedication to serve.[19]

The many doxologies in the New Testament and the many portions which are somewhat rhythmic in the early manuscripts seem to indicate that early Christian worship was characterized by reverent order. Certainly the worship scenes which are pictured in the Book of Revelation portray dignity and form. If the welter of individual experiences are to move together in unison and power, some structure is necessary.

Some worship leaders turn toward the people when they are attempting to be a voice for God's Word to His people, and then turn toward the altar when they seek to articulate for the congregation their answering word to God. This helps to accent the dialogue nature of true worship, but is unacceptable to free, nonliturgical worshipers because it suggests that God's presence is uniquely localized at an altar. Other worship leaders stress the sacrificial acts of the human worshipers when they offer up to God their confession, their prayer, their praise, their confession of faith and creed, and their offering. These are man's response to God's sacramental acts of cleansing and His coming to man in Scripture, sermon, Lord's Supper, and benediction.[20]

McNutt lists patterns of worship advocated by a number of men who write about the leading of worship. A. P. Fitch says that worship should move through experiences of awareness of God's presence, adoration, peace, and purpose. E. S. Brightman advocates a sequence of contemplation, revelation, communion, and fruition. McNutt himself suggests a progression from awareness of God and attention to Him through vision, humility, contemplation, assurance, dedication, fellowship, peace, and power, and service.[21]

A complete act of corporate worship should include a freshly awakened sense of God's presence and a fresh glimpse of His glory, this to be followed by a confession of need and sin and a renewal of cleansing and forgiving grace. Central in the entire service should be the act of listening for God to speak His living Word of guidance for obedient living. Praise should have a prominent place and the entire service should climax with an act of dedication and self-sacrifice on the part of every worshiper. In some of the group worship experiences there should be a time when every member prophesies, that is, speaks to exhort, edify, and comfort the congregation. As worshipers share what the here and now operation of God's grace is doing in their own lives, and give their word of prophetic admonition to the congregation, the whole experience may be one of reverent worship and God encounter.

VI. God's Servants Should Claim His Pardoning Grace

Worship should bring to sincere believers a new flood of enabling grace. But in spite of this, when the ministering church comes before her Lord and God in worship, she becomes aware that at best she is still an unprofitable servant. Because God is so absolutely holy, perfect, and sinless, and the church is not yet fully like God in this perfection, the encounter between God and His people always causes their unclean lips to show up afresh. When any worshiping person confronts the living God, he is overwhelmed with the fact that the only basis upon which he can live before the face of God is that God graciously forgives. Worship, if it is a real encounter, should always wring from the lips of the worshiper a fresh confession of his need and a fresh claiming of God's pardoning grace. Jesus included the plea for forgiveness in the prayer which He taught to His disciples, and declared that only the worshiper who cries, "God be merciful to me a sinner," goes down to his house justified. Because every failure of the Christian is his own fault and not God's, and is in the final analysis inexcusable, he is thrust more completely upon the unmerited grace of his forgiving God.

The Christian church has always demanded specific, public, individual confession for "police court" type sins and willful sinning. But for the sins of the Spirit, which so easily beset, such a coldness of heart, lack of compassion, covetousness, unbelief, lovelessness, and coming short of God's glory, the church has always sought cleansing in the midst of her worship. This honesty before God in group worship should help to prepare worshipers to confess their faults in private to one another in humility and love as God's Word commands them to do.

If worshipers appear before God repeatedly without admitting how completely they are dependent upon His forgiving grace, they are likely to grow pharisaical under this hypocrisy and pretense. They will be tempted to shrink down the demands of God's absolute righteousness to a list of rules which they think they can keep. Then they can feel self-righteous and begin to thank God that they are not as other men.

The worship leader should make some provision for believers to confess together during worship. Confession should not be relegated to a side business of work of merit, as the Roman Catholics have done. It should not be shifted entirely to pastoral counseling or to visits to the psychiatrist, as seems to be the practice among too many Protestants. Neither should confession become an outlet for morbid exhibitionism. The general confession of sins of the Spirit which is engaged in by every believer during corporate worship should help each one to fill in the details as they apply to his own life.

Should confession be structured into a liturgy, in set sentences to be repeated in the same way every time? This is the way it is done in a number of the much used liturgies of Christendom. However, a more living and vital way may be to vary the form in which the congregation makes her confession. Sometimes worshipers can identify deeply as a penitential psalm is read in the devotional Scripture, and make this confession their own. Other times the pastor will gather up the cries of the people in a prayer of confession. Other times worshipers may confess both their sins and their faith in God's forgiving grace as they make a hymn writer's words their very own. Christians should not confess in the melancholy mood of a wailing wall, but in a glad and reverent claiming of God's marvelous grace.

In any case the church is certainly not wise to relegate confession to an annual "housecleaning" at revival meeting time or a semiannual preparatory service held just prior to communion. If believers in every worship encounter will "quit their bluffing" and pretending a perfection which both they, their children, and the watching world know they have not really achieved, it will be easier for their children and the world to believe. If believers will honestly admit their need of God's forgiving grace, then they can experience a renewal of God's enabling grace for a more perfect obedience in the future. When they dare to own up to their imperfect performance as God's sons, yet claim the wonder and reality of God's grace that accepts them in their immaturity, then they are free in spirit and newly enabled to claim God's grace for growth.

VII. Scripture Readings Constitute a Vital Part Of the Worship Service

The entire worship service may be paced or punctuated by readings from Holy Scripture. If the call to worship is a passage of Scripture, the call to present the tithes and offerings makes use of a second one, and the benediction is pronounced in the words of another Scripture passage, then three recitations of Scripture have already been woven into the very fabric of the worship service.

A devotional reading of Scripture is also in order early in the movement of worship. The Scripture passages can be chosen so as to be consistent with the Christian year. They can also be chosen so as to emphasize salvation history. An Old Testament passage can portray preparation for the coming of Christ, a passage from the Gospels can show the very words and deeds of Christ in saving action, and a passage from the Acts or the epistles can show believers living together in a fellowship in Christ.

The psalms, the ancient worship book of God's people, should also be read in Christian worship. The psalms were originally meant to be sung, and the chanting of a psalm can replace reading if a choral group is prepared to sing it with reverence and beauty.

Responsive reading of Scripture passages can help to increase involvement and participation. The dialogue element of Christian worship can be accented if appropriate passages are read antiphonally. Some passages lend themselves to a reading in which the congregation echoes the same answer to every assertion. Psalm 136 is such a passage with its recurring refrain, "For his mercy endureth for ever." This pattern of responsive reading of Scripture is called a litany.

The reading of Scripture in unison is difficult to achieve unless worshipers have had some practice in choral reading. For those congregations which are willing to learn to do it well, the choral reading of Scripture can be a deeply rewarding worship experience. Because of the variety of Bible versions carried by individual worshipers, the passages to be read in unison must be printed as worship aids in the hymnal.

Many ministers select for reading a passage which serves as background for the sermon. This can show the wholeness and larger context of a given truth. But the reading of Scripture, done reverently and so as to interpret its inner meaning, should remain as an act of corporate worship in its own right. Selected passages which support a central theme or truth may also be read with profit as an act of worship.

VIII. God's Servants Need to Be Led in Their Corporate Praise

Because the responsibility to lead the congregation in their united praise is not primarily the minister's work, this aspect of worship will not be treated in any detail in these lectures. Other servants of God's servants should lead them in their singing. The service of worshiping God in sacred song is as sacred and central a ministry as God's ministering people ever render. In heaven when it is said that "his servants shall serve him," a large part of their service is to praise God in song.[22]

It must suffice to say in these lectures on the work of the minister that he should encourage worship in song, urge improvement at every opportunity, pray for, and give his moral support to those who serve the congregation by leading their united praise. Even though he may never lead directly in the ministry of sacred song, he should know his hymnbook almost as well as he knows his Bible.

The minister should honor and cherish the ministry of sacred song in the congregation, knowing that many of the most exalted moments of worship which Christians will ever know may come to them during their united praise. When redeemed men praise God in song, they seem to be leading all creation, voicing for the stars their wordless adoration. It is during the praise experiences of Christian worship that worshipers often feel most keenly that they are drawing near to the spirits of just men made perfect, blending voices with loved ones who have gone on before.

The minister will be alarmed if the corporate worship in song starts to grow lifeless. The heart of worship died out of the worship of God's people when they hung their harps on the willows in Babylon. The minister will know that praise is to spiritual life almost what breathing is to the physical life. Passivity is always the deadly foe of worship, and if "spectatoritis" takes over in the congregation's worship in song, the situation is serious indeed.

The minister should counsel very closely with those who lead the congregation in their ministry of sacred song, because he knows that the hymns of worship can literally carry the movement of worship. They can express the answer of the congregation to the Word of God, can help convey the evangelistic invitation to the unredeemed, and can help to mold any stragglers into the worshiping group. The hymns which the congregation sings frequently become the real creed and theological textbook of the laity. Through the hymns much of the Word of God can live on in their memory. In hymns the beauty of music and poetry are brought into the service of God, and a safe and sane outlet and expression of Christian ecstasy is provided.

Whenever possible the minister should ask the song leader or minister of music to choose the hymns and plan the musical responses for the worshiping congregation. This helps to actualize team leadership, and to draw more Spirit-given gifts into the service of the congregation's worship. This requires, however, a song leader with whom the minister can discuss in depth the dialogue of the worship hour. He must be a mature Christian who can feel deeply, not only the word which the living God desires to say to His people, but the cry of response which the congregation will want to make. The song leader must be a spiritually sensitive person who can understand the degree of maturity of the congregation, and can anticipate the level of response which they may be prepared to make. He must choose hymns which articulate for God's people exactly what their hearts long to say. Hymns may well move on the "high side" of a congregation's readiness, and help to lift their aspirations and response.

If the minister who leads worship is not so fortunate as to have the co-operation of a song leader who possesses deep spiritual discernment into the very nature of worship, then the minister will need to choose the hymns himself. This may be true, even though the song leader is highly skilled in the mere mechanics of music and choral conducting.

IX. God's Servants Need to Hear God's Word in the Sermon

The minister is tempted to shrink from insisting that the highest point of the worship hour should be the sermon, because he himself is to preach it. Who is he to thus speak words which shall mediate immediacy, that shall make possible a personal meeting of the living God with His people?

The minister must believe that God in His sovereignty has chosen to come to meet man through His Word. God's people have always believed that a word which proceeded out of God's mouth could mediate His omnipotent power. He spoke a word to create the worlds[23] and the heavens are still sustained by His Word.[24] God's Word beats against man's hardened heart like a hammer which breaks rocks in pieces.[25] Cultures and civilizations of man can rise and flourish awhile and then wither away like mown grass, but the Word of Jehovah ever rises up into all eternity.[26] God sent forth His Word like His representative to perform an errand.[27] "The Lord sent a word into Jacob, and it hath lighted upon Israel."[28]

Because Jeremiah was speaking God's Word, his message was

sent over history, to cast down or to build up kingdoms.[29] God's sovereign will for man was set forth in ten words, the Ten Commandments. God promised that His Word should not return to Him void but would prosper in the thing whereto He had sent it.[30] Even scheming Balak knew that God's Word was stronger than any army of men.

But the minister must also believe that God can make His very presence real through the Word. God enables the word which He speaks to convey the warmth of His personal life and love. Bible writers believed that God could come in His Word with a personalness almost like His coming in His incarnate Son.[31] "The Word was made flesh, and dwelt among us. . . ." Jesus rebuked the Pharisees because they sought eternal life in the words of Scriptures themselves, and did not allow the Scriptures to testify of Christ until these Pharisees could have come to Christ Himself. Jesus believed that they could have come to Him personally in the Scripture, just as really as they could come near to His bodily presence.

God's Word always is God as a person calling man into covenant response as one person to another. His first word of the Ten Commandments was, "Thou shalt have no other gods before me." The devout worshiper in Old Testament times believed that God's Word bore the very redeeming life of Jehovah which pressed toward men as powerfully in words as it did in deeds. The minister must also regard God's Word as "Thou truth," the bearer of God's life, rather than merely of propositions about God.

The minister must be convinced furthermore that God has given the inspired Scriptures as the bearer of His own living Word by which He confronts persons with His own person. Jesus assigned to the Scriptures, "it stands written," the capacity to convey God's life and will and power. He turned to the Scriptures with the same reverence with which God's people had always listened to the prophets cry, "Thus saith Jehovah." Jesus used the words of the Scriptures to defeat the tempter[32] and to cause the hearts of the Emmaus disciples to burn within them as He revealed Himself to them.[33] One of the later prophets,

Ezekiel, although greatly concerned about the restoration of temple-type worship, needed to get his very call and message from God by eating a book.[34]

When God wanted to reveal His person to worshipers who came out of a Greek background He seized upon their word *logos*. *Logos* had meant "the essence of being within man and the cosmos, which comes to man as he meditates intently upon it."[35] God guided John to point out that Jesus Christ, God's Son, is the supreme disclosure of the central reality at the heart of the cosmos.[36] Other inspired writers asserted that the Gospel can become this same *logos*, this personal revelation of God.[37]

The minister should expect God's person-revealing, life-giving power to come as worshipers ponder the redeeming deeds recorded in Scripture. God often came with His person and Word while a devout believer was meditating upon God's past deliverances of His people. As Balaam gazed upon the tents of God's pilgrim people, he waited for a word from God and declared, "Have I now any power at all to say any thing? the word that God putteth in my mouth, that shall I speak."[38] Moses meditated upon God's leading and said, "Remember all of the way which the Lord thy God led thee . . . and know that man doth not live by bread only, but by every word that proceedeth out of the mouth of the Lord doth man live."[39] Even though Elijah had just come from Mt. Carmel where God had revealed Himself by fire, Elijah did not expect future revelations through either fire or storm, but through the still small voice which told of God's love and leading.[40]

In Samuel's day the inspired writer says, "The word of the Lord was precious [rare] in those days . . ." and while Samuel brooded with God over the situation, the Lord's word came to Samuel, "Behold, I will do a thing in Israel. . . ."[41] Jeremiah grieved before God because of Israel's shallow religion until even a sign from nature, the budding of an almond tree, evoked a word from God. "I will hasten my word to perform it."[42] It was as Ezekiel sat astonished with God's captive people in Babylon that the word of God came, "therefore hear the word at my mouth."[43]

The New Testament continues the same belief that God

engages in saving action through a Spirit-guided word. Jesus was as mighty in word as in deed[44] so that He needed only to speak a word and miracles happened.[45] Amazed worshipers in the synagogues at Capernaum asked what manner of word this was.[46] Although Jesus claimed to be God's very Word and truth, yet He also promised to project His will through words, so that the Holy Spirit could later bring them to a disciple's remembrance and so that they might judge men at the last day.[47]

The disciples preached in words which God confirmed with signs following.[48] Even the nameless seventy who went out in visitation evangelism found that they could stand in a doorway and by their Gospel greeting make the very kingdom of God to come nigh to that household.[49] When the revelator pictured believers in their final triumph over Satan, he said that they triumphed by the word of their testimony, and he lists their word alongside of the blood of the Lamb.[50]

Many writers of the New Testament imply that through the message of the Gospel the Word of God can come. They regard this Word as a dynamic expression of God's life and power, just as the Old Testament writers did. Thus the Gospel message becomes a deposit which lives and grows like a seed does,[51] a power which shakes the place when it is presented boldly,[52] and a determiner of history which God's servant labors to help to fulfill.[53] The preached Word can become part of God's conflict with and triumph over Satan.

As New Testament worshipers pondered the facts of God's saving acts in Christ at Calvary, the resurrection, and at Pentecost, God Himself confronted them. Paul believed that when the Gospel was preached, then the same God who once made light to shine out of darkness on creation morning would give the light of His glory in the face of Jesus Christ.[54] Paul believed that by the Holy Spirit's help preaching could be lifted above the level of mere talk, but that the preaching of the Gospel could cause the kingdom of God to move in in power.[55] The Christian minister should believe, along with Old and New Testament leaders, that God can make the preached Word to participate in the very power about which it speaks.

By preaching and teaching the meaning of God's past encounters with men, encounter becomes possible in the present
moment. Calvary's cross and the open tomb can become realities
in the worship service as the Gospel is preached. "Say not in
thine heart, Who shall ascend into heaven, (that is, to bring
Christ down from above:) or, Who shall descend into the deep?
(that is, to bring Christ again from the dead.) But what saith it?
The word is nigh thee, even in thy mouth, and in thy heart: that
is, the word of faith, which we preach."[56] Barriers of time are
transcended and the realities of time and eternity are made
contemporary in Christian preaching. When God's Word is coming in Holy Spirit power, then judgment is beginning at the
house of God. These are moments of time filled full with
eternity's meanings.

The miracle of the new birth should be expected to occur as
the Gospel is being preached, and the Word of God which liveth
and abideth forever is coming afresh to the hearts of men.[57]
Lives can be cleansed from sin by the washing of water by the
Word.[58] Worshipers can hear Paul's letter to the Thessalonians,
not only as the word of a man, but as the very Word of God.[59]
A sin-burdened listener can hear Christ speak His Word of forgiveness during the preaching of the Gospel, just as really and
personally as anyone heard Christ during the first century. As
the Bible narrative describes a needy person's encounter with
God, the need of the worshiper may be probed in a similar tender
spot. God's redeeming help may come to the worshiper as he
reaches out to God in faith. The Word of God always includes
God's offer of a "peace treaty," in the offer of unmerited forgiveness in Christ.

The minister should deliver his sermon in the midst of
worship with humility and yet with awe and holy joy. He should
dare to believe that God has chosen to speak in the "empty
space," between the ascension and the Lord's return, by means of
Christian preaching. He should believe that as the Holy Spirit
enables him to expound the Gospel from the Scriptures, then
God's living Word will come to listening hearts in a little preview of the judgment day. Sharper than any two-edged sword,

God's Son through God's Word will lay bare the very thoughts and intents of hearts.[60] The minister should tremble lest his preaching be not in demonstration of Spirit and in power. The minister should be living within the reality of God's redeeming action as he describes God's saving action upon other men in other times and places. Hearers should identify deeply with persons portrayed in the Bible, with both their "horns and their halos."

The minister, because of his deep reverence for the inspired Scriptures from which he preaches, must be careful lest he deify the Scriptures, thus creating a new Trinity: Father, Son, and Holy Bible. God is not "there" in the Scriptures, whether anyone hears Him or not, in exactly the same way in which God was there in the incarnate Son, whether anyone was listening to Him or not. Jesus Christ was and is God's most fully alive Word. God's Word only became incarnate once, and that was in Jesus Christ. Bibliolatry would be idolatry.

But the minister believes that God has chosen the inspired record of His saving action in Jesus Christ as His special instrument by which to confront men with His own person. Here is where God intends to keep rendezvous with men. God Himself is waiting, or one might almost say crouching, within the inspired Scriptures in His unceasing effort to call and redeem men.

But both the minister and the congregation should be sobered by the fact that confrontation with God is not automatic nor guaranteed, even though the Scriptures are being expounded with Holy Spirit unction. God can speak, but man can stuff his fingers in his ears.[61]

If the minister has trouble accepting the fact that his preaching cannot force a given worshiper to actually hear God's own personal Word, he should remember that God Himself once spoke from heaven to His Son, but the Jews and others who were nearby only heard noise and thought that it thundered. Jesus told the Jews that they could not understand His sayings because they did not really want to be confronted by His Word (logos).

Worshipers need to be attentive and receptive or, like the

Jews of old, their hearts may be veiled while Moses is read and they hear nothing from God at all. James warned that the engrafted or implanted Word must be received with meekness.[63] Peter warned that worshipers must long for the Word with a desire like that which a baby feels for milk. Furthermore, Peter asserts that the worshiper must lay aside all guile, malice, gossip, or envy if he is to hear God's Word.[64]

X. God's Servants Need to Present Their Lives to God Anew

The minister should be certain that the worship service climaxes in self-sacrifice. As Abraham set out to offer up his son to God on Mt. Moriah he said, "I . . . go . . . and worship."[65] God offered His own Son in love to the death (as a lamb slain) before the foundation of the world. All worship since then has been climaxed by the giving of the very best, even to life itself, back to God in response to His great love. The beloved pet lamb which a Jewish family offered to God was to portray the pouring out of their life and love to God in answer to God's redeeming love and deeds.

The prophets chorused their protest against the giving of other sacrifices unaccompanied by the giving up of the worshipers' own life to God. Samuel warned, "To obey is better than sacrifice." Isaiah asked, "To what purpose . . . is your sacrifice?"[66] Jeremiah, Micah, Amos, and Hosea all insist that God longs for man to love Him with all of his heart, soul, mind, and strength. Jesus said that when a worshiper once grasps this, he is not far from the kingdom.[67]

The Bible is clear that Christ died once as a sacrifice for sins, and that worshipers should not try to crucify Him afresh. Rather, the worshiper should present his own body, his entire personality, and all that he has or ever hopes to be, as an offering to God in response to Christ's love. The climax of worship is reached when each worshiper presents himself to God as his act of reasonable service or liturgical response. When the entire personality has been rededicated to God, then God promises to transform the worshiper's character. His mind will be renewed so that he can discern the holy and perfect will of God and at the same time refuse to take the print of or be conformed to the sinful world.[68]

The minister, as he leads worship, should sometimes suggest practical expressions which sacrifice might involve. In the midst of worship, as believers are ministering to the Lord, the Lord may ask the congregation to sacrifice some friends or workers to go out in world missions.[69] Their gifts become an odor of sweet smell, a sacrifice acceptable and well pleasing to God.[70] Every glimpse of the living God in worship reveals again His perpetual passion for world evangelism, and the worshiper must be willing to sacrifice all selfish ambition. When the Lord's question, "Whom shall I send?" is heard anew, every worshiper must answer, "Here am I; send me."[71]

The worshiper may not linger mesmerized before the "Old Rugged Cross" but must take up his own cross of martyr obedience. The culmination of worship comes in the life poured out in sacrificial service for others. "But to do good and communicate forget not: for with such sacrifices God is well pleased."[72]

The minister, as he leads the people of God in worship, must remember that God's offer of forgiving grace and power to His people is at the same time a call of evangelism. This mighty climax of worship, when every servant of the Lord is renewing his surrender, and in his heart is crying, "Yes, Lord," can have a strong evangelistic influence upon any unredeemed person who is present and is still saying, "No, Lord." As the whole worshiping congregation present again their personalities to God as a living sacrifice, the unsaved person in the midst cannot help feeling that it would be the only reasonable service if he too would show some decent appreciation and response to God's love and grace. The most profound experience of worship on the part of believers should precipitate the most powerful evangelistic appeal to unbelievers at one and the same time.

XI. The Presentation of Tithes and Offerings Should Be an Act of Worship

When worshipers present their very lives to God as a living sacrifice during the worship service, it is fitting that they should present their tithes and offerings to God at the same time. The one tenth (or more) which is presented to God in the offering can symbolize the entire week's livelihood and service. The giving of the offering should be done as a sacred act of worship. The New Testament epistles, likely read in their entirety as the very body or framework of the worship service, usually include mention of the giving of money near to the close of the epistle.[73]

The minister may well "frame" the presentation of tithes and offerings with appropriate readings from Scripture. As the offering is announced and the congregation is invited to lay their gifts before God, Scriptures such as the following may be read.

Ps. 116:12, 14: "What shall I render unto the Lord for all his benefits toward me? . . . I will pay my vows . . . now in the presence of all his people."

Prov. 3:9: "Honour the Lord with thy substance, and with the firstfruits of all thine increase."

Mal. 3:10: "Bring ye all the tithes into the storehouse, that there may be meat in my house, and prove me now herewith, saith the Lord of hosts, if I will not open you the windows of heaven, and pour you out a blessing, that there shall not be room enough to receive it."

Matt. 6:19-21: "Lay not up for yourselves treasures upon earth, where moth and rust doth corrupt, and where thieves break through and steal: but lay up for yourselves treasures in heaven, where neither moth nor rust doth corrupt, and where thieves do not break through nor steal, for where your treasure is, there will your heart be also."

Matt. 10:8: "Freely ye have received; freely give."

Acts 20:35: "I have shewed you all things, how that so labouring ye ought to support the weak, and to remember the words of the Lord Jesus, how he said, It is more blessed to give than to receive."

II Cor. 8:9: "For ye know the grace of our Lord Jesus Christ, that, though he was rich, yet for your sakes he became poor, that ye through his poverty might be rich."

II Cor. 9:7, 8: "Every man . . . as he purposeth in his heart, so let him give; not grudgingly, or of necessity: for God loveth a cheerful giver. And God is able to make all grace abound toward you; that ye, always having all sufficiency in all things, may abound to every good work."

The congregation may well sing from memory certain hymns of praise or consecration while the offering is being lifted. Appropriate numbers may be sung by the chorus if they have such numbers prepared.

The congregation can symbolize its involvement in joyous giving if they will stand and sing, "Praise God from Whom All Blessings Flow," or "We Give Thee but Thine Own," while the offering is being carried forward. Any prayer of thanksgiving and consecration which the minister prays should be brief and to the point.

A sufficient number of ushers should serve so that the offering may be gathered quickly, quietly, and reverently. Stiff formality should be avoided. The regimented lock step of solemn-faced ushers wearing carnations in their buttonholes may detract rather than contribute to the real spirit of joyous worship in giving.

XII. Prayer May Well Climax Each Movement of Worship

Prayer may well be offered near to the climax of the approach, the listening, the giving, and of each major experience of the corporate worship. Prayer is close to the heart of the total worship experience and the one part of worship which is seldom if ever omitted. Prayer calls the worshiper to stop speaking or reflecting about God and to address Him directly. For many worshipers prayer provides the most personal, face-to-face, immediate encounter with their God which they ever experience. The worship leader should be totally immersed in the reality of prayer himself as he seeks to lead worshipers in their sacred and secret "dialogue of the heart" with their God.

Even when a prayer punctuates each phase of worship, and the content of the prayer is suggested by that phase, there should be order and form within it. Christ taught a pattern of prayer and it is fitting that the most free and spontaneous prayers should still follow a pattern something like the one Jesus gave. In audible prayer the leader may follow the progression suggested by the letters A, C, T, S. These letters remind the leader to begin with adoration, move to confession, follow with thanksgiving, and conclude with supplication.[74]

Even the corporate prayer of God's people should be seen as response to God's help and grace. A worship leader should remember that the Spirit must help his infirmity if he is to know what to pray for. Always the worship leader's attitude and spirit should show that he is aware that through Him we "draw near,"[75] and through Him we "have access."[76] The prayers of corporate worship may often represent the "sacrificial act" of response which the congregation makes to God's grace which has come to them in Scripture, fellowship, sermon, or song.

Worship leaders should carefully premeditate their prayers. Free prayers too often lack clarity, order, comprehensiveness, and dignity. A disordered array of unrelated petitions and praise becomes extremely hard for a congregation to follow and to make their very own. A worship leader should never merely have his private devotions in public. He should carefully avoid the temptation to lecture either the congregation or God. He should not use sentimental phrases, clichés, chummy talk, or slang.

The worship leader who has mingled with the congregation all week will know the aching needs which cry out to heaven from the hearts of the people. He will seek to gather up the heart cries of the entire congregation and to articulate them. Worshipers may well respond with whispered or even audible "amens" as the corporate prayer proceeds. This intercession for the needs in the congregation usually is included in a "long" or "pastoral" prayer.

Prayers which focus upon one specific petition may well be in the "collect" form. The collect begins with some attribute of God which becomes the basis of the petition, some cry of adoration because of that attribute, some specific petition, the purpose or grounds for making the petition, and a word of ascription or praise to God for His goodness in granting it.[77] Prayers within worship such as the offertory, the prayer for illumination just before the sermon, or the prayer for the sick members of the congregation may well be collect prayers.

For variety in the corporate prayers the leader may call upon the worshiping congregation to pray a refrain after each petition. An example of this might be if the leader would pray, "Oh, bless the Lord, my soul," and the congregation echo after this and each subsequent petition, "All that is within me, bless His holy name." Other refrains sometimes prayed by the congregation include, "Have mercy upon us, O Lord." This "litany" form of prayer goes back to the synagogue worship.

Still another form of public prayer is the "bidding prayer." In this form the minister first explains that he will suggest a prayer concern and then wait silently while each worshiper fills in the details as his own heart desires and in his own words. This is an effort to bring the personalness of private and silent prayer into the midst of the group-worship experience.

XIII. The Lord's Supper Should Be a Sacred Act of Worship

Even though God has chosen to use words as the central sacrament of Christian worship, He has not limited His people to the use of the verbal symbol. In both Old and New Testaments God instructed His people to use dramatic symbols. These were acts by which worshipers refreshed and intensified their grasp of the great realities of their faith. God also commanded the use of material symbols (bread, water, wine) to bring spiritual realities more vividly to the total person through sensory experience. No other acts and experiences of worship place such a high demand upon the worship leader. God waits to reveal and offer His very person, life, and power through dramatic and material symbols, if they are received in faith, just as much as through the verbal symbols or words. Therefore, ordinances should be observed with great reverence and awe.

God's acts of sovereign grace at the Red Sea and Mt. Sinai overwhelmed and conquered His people, almost compelled their response of love, and so Israel entered into covenant with God. They promised to keep responding and living like His people in the earth. The symbolic ceremony of the Passover was to help new generations to enter into the same awesome encounter with God, and to make from the depths of their own being the same covenant to live in loving response. The law was merely some detailed guidance to show the ways in which the covenant believer's response of love might best be made.

God's astounding grace broke in upon mankind in its fullest display when God acted in Christ. By the spectacle of Calvary, the resurrection, and Pentecost, God called men to enter a new covenant. Those who responded with their total being found a miracle taking place within them. Under this new covenant their personality was invaded and seized at its deepest levels. God's law became engraven on their very hearts. Holy Spirit indwelling made possible a new abandonment and power in their response to their God. Prophetic passion and unction, once limited to prophets and a few leaders, now came upon all, even sons and daughters. Powers from the coming aeon continued to break in in waves which almost overwhelmed their minds. Spontaneous joy sprang forth and stolid souls lost their inhibitions until astounded observers thought the worshipers were drunk.

The minister and his helpers (likely the elders or deacons of the congregation) should lead the observance of the Lord's Supper with the fervent prayer that through it God's redeeming act in Christ may become again as new and overpowering as it was in the first century. By observing the Lord's Supper the worshiping congregation seeks to "bind time" and to bring the wonder and the power of Calvary, the empty tomb, and Pentecost over against the present moment. The Negro spiritual song asks so fittingly, "Were you there when they crucified my Lord?" By observing the Lord's Supper the worshipers are helped to be there. It is to mediate immediacy. The intervening centuries should lose their power to insulate the soul from first-hand experience.

As the bread is broken the worshiper is there, again surveying the wondrous cross upon which the Prince of glory died. While bread is broken—in "remembrance of me"—the worshiper sees and hears again the cry, "Father, forgive," while the enmity and sin of mankind is breaking the very body of the Son of God. The worshiper dares to believe anew that such dying love can absorb his own enmity and sin, even his, as great as it is.

As the wine is poured out the worshiper sees again that God loves even to the death. He understands a little more clearly how that God Almighty actually poured out His very life to absorb and forgive men's hostility and enmity. He stands smitten before the unparalleled love of his dying God. He sees that, even while man's sin was piercing the veil of flesh which God wore, lunging its hate and rebellion toward the very heart of God, in that moment God was opening wide the veil which had barred man from His presence in the holy place. In response to man's most diabolical hate, God poured out His love and lifeblood. He absorbed it all in nonresistant forgiving love, and invited all who will accept His love to enter the holy place with Him. Thus the spectacle (of God pouring out His life in forgiving love of His enemies on Calvary) which once created the new covenant people the church now recreates the church in its covenant of love to Christ.

As the bread and wine are eaten and drunk, the worshiper declares his desire and intent to eat Christ's flesh and drink His blood by faith. He draws upon the very life of God for his continued existence as a Christian. He does not imagine that he automatically partakes of Christ's life because a magical transubstantiation has occurred and he is actually grinding up Christ's flesh in his teeth. He knows that mere flesh profiteth nothing. The words which Christ speaks are the supreme bearers of Spirit and life. But, having received Christ's word by faith, he can also have Christ's life renewed within as he partakes in faith of the symbols of His body and blood.

The worship leaders must remember that God's invasion at the Red Sea and Sinai produced separate people. Again, God's inbreak in Christ created the new people, the church. Even so, the dramatization and remembrance of God's saving work in Christ should recreate "a people." Believers cannot remain isolated individualists. Christ never joins a person to Himself without at the same time joining him to the brother who shares Christ's life. And so, those who eat of the Lord's Supper should be one bread, one loaf, one body, and a band of disciples united in faith and mutual concern.

It is not enough to discern Christ's "then body," the one He wore and which was broken on Calvary. The worshiper must also discern whether any carnality and rivalry is breaking the "body," the congregation. The worshiper will eat and drink unworthily, and eat damnation rather than blessing, if he fails to discern Christ's "now body" as well. In Corinth worshipers broke Christ's "body" by party spirit and by the rich members ignoring the hungry poor members. Worship leaders should call upon members of the congregation to examine themselves as to the reality of their personal faith, and to examine their depth of love and concern for the body, the church.

Worship leaders, and congregations, should not exclude from the Lord's table anyone who is joined to Christ and to His body, merely as a pressure device to force conformity to cultural applications currently cherished by the leaders. Christians should examine their right to exclude from the Lord's table other believers who do not share their opinions as to the correct mode of baptism, ordination, liturgy, ordinance observance, or creedal expression. Difference of race, color, sex, language, or culture make no difference at all to Christ the Lord, whose Supper it is, and who invites His own to come. Woe betide any proud mortal who takes it upon himself to exclude a brother whom the Lord has accepted and invited.

On the other hand there are good reasons why the Lord's Supper should be shared by those who share their total lives under Christ's lordship. The passover was shared by members of a family who could relate their separation unto their God to all of their life experience. They were a community of concern and love.

There is strong evidence that Christ and His disciples were

a "Chaburoth" group, a small intimate "prayer cell" of male friends who met to converse upon the things of God. In addition to "looking for redemption in Israel," these groups would hold a religious meal together. These weekly suppers were often held on the eve of Sabbaths or holy days.[79]

"Bread-breaking" became a sacred rite symbolizing deep sharing. Although devout Jews had prayer and bread-breaking at every meal, it was only in the Chaburoth, "cell group," "pot-luck meals" that the "cup of blessing" was always shared. Luke, a Gentile writer, likely was not familiar with the life of Chaburoth groups, and he alone omits mention of the "cup of blessing."

Many serious students of Christian worship are convinced that the disciples knew their risen Lord "in the breaking of bread" because He had developed a unique way of doing this during their many meals together.[80] If the Lord wanted His Supper to be observed within a group who shared deeply and cared vitally for one another, then there may be good reason now to limit the Lord's Supper to members of the congregation who are committed, not only to Christ, but to one another. Christ made an effort to have the traitor to excuse himself before the faithful few observed the sacred rite together.

For these and other reasons it seems most appropriate that the Lord's Supper should not be a completely open act of worship in which any visitor can join, just as he may share in the hymn singing, the offering, or the listening. The group is to be joined together as one loaf, one bread. The people of the new covenant are called to live together in a common obedience to their Lord. The true church is not known by a chorus of "Lord, Lord" cries, or even of sacrament receivers. The new people of God are known in history by their fruits. Where faith and Holy Spirit power have moved within a group of people until their martyr obedience has produced a separation from the ungodly— this, and only this group, is truly the church. And the group who have covenanted their lives, not only to Christ in an individualistic pietism, but to one another as to Christ's body on earth, this group should observe the Lord's Supper together.

It is supremely interesting that the writer of the Gospel of John, who wrote later than the synoptic writers, did not picture Christ making His presence real to His followers through bread and wine at an altar in a worship service. Christ ministered bread and wine to people in daily situations of human need. The Christians who are banded together to embody Christ's power as a ministering, obedient congregation—they are the ones who should observe the Lord's Supper together, if its deepest reality is to be experienced.

The worship leader should also associate the Lord's Supper with eschatology. The risen Christ, who first revealed Himself to His own at bread-breakings, promises to consummate His wooing of them in the future marriage supper of the Lamb. Just as the Supper helps to anchor worshipers back into the earthly life of their Lord, it also anchors their life and hope in the Lord's return.[81] Believers "ate with gladness" because every bread-breaking or love feast reminded them of earlier meals with their Lord. But they felt joy also because He who now came in to sup with them intended to present them faultless in the presence of His glory with exceeding joy. Feeding upon Christ's life was indeed tasting of "the powers of the world to come."[82], [83] The Lord's Supper was already a partial fulfillment of Christ's eating "it new with you in my . . . kingdom."

How frequently should a congregation observe the Lord's Supper? Almost all students of early Christian worship are agreed that the Lord's Supper was the goal of every gathering, and that Christians observed it at least once each week. Almost all of the great leaders of the Reformation hoped that the Lord's Supper might be restored to its place as a weekly ob-servance. Why should the church be so reluctant to practice the Eucharist regularly? Methodists have elected a form of their class meeting to become their regular worship and Anglicans have elevated a prayer hour in the same way. By one means or another most brotherhoods limit their observance of the Eucharist.

Some worshipers may argue that they limit their observance of the Lord's Supper lest frequent repetition should lessen its sacred meaning and power to bring blessing. But why not limit the practice of prayer for the same reason? Although few who wish to limit the observance of the Lord's Supper ever give their reasons, it may well be that the real reason lies in a feeling of unworthiness.

By combining the verbal symbol, the word, with the material symbol, bread and wine, and with the dramatic symbols, breaking and eating, the combined impact upon the heart and mind is terrific. People shrink from being so near "when they crucified my Lord." Worshipers wish to stand a little farther off when Golgotha's awful hour is dramatized. Believers tremble to be reminded so vividly that it was their sin which broke the body of God's Son. They hesitate to affirm too often the stark reality which lies at the center of living as a Christian. "He that eateth me, even he shall live by me." It seems almost too much to declare that one is living one's life, moment by moment, by feeding in faith upon the divine life of Christ.

Infrequent communion can only be overcome as believers become willing to draw near more boldly to the sublime and central realities of their faith. Worship leaders may well encourage congregations to climax their joyous occasions with the Lord's Supper. Certainly the celebration of Christ's coming at Christmas time might well be climaxed with the Eucharist because He came primarily to give His life. Good Friday might well be another appropriate occasion. Times of baptizing and receiving new members might be appropriately consummated by the Lord's Supper. Occasions when backsliders are reclaimed and reinstated into fellowship should also suggest sitting down together in the Father's house at His table. A series of renewal meetings in the congregation, a missionary conference or series of Bible studies, a home-interests conference, a homecoming, or a farewell service for students going away to college: these and other happy crises in the congregation might well be climaxed by the observance of the Lord's Supper.

XIV. A Benediction Should Send God's Servants
Out Again to Their Work

After each worshiper has presented his body to God as his reasonable service or liturgical response, and has invited God to send him out in evangelism and mission, then the worship leader seeks to symbolize God's sending in a solemn ceremony of benediction. By raising his hand during the benediction the leader can symbolize the "laying on of hands" upon the entire laity, "ordaining" and commissioning them anew. Because the living Christ has been present through His living Word in their midst, the congregation moves out to assert and actually seek to implement His lordship in all social relations. Because they have been with Him on the "holy mount" of group worship, they move together into the valley as a disciple band, determined to be the new people of God in the midst of the earth. By group decisions they seek to discover and to say their united word of prophetic rebuke to the sins of encircling society. In their life together they seek to demonstrate the miracle as to what life can be like when mortals live together in divine love. As individuals they seek to enter the arteries of a sick society as personal embodiments of Calvary's love and power.

Some worship leaders suggest that the benediction be pronounced with the simple words long used in the western church, *Ite Missa est*—"go, it is finished." Others urge that a closing prayer should be for the whole universal church of the Lamb, thus symbolizing that, when God's people gather around His throne in worship, all man- or Satan-inspired divisions will finally be transcended.

The benedictory prayer can probably do no better than to quote one of the great benedictions of the Bible. The Aaronic blessing of Num. 6:24-26 is solemn and beautiful. The triune-God benediction of II Cor. 13:14 is unsurpassed for clarity, scope, and brevity. The note of doxology and adoration is central in the benediction recorded in I Tim. 1:17. Calm confidence in God's ultimate triumph is dominant in one cited in Eph. 3:20, 21. The whole personality of man is committed to the divine care in the one recorded in I Thess. 5:23, 24, and 28. The benediction should symbolize that the church which has been gathered for renewal and fellowship in the life eternal is now being sent out to be the church scattered, at work for Christ in His world.

Because true worship points toward consummation and is a preview of the final day, it is fitting that the note of eschatology should appear in the benediction. It is good to close worship with the triumphant cry which ends the benediction cited in Heb. 13:20, 21—"to whom be glory for ever and ever." The Jude 24 and 25 benediction links the present worship with divine presentation and eternal glory. "Now unto him that is able to keep you from falling, and to present you faultless before the presence of his glory with exceeding joy, to the only wise God our Saviour, be glory and majesty, dominion and power, both now and ever. Amen."

The buzz of conversation which comes after the benediction can be either a distracting intrusion or a sharing of the concerns of the common life as it is to be lived under Christ's lordship. If the conversation is completely secular chatter, a talking about human affairs oblivious of the way in which the sovereignty of God must impinge at every point, then it is unseemly for the Christian at any time and doubly so in the house of God.

XV. Announcements Should Be Made Between Church And Sunday School

Announcements often come as a distraction into the midst of the worship service. Worship should be something of a dialogue. The coming of God's Word is answered by the response of the believer. The worshiper receives God's grace through His Word and then offers his sacrifice of praise or offering in response. This rhythm should not be interrupted by a list of tedious announcements, many of which divert the mind away from the soul's present dialogue with God.

Announcements should be kept to a minimum, and the necessary ones may best be made at the bridge between Sunday school and the worship service, regardless which one comes first. Make announcements concisely and without apology.

"Concerns of the church" may well be the way announcements are listed in the bulletin and the spirit in which they are presented. The needs of sick members, the important tasks ahead in the congregational program, and the good things which are ahead for God's people to enjoy together—these announcements should all be made with anticipation and shared concern.

XVI. Other Worship Services of a More Subjective Character Are Needed Too

The pattern of worship implied in this lecture is one of reverent dignity, with order, movement, and climax. It is more objective than subjective in focus. This is intended to be the suggested pattern for the Sunday morning worship. It is a service of adoration, reverent listening, and Thou-centered praise. It would use the older, majestic hymns and rely upon a profound, exegesis-based exposition of Scripture. Responsive readings from Scripture would fit into this mood and pattern of worship. But subjective worship is valid and rewarding too. The congregation should gather at other times for meetings in which believers testify to one another of their experiences of the grace of God. Better type Gospel songs and topical preaching would fit here. Special music, quartets, solos could have a place.

In addition to and beyond the corporate prayers in which worshipers unite when responding to God during their more formal worship services, it is important that there be informal "prayer meetings." Believers need to share in periods of intense intercession for one another and for concerns of the kingdom of God. In informal prayer and worship services each worshiper should at times lead out in audible prayer. In these periods of free and spontaneous worship the service may shift almost imperceptibly from prayer, to praise, to testimony, even as is suggested in many of the psalms. The ordered worship service should not be presented as an alternative to the prayer cell or informal worship. Every congregation needs both types.[84]

Chapter 5

The Minister Assists God's People In Their Service to Men

I. The Minister Must Also Help to Administer

The church should allow her pattern of administration to be shaped partly by the task which the need of the world thrusts upon her. Rapid changes brought about by urbanization and the space age may make time-honored patterns of polity inadequate. As the ministering congregation seeks to take the servant posture of her Lord toward human sin and need, the Spirit of God will be faithful to guide the church into appropriate organizational and administrative forms.

If a dedicated laity will arise in faith to claim charismatic gifts and power for ministry, this will correct many defects in the contemporary Protestant pattern. No more will the minister be forced to "do everything that gets done." Although the layman's primary task is to do the church's work while she is scattered, the gifts which the Holy Spirit bestows upon him for ministry should find an increasing place in the life of the church while she is gathered. But the ministering congregation will not be renewed for her task in the world unless the minister of the Word has courage to really give himself to his central preaching-teaching task.

Because the Word of God is central in all decision-making and work of the church, the man who is ordained, set apart, and supported to give himself to the ministry of the Word cannot divorce himself completely from church administration. He

must be related to all of the actual ministries and activities of the
congregation so that he may bring to it the counsels which
emerge from his depth level and continuous studies in the
Word.

The ministering congregation is led in its ministry to its
neighborhood and to its own inner growth by a team of lay
leaders. Church council members, elders, deacons, trustees, mission board members, Sunday-school officers and teachers, women's
missionary officers, youth fellowship officers, ushers, stewards,
song leaders, mutual aid committee members, and many other
such leaders carry, and should carry, the work of the church. In
addition to his primary responsibilities as preacher and worship
leader, the ordained minister serves as a "basin-seizer," stooping
to serve one and then another as opportunity and need arises.
He is a "chaplain" to the "Lord's ministers," a "servant of God's
servants," a "coach of the Lord's team," or a "ministerial
enabler." The congregation assists him in many ways in his
ministry as preacher and leader of worship when the church is
gathered, and he assists them in their leadership of the congregational program of Christian nurture, outreach, social witness, and
in their personal "church work" in their life all week.

The total administrative program of the congregation cannot be discussed in one brief lecture. Because of lack of time
many highly significant areas of congregational work will not be
considered. Among these are administering the Sunday-school
and Christian education activities, the training of teachers,
budgeting and financing of the church program, planning an
adequate church building, preparing publicity, and relating to
other institutions and agencies which attempt to serve the
community. The congregational program of music education,
youth activities, and women's missionary and fellowship ministries are all extremely important parts of the congregation's
work which cannot be treated here.

Several important aspects of congregational ministry, which
are too often omitted or treated lightly in most books on church
administration, will be considered in this lecture. The way in
which the minister of the Word of God serves the ministering

congregation in these areas of work which will be considered may suggest how he should relate to all of the congregational leaders in their total congregational program.

Many ordained ministers would much rather merely minister—that is, serve persons directly. But they must also help to administer, that is, serve by co-operating with and co-ordinating the ministries of many other persons. Ordained ministers should rise above any peevish avoidance of all administrative duties, whether this stems from laziness, impatience with the faltering efforts of co-workers, or a perverted notion that all institutionalized forms of church life are somehow sinful and beneath the dignity of a holy man like himself. The minister needs more genuine patience and humility to work behind the scenes, helping someone else to do the work and to get the credit for it, than he would need to do the work himself.

Even the committees which are elected to lead out in various phases of congregational ministries should see their work as that of perfecting the entire congregation in its work of ministering. The committee should be only a rallying center around which the Holy Spirit may lead the persons He is gifting to come to work together. All committee meetings should be open. It should be the expected thing that the Holy Spirit may be giving His charismatic enablement to some member of the congregation, and that this member will show up at the next meeting of the committee, seeking for the way to work together in love.

All of the preacher's high-sounding phrases about love in human relationships receive their acid test in the administration of the work of the congregation. Here the congregation learns whether the minister really believes what he has been preaching about the charismatic gifts which the Holy Spirit gives to every member.

The mature minister accepts it as an humbling judgment upon his ministry of God's Word to the congregation if the interaction of lay leaders is punctuated by pettiness, easily hurt feelings, and a "loving to have the pre-eminence."

II. Administration Reveals Both the Divine
And the Human Sides of the Church

Ordained ministers are tempted to lose patience with the humanness of the congregation. The minister of the Word is constantly studying all of the glorious pictures of the church as they are held up in the epistles. By combining all that the epistles say about the church, the minister concludes that it is to be the very family of God Himself, a colony of heaven projected across into the present temporal order, and a disciple band within which the Holy Spirit power moves perpetually as He did at Pentecost. The church is to be a people of the living God who demonstrate God's divine love, holiness, and power in their group life together. They are to function as Christ's "now body" in society, beseeching men to be reconciled to God with the same persistence and passion which once burned in Christ Himself. The minister is apt to forget that no one congregation, even in New Testament times, ever measured up fully to the total New Testament ideal. The congregation in which he now serves will be imperfect too.

The minister must continue to believe profoundly that God will never stop striving and wooing His people until they finally do reach consummation, beyond history, in "the measure of the stature of the fulness of Christ." And so, while the treasure is now held in earthen vessels, the minister sees the excellency of the power at work already amidst the sociological forms and processes of church life.[1]

The wise minister remembers that persons are all hungry for status and power, and are tempted to use church office to "baptize" this psychological drive. Rootless people want a home, and may seek to have the church become a mere "friendly church," moving along on a clublike level of buddy-buddy chumminess. People tend to seek out their own social class and will unthinkingly transform the congregation into a one-class group. Without intending to do anything wrong, leaders may "sound out the important people" before a member's meeting or bring a "hidden agenda" along to the official board meeting.

Members may too easily assume that the methods of democratic process or of *Roberts' Rules of Order* are the highest way the Holy Spirit can find to bring a congregation to consensus. The minister who has been set apart to minister God's Word must bring its principles and spirit to bear upon the life of the church exactly at these revealing aspects of congregational life. The excellency of God's power must be felt from time to time, even through earthen vessels.

The minister should not only preach about and give conceptual definitions of the charismatic life of the church, but must help her to detect it in action. The minister should call members back to the reality of the Holy Spirit impulses in present relationships. He should help to lift up the essentials of a prophetic faith until that faith can judge the very culture in which it has become embedded. He should help members find Christ's authority in a decision-making process as the group seeks to sense the solution which possesses the most inner consistency with the words and Spirit of Jesus. This becomes the supreme test of his ministry of God's Word to the church.

III. Administration Must Be Done in the Spirit of the Master

The minister, because of his constant exposure to God's Word, should have greater sensitivity to detect the inroads of "subchurch" practices. Yet he must realize that he too is human, and needs the help of his brethren in the congregation to keep congregational administration faithful to and consistent with the inner Spirit of Jesus.

Congregational leaders must remain alert and sensitive lest institutionalized forms curb the freedom and spontaneity of the Holy Spirit's working in the present moment. Persons who carry offices in the church need to beware lest they begin to play roles and wear false fronts as they interact. Christians immersed in the implementation of a "program" too readily fail to find and to meet one another supremely upon the basis of their joint participation in Christ through the Spirit.

The minister can very readily acquire too much power in

the congregation. Because his term in office is usually longer than that of the rest of the team of leaders, and because of his greater training and experience, he may be tempted to "play God" or assume omniscience. The minister will be tempted to hand-pick his co-workers, to soft-pedal complaints from the "loyal opposition," or to quote the opinions of authorities to add weight to his own opinions. It is extremely important that the minister live in transparent openness with his brethren and walk humbly with his God.

If the leaders of a congregation are spiritually mature, their experiences in administration and committee work can become some of their most moving and rewarding experiences of the here-and-now action of the life of the Spirit of God. This is ever so much better than to retreat from the demands of church admin-istration and to seek for "reality" and "life in the Spirit" in some comfortable cell or renewal group far removed from the actual tasks of the church. The very glory of God must shine out through the "wheels within wheels" of congregational life as the church organizes and co-operates to do her work in her world. The same group which faces a common task together, such as a church board or Christian education council, may well be the group to share mountaintop experiences of spiritual search and renewal.

Many if not most of the directives in the pastoral epistles apply most pointedly to the minister-leader as he interacts with lay leaders. "Do nothing by partiality," "not violent," "not quar-relsome," "not arrogant," "not quick tempered"—these and others are warnings on the negative side. The positive admonitions like-wise relate to administration. Be "dignified," "upright," "sen-sible," "gentle," "self-controlled," "above reproach," "set the believers an example in speech and conduct," "exhort an older man as a father"—these and others stress Christlikeness, wisdom, and tact in relating helpfully to people.[2]

IV. The Minister's Pastoral Calling Should Be Largely Enlistment

Many ministers revolt against the seemingly futile round of

doorbell ringing or the traditional pastoral call. Why walk around paying innocuous visits in a vast pious pretense? What strong man wants to spend his time drinking pink tea with polite ladies and saying "sweet nothings" in superficial conversations? What man of God can bear to visit a group of perpetually passive members, becoming "a docile little man encouraging docile people to be still more docile"? No minister of God's Word should ever succumb to such an empty farce.

Instead of all this, the minister should call in the homes of members as a "talent scout" for the King. The minister should seek to enlist households into the work of the whole family of God. He should not only ask each member to share with him their concerns for the work of the church, but should ask pointedly about any talents, gifts, skills, interests which might be more fully enlisted in Christ's mission through the congregation. The minister should discuss and pray with each member about their own personal pentration of the sub-Christian social order through their daily work. The minister should feel lifted and borne along by the gifts which God's grace has given to members of the congregation.

The minister may use any one of a number of methods to insure systematic coverage of all of the homes of the congregation in his "pastoral-calling" program. If he visits all of the homes in succession of those who are members of a particular adult Sunday-school class, then he can stress the importance of the adult class as a little "church within the church," and help class members to face their responsibilities in outreach through class projects and fellowship. Officers of the class can supplement or fill out the pastor's calls because usually the pastor is unable to visit in every home as often as he could wish.

If the congregation is small and the minister visits each member during the week of his or her birthday, then he can make the call intensely personal, relating it to the person's own life pilgrimage. He can ask for a testimony from the member as to the ways in which the Lord has led during the past year, of victories or defeats, and of goals for growth during the year ahead. If the congregation is too large for the minister to visit

6

each member personally each year, then church elders or other spiritually gifted members of the congregation should be asked to assist in the spiritual ministry to families.

Some ministers visit their members by neighborhoods or fellowship areas, going from one family to another in a given area of the total parish. If the minister uses this approach, then he can call members who are near-neighbors to begin to meet together informally for prayer and fellowship. The minister can challenge members to assume responsibility before God for the needs of lost persons in their own neighborhood, and can help members to get started in a co-operative effort to "by all means save some." The minister can help members in a given area to discover their own social witness in their own neighborhood.

One minister arranged for the church couples from the same neighborhood to meet in a home of one of them for an evening of prayer and fellowship. Many Christians need to learn for the first time how to carry on a spiritual conversation over a coffee cup and how to bare their hearts and their real problems before God in prayer as part of an evening's visit in a fellow member's home.[3] The church becomes a reality for some Christians for the first time when they accept responsibility in a face-to-face fellowship and service group.

V. The Minister Seeks to Awaken Greater Evangelistic Passion

The minister, guided by his constant study of the Word of God, is made aware that the congregation exists by evangelism as a fire does by burning. He knows that if the congregation ever parks or ceases her efforts to win men to faith in Christ, the church herself will begin to lose her faith and be on her way to apostasy. Evangelism is not one of the things which are optional, which a congregation can decide to omit, and still continue to be a true church.

In all of the minister's leadership he tries to allow God's Word to kindle evangelizing passion in the heart of every Christian. Every worship service should provide a glimpse of the God who is seeking to send worshipers out in evangelism. Every approach to the Scriptures should be made with the full awareness that it is a missionary book. Every invitation given for the Holy Spirit to invade the worshiper's personality to the depth should be given in expectancy that the Holy Spirit will generate within the believer the same redeeming passion which the God-Man demonstrated at Golgotha. The minister hopes and expects that when a worshiper meets the living Christ in the fellowship, the Word, or the worship, then Christ will commission that worshiper personally and overwhelmingly with His own sovereign sending: "As my Father hath sent me, even so send I you."

VI. The Minister Helps the Congregation to Face The Problems in Evangelism

The minister who has had a broad liberal arts and theological training will be almost overwhelmed with the complexity of the problem of communicating the living Word from Scriptures to the "tower of Babel" of today. He will be nearly daunted by the magnitude of the semantic problems involved. He will ask how modern man himself can be still and know that God is God, amidst the crashing of empires, the orbiting of enemy scientists overhead, the stunning acceleration of catclysmic changes, and the din of moronic-level amusements.

The trained minister will be tempted to ask how any church can give her verbal message convincingly when the professing church has so largely given the lie to her Gospel message by condoning war. Can the heathen really hear of God's love for enemies if "Christian" nations alternate their plane loads of Bibles with plane loads of bullets and bombs? Can Western Christianity, so vastly secularized, have anything convincing to say as opposed to the secular "religion" of communism? Can the Christian church in America, impotent to either repent from or change her own sinful record in racial discrimination, really be heard in a world in which the colored races may soon be the dominant majority? Can persons from the streets of American cities so largely given over to a pursuit of sensuous pleasure and amusement really hear and respond to Christ's call with ultimate concern and seriousness? Can a man who expects miracles only from science and "miracle drugs" really come with saving faith to receive the miracle of the new birth?

But the minister who knows in part the magnitude of the problem of reaching modern man with the Gospel must also know and believe in childlike faith that the living God can break through any barrier mankind can create, and can still save those that believe. Jesus Christ first came to earth in an hour so horrible that babies were being systematically murdered by government decree. While Rome was falling, God was giving to Augustine a vision of the city of God. When Ivan III was giving Russia its start by freeing her from the Monoglians, God was giving to a frightened monk, Martin Luther, a grasp of justification by faith. When mobs threatened civilization and stormed the gates of the Bastille, a man named Wesley was finding his heart strangely warmed and set out on horseback to evangelize England.

No, the minister who can match faith with the prophets who spoke in the Scriptures will survey his own community and will always be looking for the "cloud the size of a man's hand" on the horizon. He will help the congregation to brood with the redeeming God over their neighborhood until they do find God's way to penetrate it with the Gospel. He will not do the planning of evangelistic efforts himself but will see to it that the congregation has a missions committee which does lead out in this work.

VII. The Congregation Should Plan Its Strategy For Penetrating Its Neighborhood

Every service of worship should serve as renewal and preparation for the "church work" of the members. The minister should seek to help to prepare members of the congregation to do their real "church work" as they penetrate the arteries of the sin-sick society through their daily work and professions. One member may seek employment in each factory of the area, or department of a large factory, so that he may serve and witness there as a representative of God's love and power. Another member may move into a professional group, such as a medical society, with the conscious purpose of witnessing to these persons of Christ's lordship and redeeming power for the life of every man. The congregation, as God's realm of redemption in the community, likely needs a representative in each major industry even more than does the city bank or community hospital board.

A consciously chosen strategy of penetration should be constantly held before the congregation. The minister should help to provide times when each "runner" or "representative" of Christ's church might bring to the congregation a report of his progress and problems in his work as a witness. Worshipers need to report just how their love of God is affecting their love of neighbor. The work of the church while scattered should be honored almost more than the work of the church gathered.

The minister, as he expounds the living Word of God from the Scriptures to the members of the congregation, hopes that they will regard their daily work all week as a vital part of the total answer which they bring to God's gifts of charisma and Word. The minister should portray daily toil, not as a necessary nuisance whereby Christians "make expenses," but as a real laboring together with God in the midst of human relationships. On the job the member of the congregation constantly confronts problems which surpass his human resources, and finds the loudest calls for a life of self-denial and redeeming love.[4] Even in the fixed "beehive ritual" of modern industry, the Christian worker can find outlet for his creative abilities as he seeks to enter redeeming relationships with persons.

VIII. Subgroups of the Congregation Should Engage In Fellowship Evangelism

The minister should seek to help each fellowship or study group of the congregation to accept evangelism as one of their reasons for existence. The group should prayerfully lay a loving strategy to win persons to their fellowship and then to their Christ. The group should seek to encircle unsaved persons with the warmth of their fellowship. They should constantly pray that the Christ who is in the midst of the two or three who meet in His name and nature may confront and redeem the unsaved person who may be in the midst of the meeting. Christians who open their own lives to the power of the Holy Spirit's renewing and convicting action can create a fellowship which can be God's realm of redemption for a non-Christian. Every subgroup of the congregation should be engaged in fellowship evangelism twelve months of the year. The minister should not rest until the congregation has a plan to implement this goal.

For instance, every adult and youth Sunday-school class should have a teacher who leads them in their goal of mutual nurture, but they should have another person, possibly a class president, who leads them in their goal of evangelism. The president should lead the class in its strategy of winning new persons into the fellowship with the same persistence and seriousness with which the teacher leads them toward their goal of Christian education. If Christians will quit bluffing, and will admit their hourly need of God's grace, guidance, and forgiveness, then the unsaved friend in their midst may be led to believe. Pastor, parents, and Sunday-school teachers should evangelize children who grow up within the life of the congregation, leading them to a conversion experience during their early teens.

IX. Evangelism, Worship, and Fellowship Should Be Blended

The minister should keep alive in his own soul, and help the congregation to believe, that the preaching of God's Word always can create a situation in which the living Christ can confront men. The Gospel of Christ is God's power to save men who believe. The congregation should never gather to hear the exposition of the meaning of Scripture without living in the trembling expectancy that the Word of God may come into someone's experience as a leaping and powerful, renewing, regenerating reality. Every time the congregation is hearing the Word of God the Holy Spirit's convicting power for evangelism should also be expected in the meeting. Many, if not most, of congregational meetings should include a quiet but deeply earnest invitation for any wandering one to come home to Father's house through faith in Christ. The convicting Holy Spirit is ever saying, "Come," and the church which is truly the bride of Christ will not hesitate also to say, "Come." The minister should give the evangelistic invitation in the name of the congregation and its total ministry, even though the particular sermon may not be focused toward an evangelistic call.

No "ready-made package" of the evangelistic techniques should be sought by the local congregation nor used in toto if a "package" is suggested by experts. The local congregation must prayerfully seek those "bridges of God" or avenues of penetration into the hearts and lives of persons in their own neighborhood. If ministering among a people where family linkage is strong, as it is among some Spanish-speaking communities in large cities, then the congregation may well concentrate upon each member "bringing his own brother Simon." In situations where mass evangelism is really relevant, the congregation should not refuse to co-operate in a community-wide "festival of evangelical faith." At least once each year the congregation should contact its community in vigorous visitation evangelism.

X. Church Fellowship Should Prepare Members For "Evangelistic Dialogue"

One of the purposes of congregational fellowship, study, and testimony is to prepare members for evangelistic dialogue and witness. The member who learns how to discuss spiritual realities with naturalness and conviction while in the midst of the congregation will be better prepared to open a spiritual conversation at the shop or schoolroom. The minister should encourage members to seize every opportunity, as the Spirit of God opens the way and prompts, to speak to one another about God's working in their own lives, and thus be preparing themselves to speak to the unredeemed person they may meet in the restaurant or on the golf course.

The members of the congregation should not limit their witness to "safe" situations where the hearer cannot talk back

and challenge their testimony. Too often congregations go only
to convalescent homes, prisons, and rescue mission where a captive audience must listen. Or they do their evangelism safely by
proxy, paying a radio speaker to contact lost persons at the safe
distance of a remote radio receiver. It is also quite safe to send
some literature to a distant person, or to leave a tract on a door-
step and move away quickly. The Christian must have the holy
boldness to enter dialogue with actual lost persons in his own
daily life situations. Until a congregation is willing to evangelize its own front door, all efforts by proxy at a safe distance
need to be suspected as comfortable evasions.

XI. Just Being a True Church Will Arrest
The World's Attention

The church can evangelize her community also by just being
a New Testament church. When God's Spirit moves in unex-
plainable power in her midst, then "explanation evangelism" can
happen again. When transforming power and intoxicating joy
are obviously moving in a church fellowship, then the astounded
outsiders will come asking for the secret, and the situation is
ripe for "explanation evangelism." When members go from
the group worship and sharing experiences out into the common
life feeling that they are a "diplomatic outpost of heaven," then
the unredeemed may begin to take the church seriously. When
in the lives of members the demands of the kingdom of God
replace expediency, caution, and the *status quo,* then the world
may want to hear the Christian's verbal message.

It is quite true that alongside of the massive powers of big
business, big government, and big labor the congregations seem
to "present a picture of limp futility." But if Christians could
meet together overwhelmingly convinced that in their fellowship
the new age had dawned, then they could disperse to walk among
men as children of the resurrection. The astounded world might
again exclaim, "These that have turned the world upside down
are come hither also."

XII. The Congregation Should Engage
In Social Witness and Action

As the minister preaches God's Word in the midst of the gathered people of God, neither he nor they can escape the conclusion that the church is to penetrate society redeemingly. Many analogies, such as light, salt, fire, and leaven, suggest that God's people are to be a powerful force in the social order. Christians simply cannot declare that the ascended Christ is already the unrecognized Lord of men and nations, and then not give a word of prophetic rebuke to the sub-Christian social order. However, the New Testament does not suggest that the church should try to become one of the countervailing powers in society, so that "big church" can bargain with big business, big government, and big labor. On social issues the church speaks to its members more often than it speaks for its members to the world.

First of all, the minister and congregation seek to redeem individuals from within the social order. But beyond this they should seek to solve, by divine power within their own fellowship, some of the persistent problems of society, such as class conflict, racial tension, parent-child conflicts, misuse of leisure, confused sex roles, or conflict between employer and employee. The Christian believes that God by His Spirit makes available to an obedient church, when they are "up against" a real problem, His own divine guidance and wisdom. In the church believers are to learn "to apply to all of the affairs of time the judgments of eternity." If Christians have the courage to follow Christ in obedience in the way of the cross, then they need not lament the "tragic necessity" of having always to choose "the lesser of two evils."[5] God is abundantly able to lead His people in a redemptive witness in society if they have the courage to obey in a martyr faith.

In addition to his primary task of preaching and teaching God's Word, the minister should help the congregation to wrestle prayerfully with the burning issues which are too often only discussed in top-level committees and remote study conferences. Issues of race, capital punishment, conspicuous consumption, cut-throat competition, corruption in politics, smut on the newsstands, inadequate care for the aged, and a redemptive program for delinquents should be discussed from time to time, as one or another member confronts them in his daily work. Members should bring the pressing problems which they encounter in their vocational ministries along back to the bosom of the local congregation for discussion and words of guidance. Then the individual Christian can return again to his work, infiltrating the arteries of a sin-sick society like a "spiritual corpuscle." The congregation should not attempt to set up a completely different social order, but should seek to work redeemingly within the one in which it finds itself.

At times the living Christ who moves and acts in the midst of and through His obedient church may guide the congregation to give a corporate word of prophetic rebuke to a given sinful situation. Thus, if a well-meaning but misguided radio preacher is preaching nationalism and hate in a perverted campaign against communism, a minister may well lead the congregation to frame its corporate word of kindly but pointed rebuke. A members' meeting may be led to frame its letter of concern to the editor of the local paper about the all-night prom, the Sunday races, or the practice of selling liquor in the grocery store. If racial discrimination raises its horrible head in the neighborhood, the congregation must find a way to speak in God's name with resounding and thunderous voice against it.

XIII. The Congregation Should Engage In a Ministry of Mutual Aid

The minister who works deeply and constantly in God's Word and who seeks in all seriousness to bring its principles to bear upon the practical issues of congregational life will be appalled at the way secularism and selfishness have replaced caring and brotherly sharing among the people of God. He will remember how that the Old Testament prophet was horrified at the spectacle of rich and poor existing side by side within the same covenant life before Jehovah. The canceling of debts,[6] the refusal to charge interest to a brother,[7] the grain left ungleaned for the poor or the widow,[8] and the return of lost land to the original household at the year of jubilee—all of these were practical provisions which God ordained to guide His people in this mutual aid. Furthermore, any ministry of God's Word which follows faithfully in the tradition of the great prophets of Israel will necessarily thunder out against neglect of the poor or the widow.

The minister who is honest in expositing the total message of Scripture will find the evidence from the New Testament even more demanding in its insistence upon "unlimited liability" of the members of the Christian disciple band for one another. Christ declared that the rich ruler could not even receive eternal life until he was willing to become sacrificially concerned for the poor.[9] He promised those who did leave all to follow Him that they would find one hundredfold waiting for their need when they fled like a refugee into the arms of the congregation.[10] Christ presented the desire to give alms as a very natural reason why a Christian would sell property.[11] Christ warned men that they can know in advance that in the final judgment day one of the tests will be the amount of sacrificial concern which they have shown for "one of the least of these my brethren."

The minister of the Word knows full well that in the early church the very first organization was for natural aid.[12] One of the first tests of a professing man's faith was his readiness to meet a brother's need.[13] The first reason why a Christian should work was so that he might have to give to one in need.[14] The first mention of fund-raising in the church was for mutual aid.[15] The first conference resolution sent to younger churches included the exhortation to "consider the poor."[16] One of the outstanding characteristics of the church of Pentecost was that no one felt that ought which he possessed was his own, but they had all things common.[17] But how can the crowd of near strangers who gather to hear a sermon together on their day off ever be led to become the family of God, caring and sharing for one another to the point of sacrifice?

The minister will need to give high priority to encouraging

the caring ministry of the congregation. The Apostle Paul considered the mutual aid program of the church so important that
he interrupted his evangelistic and church-founding campaigns to
personally supervise the gathering of gifts for the poor saints
in Jerusalem. In fact, Paul placed mutual aid above even the
"Good Samaritan" ministry which Christians owe to their unsaved neighbors in need. He said, "Especially unto them who
are of the household of faith."[18] Even in plush, pampered, flesh-
pot American culture many needs will call for sacrificial sharing,
and many poor people will need help who should not be shunted
off to the Salvation Army or Welfare Department for help.

The minister will need to teach the truth of God's Word
long and patiently before the average American Christian begins
to comprehend the importance of mutual aid in the church. Raw
individualism, pietistic Fundamentalism, and reliance upon
secular insurance agencies are so widespread in their influence
that many Christians can scarcely conceive of a congregational
life so joined in loving concern that when "one member suffer,
all . . . suffer with it." The average board of church elders would
be mystified and embarrassed if some modern Barnabas, filled
with Holy Ghost compassion, would sell a property and bring the
proceeds to the mutual aid fund of the congregation.

XIV. Members with Business Experience Will Need to Administer The Mutual Aid Ministry

The minister should not leave the ministry of God's Word
for which he was ordained to serve tables in mutual aid. All of
the sanctified imagination of dedicated businessmen of the congregation will be needed to plan and implement a procedure of
mutual aid for the modern urbanized congregation. The mutual
aid program among God's people, designed to be a channel of
divine love, will differ in many respects from even the best com-
mercial insurance company. It will not sue to collect damages.
It will not seek to make money from the tragedies which people
suffer. It will not use salesman methods to get the members
to enroll. It will not provide luxurious salaries for the persons

who administer it. It will not invest any reserve capital in character-destroying organizations, such as the liquor industry. It will not refuse to cover chronically ill members because they are poor risks. It will not operate upon the profit motive. It will seek to provide a workable arrangement whereby the members of the family of God may express the more-than-human caring which they need to feel for one another.

When members are of necessity involved in welfare and insurance programs provided by industry, the congregation will seek to supplement these provisions. But much more than this, the congregation as a fellowship of divine love will seek to meet the deepest needs of persons which no guaranteed security and welfare built into the economic order can ever touch.

The congregation should consider co-operating with a church-wide mutual aid program. In the Mennonite Church a nationwide program of brotherly Mutual Aid has been developed. Through this channel the congregation can enroll and cover its poor or "poor risk" members and pay their share for them. Through this wider base of sharing larger needs can be met by brotherly sharing and caring.

XV. The Minister Should Help the Congregation to Perfect Its Ministry in Life's Crises

The Word of God offers profound insights into the meanings of both the happy and the solemn crises which come into life's pilgrimage. God's Word can interpret life's sweetest joys as well as the significance of suffering. The minister, as he exposits the teachings of Scripture, should also help the congregation to meet suffering and even death in a way commensurate with the deep meaning which they have in the Creator's intention.

Because God found a way, supremely at Calvary's cross, to make suffering a redemptive thing, the family of God should seek to allow it to be redemptive as it comes into the experience of members. Members steward the comfort (by which they themselves have been comforted by God) to one another as a given member has need. The family of God live in their heavenly Father's world, and all of life can have sacred meaning, including providential circumstances which involve tragedy and suffering.

The pastor should teach the Biblical truths relating to the "boundary situations," the happy or sad crises which come to persons. But he should also help the congregation to become a functioning community of concern and spiritual ministry to one another. When sickness strikes he is not the only one who cares, calls upon, and prays with the sick members. Adult Sunday-school classes or fellowship groups should be poised, ready, and eager to perform this ministry of love.

Persons who become seriously ill are confronted with their own finitude, helplessness, and even with the possibility of death. Pain isolates the sufferer on a little island of misery. The resulting feeling of social distance and loneliness causes deep anxiety and insecurity. There may also be feelings of resentfulness, rebellion, with resulting guilt feelings. The person who is critically ill begins to ask life's fundamental questions.

In addition to the best care which doctors and nurses can give to the body, the congregation as the fellowship of divine love needs to be constantly active, offering the spiritual help which the suffering person needs most of all. Christ reveals Himself afresh to the suffering Christian in the midst of his misery, and also meets the member who comes to minister to the fellow member in love. "Ye did it unto me" often comes as a glad surprise to Christians as they minister to the sick.

Simply because medical care is improved for the care of physical illnesses, the congregation should not forget that God often purposes to meet His children in spiritual renewal when sickness brings a pause along life's pathway. Christians should not conclude, as Job's friends did, that all sufferers are sinners, but should discover as Isaiah did that a sufferer can also be a savior. Profound spiritual insights should flow back into the conversations of the congregation from the bedsides of the sick.

The congregation should provide some deeply spiritual member to keep watch and prayer vigil by the bedside of a member who is terminally ill and whose life is ebbing away. A Christian who has faced many smaller "deaths to self" can face the final death experience without fear. A believer who lives already in resurrection power can affirm a larger life and even welcome death as the way to begin life with Christ, which is far better. A Christian within whose personality eternal life has already begun does not need to deify or absolutize finite existence. "Into thy hands I commend my spirit" may be a Christian's supreme act of worship.

If the minister has been faithful in teaching God's Word and its truths regarding life and death, the members of the congregation should be prepared for their own experience of death and also prepared to support one another. The terminally ill member cannot be expected to "think it all through" in the last hours. He is busy then redistributing his energies to fight disease. He will not likely change his philosophy of life to include a realistic view of death, if he has not learned to do this while he was in good health. However, the understanding Christian who ministers at the bedside of the terminally ill person will not be surprised if the dying person attempts to "bargain with God" or offers some "deathbed confession." These are characteristics of man's humanness and weakness and should not be belittled.[19]

XVI. The Minister Should Bring God's Word— When Death Claims a Member

The congregation of believers needs to hear the Word of the living God to their situation when death invades their midst. The death of a loved one causes time and eternity to seem to meet. The loudest sermon a congregation can ever preach to its community may be by the attitudes, spirit, and emphases which accompany a funeral. The faith of the church may become real in depth to a nominal Christian for the first time when death has claimed a loved one. The congregation would be wise to select a committee of qualified persons to assist and give counsel to the grieving family at times of death and the funeral. Society has a way to dispose of the body of a departed loved one. The state, through its coroner, knows how to dismiss a citizen. The mortician, through his embalming and cosmetology, knows how to care for a corpse. But only the Christian church can speak to the real anxieties which death arouses in the human heart.

The Christian congregation should assume control of the observance from start to finish. The mortician should be regarded and honored as an efficient tradesman who has caskets to sell and who can oversee a sanitary and respectable disposition of a body. But the church is the real "home" of the Christian, and at time of death no "funeral home" should be allowed to offer a streamlined service which reduces the family of God to mere spectators. If the mortician is a devoted churchman, his services in times of sorrow are still more valued and helpful. Although the congregation controls the funeral, the mortician's expert counsel should be sought on matters of death certificates, cemetery regulations, permits to bury, government allowances for burial expenses, and many other matters. The mortician deserves the prayers and appreciation of the congregation for work done with sensitivity and concern.

The pastor, with congregational leaders and family, should plan a funeral service which affirms the undying faith of the church. Because the emphasis is upon the going of a member of the family of God on earth to join the family of God in heaven, the focus of attention should not be upon the dead body. The body may well be committed to the earth in a simple service before the public service of worship and memorial is held in the church building. At least, any viewing of the remains should be done at the funeral parlor and the casket reverently closed before the service of memorial and worship at the church. The congregation should firmly refuse the participation of lodges or other fraternal or secular organizations in a funeral service of worship in the church. It is cruel to ask a grieving widow to do her final viewing of a departed loved one before a crowd of spectators.

In the funeral service itself the emphasis should not be upon fullsome eulogy or praise of the departed. In a manner consistent with Christian humility worshipers should offer their gratitude to

God for the blessing of having known and having been enriched by the life and ministry of the departed. The great facts of the Gospel, especially as they relate to the resurrection and life everlasting, should be reasserted with clarity and force. The service should also symbolize the way in which the family of God is closing ranks around the sorrowing family.

Great hymns of faith and trust should be sung by the worshiping congregation with a note of triumph. Sentimental nonsense like "Beautiful Isle of Somewhere" has no place in a Christian funeral. The service should include plentiful reading from God's Word, and should be a bit more stately, dignified, restrained, and even liturgical than other worship services to which the congregation has been accustomed. This will help the sorrowing ones to control their emotions and to maintain reverent Christian dignity. Hymns like "O God, Our Help in Ages Past, "Guide Me, O Thou Great Jehovah," or "Lift Your Glad Voices in Triumph on High" are suitable for a Christian funeral. Portions of *The Messiah* might well be rendered by a choral group or choir. How better could a congregation climax a funeral service of worship than by singing together, "The strife is o'er, the battle done; the victory of life is won; the song of triumph has begun. Alleluia!"

Christians may well consider bequeathing their bodies to the cause of medical research. Eyes can be bequeathed to an eye bank first if desired. By such bequeathing a Christian can dedicate his body to the service of mankind in death, even as he did in his lifetime. This practice is being regarded with increasing favor by Christian thinkers. Information may be found in *Manual for Simple Burial*.[20]

Concerned Christians have been asking in increasing numbers about the right or the wrong of the practice of cremation. Early believers tended to want to be buried in rock tombs because Christ's body was briefly buried thus. Later on, Christians tended to view cremation with dislike because so many of their martyred brethren perished in the flames at the stake.[21]

Still later on in church history, some believers disliked cremation because a few infidels had their bodies cremated and their

ashes scattered as a tribute to their scorn of the doctrine of a
bodily resurrection. But the recollection of the cremated martyrs
helped offset this emotional bias. Surely God would raise the
martyrs!

Few churches have spoken out officially about cremation,
but as urbanization has increased, the matter of finding sufficient
graves on the hillsides around large cities has become a problem.
Christian leaders have begun to express themselves on the matter.
From communions as diverse as Quakers, Roman Catholics,
Presbyterians, and Episcopalians, leaders are saying that cremation is a clean and orderly way to return a body to the elements, and that there is nothing in Christian faith to forbid it.[22]
However, if individual Christians have an emotional dislike for
it, these feelings should be honored.

XVII. The Congregation Should Perform Its Spiritual Ministry
To Bereaved Members

The minister who seriously intends that the principles of
Scripture shall actually guide and mold the practices of congregational life may encourage the congregation to adopt some standards for the conduct of funerals. These might well include such
things as (a) agreement to use only inexpensive caskets, and
funeral services, in the interest of a memory picture of simplicity
and stewardship; (b) limiting floral displays to one or only a
few wreaths, with other gifts directed toward a memorial fund,
usually some cause in the church which was dear to the heart of
the departed; (c) agreement to use simple, possibly even uniform,
plaques to mark the graves of members of the congregation. In
death as in life the congregation should stand together against
conspicuous consumption, status seeking, and the accent upon
luxury which blights affluent society.

The congregation, rather than the mortician, should provide
the emotional and spiritual ministries to the bereaved. The
minister (and the responsible committee of the congregation)
should be first counselors in the selection of pallbearers, selection
of burial clothes, and the selection of hymns for the memorial

service of Christian worship. The congregation should provide, without any cost to the family, the extra cars for the funeral procession, the hospitality and meals for friends from a distance, and any other services of love which may be appropriate. The congregation should stand by as a fellowship of concern while the grieving member "does his grief work." The entire congregation should be the bearer of pastoral care in this as in all other crises in the lives of members. By gathering to talk together about the much appreciated ministries of the departed loved ones, as the early church did in the case of Dorcas,[23] the congregation is engaging in the very best "grief therapy."

XVIII. The Minister Should Bring God's Word—
When a Child Is Born in a Member's Home

The evangelical Protestant churches have too largely ignored the sacred event of the birth of a child into a family of the congregation. The Hindus have given solemn significance to the event by their doctrine of reincarnation. The Roman Catholics have brought awe and mystery (and magic) to the event by their insistence that the newly born infant must be given sacramental regeneration by baptism lest it go to limbo if it should die while yet in innocence. The *Prayer Book* includes a service for the Churching of Women, but this likely seems quaint and medieval to most modern American parents. Even the practice of infant baptism as it is carried forward by respected denominations within the evangelical tradition fails to be convincing for many Christian thinkers. Early Israelites wanted a child so that they might achieve immortality through the child, and so transcend their own finiteness and death. But few moderns know why they desire a child in their home. The Christian church's word on the subject has been unclear. Even the duty to replenish the earth, which had been cited in earlier years, has lost its meaning in days of population explosions.

While the churches flounder along without a clear statement about the theological significance of birth, other specialists examine the phenomena. Medical doctors discuss how the physical act of birth may be accomplished without fear or danger of infection. Psychiatrists such as Otto Rank and Alfred Adler examine the effects of this "fall of man," when the person is thrust out of his "paradise" where all needs are met, temperature is even, and no other sovereign ego ever collides in competition.

Economists become optimistic as they predict the buyers' market which the newly born babies will create. Sociologists become apprehensive as they ponder the "population explosion" and talk of the "squalling of one hundred million babies around the world."[24] Psychologists of personality ponder the trauma which the unwanted or deformed child experiences.

As medical science has gradually lessened the physical danger and fear of death which had surrounded the experience of birth in earlier years, society is left with a more terrible fear. This is the fear of launching into existence a life which has no meaning, no real reason for being, no sense of direction, no bond of relationship to ultimate reality in the universe, and no hope for eternity.

Few persons refuse to believe in some version of immortality, that is, that the new life they help to launch into existence will exist forever and ever. But an unverbalized horror grips the spirit of thoughtful persons as they ask a newborn child to take the weight of eternity upon its shoulders and yet feel unable to say a strong sure word to the child about the eternal meaning and dimension of his existence.

The minister of God's Word to God's family, the church, must include clear teaching, in public, about the sacred significance of birth. Parenthood should be presented as the acceptance of God's offer to come up and join Him in co-creatorship. God uses the union of parents to produce the new life. God acts again as He did on creation morning, imparting to the newly formed organism an immortal soul.

But parents need to be reassured that they are not, by their union, transmitting a damning depravity to an innocent and helpless person, who might be doomed to eternal hell through a depravity which they force upon him. Rather they need to believe that the last Adam has entered into humanity so redeemingly that all innocents (even the children of Hottentot parents) belong to the kingdom of heaven.

Parents need to believe that, even though their little family-kingdom of love is called upon to miniature God's perfect kingdom of love (and they know only too well that their love and family relationships are imperfect), yet God can work through their imperfect lives and home. If they will walk humbly with their God, admitting their daily need of both enabling and forgiving grace, then God can make their imperfect relationship His sacrament to transmit His perfect, omnipotent, redeeming love to the innocent child. Jesus said that innocent children are already in the kingdom (until they choose to walk out in defiance when they reach the age of moral accountability).

Parents should welcome in awe and wonder the little citizen of heaven's kingdom into their home. The same God who put into the bodies of parents the ability to procreate can also work through their human relationships to convey His love, strength, and grace to the children. Children who are welcomed into the home in awe, gratitude, and wonder will likely feel all of their lives that God was indeed present at their birth, separating them from their mother's womb and calling them by His grace.

The minister believes that God requires all of His people to be a ministering congregation. Therefore, the minister should encourage the congregation to appoint a cradle roll department or other responsible group to assist in the spiritual ministry to parents when a child enters the family. Part of the minister's task is to share his insights from his study of the Bible and Biblical theology with this responsible committee of the congregation, so that their ministry may be informed and controlled by the deepest truth from God's Word.

The minister (and or cradle roll department) should lead the parents in a sacred worship service during the first call in the home after a child has been born. If the parents are sensitive Christians, they are probably crying out in their innermost hearts the cry of Manoah to the man of God: "How shall we order the child [which God has given to us?]" The minister should reassure the parents of God's grace for their sacred task of bringing up the child in the nurture and admonition of the Lord. He should challenge them to dare to be a partner with God in His re-creating work even as they have been in His creating work.

The very existence of a child, sharing the physical features of both parents, offers a permanent reminder of the way in which their lives are to complement one another and to be one. Even as God has used the uniqueness of each parent to create a new person, so God desires to use the spiritual contribution of each parent's unique faith and experience as an instrument of His grace in the molding of their child to become a mighty man or woman whom God can use.

The simple service of worship in the home might well include a recognition of God's sovereignty and ownership as Creator, a humble thanksgiving for His gracious gift of a new life, a claiming of Christ's universal atonement which covers the soul of the innocent child, and a promise to rear the child in the nurture and admonition of the Lord.

Because American fathers have so notoriously abandoned their God-given place as head of the home, the minister may well use the occasion of the birth of a child to call the father to face his spiritual responsibility. The Biblical record reports that man began to call upon the name of the Lord when Seth named his firstborn son Enos (which means frailty).[25] It further reports that Enoch walked with God after he begat a son, Methuselah. Parenthood should be a time of sacred and intense God-confrontation.

Some fathers need to be reminded that what they are as a human father will mold their child's concept of God when the child is told to pray to God as a "Father." Some fathers should be told the story of the man who stepped up and offered to catch a child which a fireman wished to drop from a third-story window of a burning house. After holding up his arm and declaring his readiness to catch the child, he lost his nerve at the crucial moment and stepped back, allowing the child to crash to its death on the pavement. Fathers need to be reminded that they have no right to open their arms and to invite the creating God to entrust into their nurture an immortal soul whom God desires in His fellowship throughout all eternity, and then through cowardice or laziness to fail to nurture that child for both time and eternity. The minister or cradle roll department visitors need holy boldness to confront American fathers with their spiritual responsibilities. Fathers need to be reminded kindly but firmly that evasion of their nurture obligations is a serious sin.

XIX. The Minister Should Lead a Public Service For "Dedication of Parents"

The minister may well lead a sacred service of dedication for parents as part of a public service of worship in the congregation. This may appropriately be included as part of the annual home-interests or Mother's Day services. In this service the minister may remind the entire congregation that the infant is already in the kingdom through the universal atonement of Jesus Christ, and needs no sacrament to "save its soul." The service should rather be one in which the parents' covenant before God and the congregation to dedicate their lives without reserve to the task of bringing up the child in the nurture and admonition of the Lord. In a second part of the same ceremony the entire congregation, as the family of God, should promise their readiness and commitment to assist the parents in every way possible in their sacred responsibility.[26]

XX. The Congregation Should Minister to Members During The Happy Crisis of Marriage

In addition to preaching and teaching the standards of God's Word which should govern marriage, the minister should encourage the congregation to outline a set of "guiding suggestions" or "standards" for weddings to be solemnized in their church building. If the congregation acts responsibly and lists such guiding principles, the minister will be saved from much embarrassment when a starry-eyed couple asks for some inappropriate activity or song to be part of their marriage ceremony. The congregation would be wise to select a committee of qualified persons who could assist the bridal pair, family, and pastor in planning a wedding which is truly Christian in every detail. It may reflect a materialistic bias that our congregations have trustees to see to the care of buildings but no committees to assist at times of death, birth, and marriage.

Marriage is a holy covenant, "instituted of God, regulated by His commandments, blessed by our Lord Jesus Christ, and to be held in honor among all men." These convictions should be further articulated in guiding suggestions which might include the following points:

(1) request that couples contemplating marriage should inform the minister (and the committee of the congregation charged with the responsibility to give assistance at weddings) at least 30 days before the proposed date.

(2) Couples should consider carefully the list of "suggested hymns for weddings" provided by the music and worship committee of the congregation. This list might well suggest appropriate numbers and warn against the use of sentimental love songs or operatic-type numbers which are not appropriate for a sacred service of Christian worship.

(3) Couples should have their wedding rehearsal opened with prayer by the minister, carried through in the same spirit of sacred joyfulness which should characterize the wedding service itself. Too often one or two would-be-wits bring into the rehearsal a "carnival atmosphere" which detracts from even the wedding itself.

(4) Gift displays should be avoided, but friends who desire to give gifts should be encouraged to send them to the bride's home beforehand.

(5) The congregation, as the family of God, should rally around the family during this happy crisis. A responsible committee of the congregation should be called upon for assistance in appropriate ways. The family and couple should be discouraged from employing one of the professional "wedding directors" with their packaged programs.

(6) Every effort should be made to keep the service a reverent experience of Christian worship. The occasion should

not become a theatrical performance where florists, caterers, photographers, tape-recording engineers, dressmaker, and paid musicians compete to create a magnificent spectacle.

(7) The congregations of both parties should be on the guest list automatically, because God's family is commanded to "rejoice with those that do rejoice." More casual friends, or friends beyond the congregation, may rather be invited to the reception which follows the wedding, during which time the newly married couple symbolizes the reception of their friends to their newly founded home.

XXI. The Minister Should Solemnize Marriage In a Service Which Is Truly Christian

In the wedding service itself the minister should set forth in appropriate readings from Scripture and in a few well-chosen remarks the central meaning of Christian marriage. Emphasis in the entire service should fall upon the vows, as the very essence of the marriage, and upon the intercessory prayers of the congregation who are focusing their loving prayers upon the bridal pair.[27]

A note of grimness should be injected too. This love dare not be mere romantic love, which abides as long as the partner remains attractive. The marriage vow is based upon self-sacrificing love, love to the death, love which seeketh not her own. Partners are promising before God and witnesses to take one another through prosperity and adversity, for better or worse, "till death do us part."

The minister should omit any of the old remnants of feudal "marriage by capture." It is not necessary to ask whether anyone present can show reason why the pair should not be married. Then, too, the minister can symbolize the centrality of the church by mentioning the church first (before the state) in his formula of authorization. "I now, by the authority vested in me by the Mennonite Church and the laws of the state of Indiana, do. . . ." Furthermore, the signing of the license, which symbolizes the civil or state's authority, can be done in private, after the worship service is over.

Either the minister (or the responsible committee of the

congregation) should offer assistance in the selection of suitable announcements and publicity. If the wedding is to be a truly Christian occasion in which Christ is honored even more than the bride, and in which attention is focused upon sacred vows being made (and renewed by all married couples in the congregation), then the invitations should frankly indicate this emphasis.

If the wedding actually was a sacred occasion of vows, prayers, and praise to God for His grace in uniting two lives into one, then the account in the newspaper should reflect this spirit. The usual monotonous recital of details about the bride's dress, the ushers' ties, and the frills upon the clothing worn by the attendants are utterly unworthy in the reporting of a truly Christ-centered wedding. The pictures in the paper should include the groom standing with his bride, and should not subtly suggest that the bride's gown was more important in the wedding than was the man she married!

XXII. The Congregation Should Meet Frequently To Discuss Their Common Concerns

They who fear the Lord need to speak often one to another. If the church is to be saved from irrelevance, Christians will need to bring many of the concerns of the common life back into the congregational meeting. Committees chosen by the congregation and responsible to the congregation will need to report and give account of the way in which they are being led to work each in their particular area of church concern. If believers are to bind and loose in Christ's name, and really be communities of discernment, group decision-making will need to be learned and then practiced with seriousness.

Frequent members' meetings (at least once a month) are a necessity in a modern urban congregation because of the mobility of members. A congregation can quickly degenerate into a group of near-strangers, who are like marbles in a bag, only touching one another at one point. But beyond the sheer problem of keeping acquainted at a level deep enough to care and to bear one another's burdens, the congregation needs to meet often because the problems which it faces in giving its corporate witness in the world are so baffling and so complex.

Furthermore, the congregation needs to meet in earnest discussion of common concerns and tasks so that the prophetic word which God desires to give to the brotherhood through various members may be heard with seriousness. The all too typical "fellowship" meetings held in Protestant congregations are too superficial. The nervously poised teacups, the gushing and forced efforts to be friendly and to impress one another, the pathetic attempts at heartiness and back-slapping, the trivia and banalities which make up the conversation—these only nauseate persons who carry deep concerns for stark human needs or desperate situations in world affairs.

The minister who understands something of God's will for His people's life together must teach and lead his congregation toward an embodiment of God's will in the congregational program. God desires that His people may be able to meet and break bread together in sacred fellowship, their hearts burning within them as the presence and will of their living Lord is made real to them. Christ's church needs to attempt to bind on earth that which has already been bound in heaven, as they seek the mind of their Master for their obedience. This will require that members of the congregation regard their church gatherings as very serious and significant occasions.

XXIII. The Minister Should Supervise
The Instruction of Converts

The minister of God's Word and the congregation should take seriously and plan carefully for the instruction of new believers for church membership. If believers are given a meager, narrow conception of responsible membership, they are likely to remain narrow Christians for a long time. If only a few denominational distinctives are taught, not anchored in an adequate Biblical theology, then there is danger that the denomination will degenerate into a cult. When frontier evangelism with its theory of "instant evangelism" ceased to instruct new believers, the results were tragic for the Christian church in America.[28]

Convert instruction is needed so that believers may count the cost of discipleship, and be prepared to say a meaningful "yes" to Christ's lordship in every area of their lives. New believers need help to examine the loyalties and assumptions which they bring with them so that loyalties incompatible with Christ's sovereignty in their lives may be surrendered. Prebaptismal instruction should help the new believer to answer the question, "What am I committing myself to?"

During convert instruction the young Christian should learn how to discern the weightier matters of the law. He should learn how to recognize the guidance of God and His Spirit in decision-making, and in his ordinary life from day to day. He should be prepared for responsible dialogue in defense of his faith. While the total nurture program of the congregation could and should give help in this area of concern, the instruction of new believers should focus upon them intensively and specifically. How to answer the "tormentors" (the hostile world which forever challenges the Christian who dares to be true) might be a good pattern for convert instruction.

If the new believer is in his or her teens, then convert instruction may speak to the questions: How does God become real to us? How discover where the lordship of Christ impinges in daily life? How recognize the guidance of the Holy Spirit? How does God through Christ atone for our sins? How do we claim what God has done for us in Christ? How shall we grow in His grace? How triumph over temptation? What should church membership mean to us?[29]

If the new believer is already an adult the questions may move on to discuss: How does the redeeming God confront us now? How claim the sanctifying work of God's Spirit to free us from the grip of past habits? How does Christian faith bring meaning to existence? How relate personal discipleship to daily vocation? What is the place of the church fellowship in growth, obedience, and service? How does the Christian fulfill his social witness and responsibility? What is the way of the cross in human relationships? What is the contribution of our brotherhood to ecumenical conversation?

Converts should have "sponsors" or "advocates" among the members of the congregation. These "advocates" should take a deep, personal interest in their problems and growth, introduce them to new friends in the congregation, and explain to them the way the congregation works together at the Lord's work. These "sponsors" may well attend some of the instruction classes or seminars with the new believers, and share their own testimonies and searchings with them.

New believers should not be baptized until after the elders or members of the congregation have "judged [them] . . . to be faithful to the Lord."[30] Converts should individually ask for baptism and be received individually, when each one has reached a happy crisis in believing and readiness to take up the way of the cross. Baptism, in addition to being a seal of Christian assurance and the answer of a good conscience toward God, should also be made to symbolize the acceptance of the outpoured Holy Spirit, a claiming of one's union with Christ in death and resurrection power, and one's vow to be faithful to Christ until death as a member of His martyr band.[31] Prebaptismal instruction should be intense enough so that baptism can be made the "ordination or commissioning of the laity."

The minister may call upon the converts' parents, when they are Christians, to assist in the instruction. In Holland among Mennonites for 150 years (1527-1677) all instruction and catechism was to be done by the parents alone. Peter Janz Twisck's catechism of 1633 was intended for the parents themselves as they instructed their children.[32] In some cases a class or fellowship group may be assigned the sacred task of instructing a new believer. In this case the church group would discuss together, with the new believer in the midst, the crucial issues of Christian faith and obedience which were of deepest relevance for the new believer's establishment in the faith.

XXIV. The Minister Should Urge the Congregation To Co-operate with the Denomination

The congregation has primary responsibility under God for its own immediate neighborhood. No service abroad by proxy or by contribution of funds can be of much significance if the congregation refuses to attempt to be a faithful church at home. But having been faithful at home, the congregation needs also to co-operate with many other congregations in order to make its message and impact felt to the very ends of the earth. Practically every ministry of divine love which the congregation renders at home must be extended to others through recognized denominational channels.

Actually most of the decision and action of the Christian church does center in the local congregation. The congregation owns its own property, decides its own liturgy (in the free-church tradition), chooses its own curriculum materials for its Christian education program, elects its own staff of workers and teachers, plans its own programs of prayer meetings and members' meetings, and plans its own budget. The congregation decides when an applicant for baptism is ready to receive this sacred ordinance, and decides whether a given member is worthy to receive a church letter when he wishes to transfer to another congregation. The congregation chooses its own minister and bishop and decides what amount of financial support they wish to give to them. The congregation plans its own program of evangelism and mutual aid.

The congregation plans its own program of publicity, administers its own program of discipline, and organizes its own program for women's work, men's brotherhood, youth work, or boys' and girls' clubs. The congregation can even decide to operate a radio program or operate a Christian day school if it chooses to do so. The congregation can choose the amount of support which it wishes to give to denominational agencies.

But the congregation dare not become a little island of isolation and self-sufficiency. Through church-wide agencies the congregation must co-operate with other congregations to carry forward many avenues of service and witness which it simply could not perform alone. Probably one half of the total giving of the congregation should be shared with the regions beyond. Through both district and general conference agencies the congregation should co-operate in evangelism, Christian education, mutual aid, publication of Christian literature, Christian social action, witness against war, world-wide relief and charities, or ministry to the mentally ill. The ordained minister probably has had wider contacts than have some other leaders of the congregation and he should strongly encourage the congregation to co-operate with church-wide agencies. The church-wide agencies, by virtue of their resources of specially trained personnel, can actually help to provide leadership for the local congregation and can help her to find the way of obedience.

Church-wide agencies can give a prophetic witness to government with an effectiveness which a local congregation could not achieve. Church-wide agencies can operate a Christian college, seminary, radio program, or mental health program, and for these types of pioneering leadership and service the local congregation should be profoundly grateful. Representatives from these agencies should be invited into the congregation from time to time so that the members may understand the pioneer work which they are doing and may better undergird these agencies with their prayers, suggestions, and gifts.

Even in urging loyalty to the denominational program the minister should avoid absolutizing the denomination. Believers should be encouraged to love and to pray for the whole church of the lamb. Believers should feel joined to all who are joined to Christ the Head.

XXV. The Minister Should Lead the Congregation In Conversation with Other Brotherhoods

What should the relationship of the congregation be to other congregations in the neighborhood which belong to other households of faith? Because Christ prayed that His disciples may be one so that the world may believe, every modern disciple who cares about the same concern which Jesus cared about will be eager to strive toward Christian unity. Anything less would be callous indifference to a passionate desire of the Lord of the church.

But "working toward" Christian unity with all other households of faith does not mean that each one shall abandon its unique emphasis so as to seek union in some "least common denominator." This would mean the end of a virile, vital, vigorous faith in the land. The ease with which rapidly moving Americans join the church nearest to them is probably a sign that "Mr. Average American" does not know what is distinctive in the faith of his own denomination and cares even less to sustain it. This "ecumenics of Main Street America" can lead to a flabby faith.

Rather, all congregations (and denominations) should ask themselves what God has given to them out of His providential leadings with them in their past. What unique aspect of truth do they hold to steward and share with other households of faith? Then the congregation and denomination should prepare to enter conversation or dialogue with any other household of faith in search of a larger truth and a fuller obedience to Christ than either one of them possesses alone. Congregations should expect that differences will force them to examine the faith afresh, and that the other brotherhood will likely also have some strength from which they can learn and profit.

The only criteria for entering such conversation should be that each respects the other's right to claim to be Christian, that each one renounces any claim to be the "only true church," that the basis of the search for a larger truth which might transcend differences shall be the Holy Scriptures, and that the intent shall be to help one another find a more complete obedience to Christ.

Local congregations should carry on these conversations among the serious-minded adult groups of the respective congregations. Mass meetings with imported speakers have a little value in finding a common faith, but are less significant than face-to-face conversations would be. Joint Good Friday or Thanksgiving Day services are of limited value, since only a few from all the congregations usually attend, and face-to-face sharing is usually lacking. Joint fellowship occasions, such as picnics, have a little value but do not solve the real problem if crucial issues of difference continue to be glossed over and avoided. However, sharing on an informal level may prepare the way for serious search together about issues of ultimate concern.

XXVI. The Minister Should Share His Theological Training With the Team of Congregational Leaders

Crucial areas of congregational work could not be treated at all in this one lecture on church administration. (Church publicity, church stewardship and financing, and the Christian education program of the congregation are examples of such vital aspects of congregational work.) The fact that the ordained minister of the congregation may not carry central responsibility in these areas does not mean that he is not profoundly concerned about them. As in all other areas of congregational life the minister of the Word seeks to bring its deepest truths to bear upon the congregation's practices in these matters too. The supreme test of a Biblical faith is the way it is spelled out in a program of consistent obedience and ministry as God's people among men.

The minister of God's Word should try constantly to share his theological training with all the teachers and leaders of the congregation. He should sweep his desk clear of trivia and reserve time to serve as a teacher of teachers. For at least one hour each week he should give himself to educating the team of teachers and leaders. Lectures in church history and Biblical theology may be given periodically in the midweek meeting, the adult class periods of summer Bible school, or in the adult section of the Sunday school. At the opening of a new section of Sunday-school lessons the minister might well lecture on Biblical theology, giving Bible backgrounds and setting the lessons in proper perspective in salvation history.[33] Most lay leaders will be profoundly grateful for some help in grasping Biblical theology and backgrounds.

The minister should constantly encourage every mature member who can do so to secure some advanced Biblical and theological training. Theological understanding is for Christians, not just for ordained ministers.

If persons training for the teaching, medical, or other professions could take time out for at least a year of theological training, this would greatly increase the spiritual perception with which they could serve mankind. It would also enable them to serve in the congregational ministries with greater insight and effectiveness.

But for most ministers the task of sharing theological insights with teachers, stewardship committee, cradle roll visitation staff, mutual aid committee, worship and music committee, and other leaders will continue to be their sacred responsibility. No other opportunity to minister God's Word could be more rewarding than this one.

A minister need not waste his energies trying to be an "image buster," destroying false notions which neighbors may have about the role of an ordained person. Let him simply give himself with unswerving faithfulness to his preaching-teaching ministry and the undesirable aspects of professionalism will not fit, the image of the aloof "man of the cloth" will not apply, and the "stuffy-reverend-parson" concept will not cling to him. Let him give himself first, last, and always to his servant of God's servants role, and the "young-executive" status-seeker image will be shattered by the daily integrity of his life. Let him preach God's Word with Holy Ghost power, and people simply can not continue to regard him as either the "prayer-boy" for public functions or the "symbol of religion." Let him preach-teach God's Word in its height and depth of meaning and application, and the same Holy Spirit which empowers his ministry of God's Word will begin to empower the charismatic life of the whole congregation to go out and to do God's work in the world as the minister himself could never do it if he had stooped to become the congregation's errand boy to do their work for them by proxy.

Footnotes

CHAPTER I

1 Matt. 18:21-27.

2 Ex. 19:6.

3 Henry C. Goerner, *Thus It Is Written* (Nashville: Broadman Press, 1914), p. 17.

4 Isa. 49:1-7.

5 Psalm 2, 22, 47, 67, 96, 110, 117, 145, and 150 are among those which echo this emphasis.

6 Amos 9:12.

7 Mic. 7:16, 17.

8 Jer. 1:9, 10.

9 Hab. 2:13, 14.

10 Joel 2:28; chap. 3.

11 Ezek. 39:21-24.

12 Dan. 12:3.

13 Zech. 2.

14 Mal. 1:10-20.

15 James Smart, *The Rebirth of Ministry* (Philadelphia: Westminster, 1960), p. 11.

16 Luke 22:27, RSV; Mark 10:45.

17 D. T. Niles, *The Preacher's Calling to Be Servant* (London: Lutterworth Press, 1959), p. 33.

18 Acts 3:13-16.

19 Acts 4:24-28.

20 Acts 14:3.

21 Acts 19:11.

22 Paul S. Minier, *The Images of the Church in the New Testament* (Philadelphia: Westminster, 1960), p. 225.

23 Lesslie Newbigin, *The Household of God* (New York: Friendship Press, 1960), p. 114.

24 I Cor. 7:7.

25 Howard Charles, *The Charismatic Life in The Apostolic Church* (unpublished thesis in files of the author, Goshen, Indiana), p. 232.

26 Eph. 4:15.

27 I Cor. 14:29.

28 Jas. 5:14.

29 For a more extended treatment of healing, see Paul M. Miller, *How God Heals* (Scottdale: Herald Press, 1960).

30 I Pet. 4:11.

31 I Cor. 12:6, New English Bible, © The Delegates of the Oxford University Press and the Syndics of the Cambridge University Press 1961.

32 Eph. 4:11.

33 Howard Charles, *op. cit.,* p. 295.

34 I Pet. 5:3.

35 Harold S. Bender, *These Are My People* (Scottdale: Herald Press, 1962), p. 96.

36 See critical apparatus, Nestle's text of Greek New Testament, Stuttgart edition, 1920.

37 James Smart, *op. cit.,* p. 43.

38 Eph. 4:11.

39 James Smart, *op. cit.,* p. 12.

40 II Cor. 4:5, Moffatt.

41 D. T. Niles, *op. cit.,* pp. 73-78.

42 H. R. Niebuhr and Daniel D. Williams, *Ministry in Historical Perspectives* (New York: Harper and Brothers, 1956), p. 8.

43 T. W. Manson, *Ministry and Priesthood: Christ's and Ours* (Richmond: John Knox Press, 1957), p. 47.

44 Harold S. Bender, *op. cit.,* p. 98.

45 Acts 20:28; I Pet. 5:2-4.

46 I Thess. 5:12.

47 Acts 6:1-6.

48 Howard Charles, "The New Testament Pattern of Church Organization," *Church Organization and Administration* (unpublished study conference paper, Mar. 25-27, 1955, Scottdale, Pa.), p. 8.

49 John P. McGuire, *The Mass Presented to Non-Catholics* (Milwaukee: Bruce Publishing Co., 1958), p. 12.

50 James M. Hoppin, *The Office and Work of the Christian Ministry* (New York: Sheldon & Co., 1949), p. 354.

51 For a discussion of "Episcopal Succession," see Appendix 2.

52 J. Z. Lauterbach, "Ordination," *The Jewish Encyclopedia,* edited by Esadore Singer, Vol. IX (1912), p. 429.

53 Victor Fast, "A Study of Ordination" (unpublished manuscript in files of author), p. 6.

54 Franklin M. Segler, *A Theology of Church and Ministry* (Nashville: Broadman Press, 1960), p. 62.

55 Acts 13.

56 David Daube, *The New Testament and Rabbinic Judaism* (London: Athlone Press, 1956), p. 237.

57 J. B. Lightfoot, *The Christian Ministry* (New York: Thos. Whittaker, n.d.), p. 6.

58 See Appendix 3, "The Word-Centered Service in the History of Christian Worship."

59 I Pet. 1:25 and Acts 10:36.

60 Eph. 2:17.

61 Gal. 1:16.

62 Donald Miller, *Fire in Thy Mouth* (New York: Abingdon, 1954), p. 17.

63 Heber F. Peacock, "Ordination in the New Testament," *Review and Expositor,* Vol. XV, No. 3 (July, 1958), p. 274. (Here see Appendix 1, "The Significance of Laying on of Hands in Christian Ordination.")

64 I Tim. 5:17.

65 I Tim. 5:1; 5:22.

66 Illion T. Jones, *The Pastor, the Man and His Ministry* (Philadelphia: Westminster, 1961), p. 124.

67 Daniel Kauffman, *Doctrines of the Bible* (Scottdale: Mennonite Publishing House, 1929), p. 347.

68 *Ibid.,* p. 350.

69 *Ibid.,* p. 352.

70 Leif Eeg Olofsson, *The Conception of the Inner Light in Robert Barclay's Theology* (Lund: CWK Gleerup, 1954), p. 167.

71 Elton Trueblood, *The Paradox of the Quaker Ministry* (The 1960 Quaker Lecture of Indiana Yearly Meeting), pp. 5, 6.

72 Paul C. Clifford, *The Pastoral Calling* (New York: Channel, 1961), p. 7.

73 Roy Pearson, *The Ministry of Preaching* (New York: Harpers, 1959), p. 55.

74 Winthrop Hudson, *Conference on Motivation for the Ministry* (Louisville: Southern Baptist Theological Seminary, 1959), p. 33.

75 *Mennonite Encyclopedia,* Vol. III (Scottdale, 1955-59), p. 699.

76 Clayton Beyler, *The Call to Preach* (Scottdale: Mennonite Publishing House, 1963), p. 10.

77 Kling, *Motivation for Entering the Ministry* (Educational Testing Service, Princeton, New Jersey), p. 19.

78 D. T. Niles, *op. cit.,* p. 85.

79 Acts 20:18-25.

80 Wayne E. Oates, *Protestant Pastoral Counseling* (Philadelphia: Westminster, 1962), p. 158.

81 Walter Wagoner, *Bachelor of Divinity* (New York: Association Press, 1963), pp. 51, 52.

82 Harold S. Bender, "I Robbed Churches—Paul," *Gospel Herald* (Sept. 4, 1962), p. 773.

CHAPTER II

1 I Cor. 1:17.

2 Acts 28:31.

3 Acts 10:36.

4 I Thess. 2:13.

5 I Cor. 14:25.

6 I Thess. 5:19-22.

7 Leif Eeg Olofsson, *The Conception of the Inner Light in Robert Barclay's Theology* (Lund: CWK Gleerup, 1954), p. 194.

8 J. B. Weatherspoon, *Sent Forth to Preach* (New York: Harpers, 1954), p. 71.

9 J. L. Moreau, *Language and Religious Language* (Philadelphia: Westminster Press, 1961), p. 188.

10 James Smart, *The Interpretation of Scripture* (Philadelphia: Westminster Press, 1961), p. 147.

11 Robert H. Mounce, *The Essential Nature of New Testament Preaching* (Grand Rapids: Eerdmans, 1960), p. 77.

12 J. Stanley Glen, *Recovery of the Teaching Ministry* (Philadelphia: Westminster, 1960), p. 85.

13 Paul Tillich in Hans Hoffman, *Making the Ministry Relevant* (New York: Scribner's Sons, 1960), p. 35.

14 I. T. Jones, *Principles and Practice of Preaching* (New York: Abingdon, 1956), p. 82.

15 Webb B. Garrison, *The Preacher and His Audience* (New York: Fleming Revell, 1954), p. 165.

16 Edgar N. Jackson, *A Psychology for Preaching* (New York: Channel Press, 1961), p. 198.

17 John 3:19, RSV.

18 Frederick C. Grant in Howard A. Johnson, *Preaching the Christian Year* (New York: Scribner's Sons, 1957), p. 152.

CHAPTER III

1 Ezek. 2:1.

2 I Cor. 14:25.

3 John 2:22, 23.

4 William E. Hulme, *Counseling and Theology* (Philadelphia: Muhlenburg Press, 1956), p. 216.

5 Max Thurian, *Confession* (London: S.C.M. Press, Ltd., 1958), p. 30.

6 O. Hobart Mowrer, *The Crisis in Psychiatry and Religion* (New York: D. Van Nostrand Co., 1961), p. 102.

7 Dietrich Bonhoeffer, *Life Together* (London: S.C.M. Press, 1956), p. 103.

8 Karl Menninger, *Theory of Psychoanalytic Technique* (New York: Basic Books, Inc., 1958), p. 172.

9 Paul Tournier, *Guilt and Grace* (New York: Harpers, 1962), p. 68.

10 Seward Hiltner and L. G. Colston, *The Context of Pastoral Counseling* (New York: Abingdon Press, 1961), p. 214.

11 Wayne E. Oates, *Where to Go for Help* (Philadelphia: Westminster Press, 1957).

12 Edward Thurneysen, *A Theology of Pastoral Care* (Richmond: John Knox Press, 1962), p. 314.

13 John M. Price in *An Introduction to Pastoral Counseling*, Wayne E. Oates, Editor (Nashville: Broadman Press, 1959), p. 293.

14 II Cor. 1:2.

15 Edward Thurneysen, *op. cit.*, p. 112.

16 Conversations recorded by the author during meetings of the Academy of Religion and Mental Health, South Bend, Indiana, January, 1959.

17 Edgar N. Jackson, *A Psychology for Preaching* (Great Neck: Channel Press, 1961), p. 76.

18 Wayne E. Oates, *Protestant Pastoral Counseling* (Philadelphia: Westminster Press, 1962), p. 128.

19 Charles D. Kean, *Christian Faith and Pastoral Care* (Greenwich: Seabury Press, 1961), p. 29.

CHAPTER IV

1 Lewis Benson, *Prophetic Quakerism* (Philadelphia, Friends Book Store, 1944), p. 31.

2 Isa. 38:18, 19.

3 I Cor. 12:10, 11.

4 Oscar Cullman, *Early Christian Worship* (London: S.C.M. Press, 1953), p. 13.

5 G. Gerhard Delling, *Worship in The New Testament* (London: D. T. Todd, 1962), p. 70.

6 I Thess. 2:13.

7 I Tim. 4:13.

8 Col. 4:16.

9 A. B. MacDonald, *Christian Worship in the Primitive Church* (Edinburgh: T. T. Clark, 1934), p. 89.

10 Oscar Cullman, *Early Christian Worship* (London: S.C.M. Press, 1953), p. 16.

11 Walter Eichrodt, *Theology of the Old Testament* (Philadelphia: Westminster, 1961), p. 359.

12 Eph. 4:16.

13 Raymond Abba., *Principles of Christian Worship* (New York: Oxford University Press, 1957), p. 4.

14 Donald McLeod, *Word and Sacrament* (New Jersey: Prentice-Hall, Inc., 1960), p. 160.

15 E. R. Micklem, *Our Approach to God* (London: Hodder and Stoughton, 1934), p. 134.

16 T. S. Garrett, *Christian Worship* (London: Oxford University Press, 1961), p. 14.

17 Psalms 29, 34, 42, 46, 63, 65, 66, 67, 89, 90, 92, 95, 96, 99, 100, 103, 104, 105, 106, 107, 108, 111, 117, 135, 136, 145, 147, 149, and 150 are all psalms which begin in such a way that their opening verses might well serve as a call to worship. The opening words of greeting in many of the New Testament epistles are also suitable, such as I Cor. 1:3; II Cor. 1:2-4; Gal. 1:3-5; Eph. 1:2-6; I Pet. 1:3-5; and II Pet. 1:2, 3.

18 Albert Palmer, *The Art of Conducting Public Worship* (New York: Macmillan Co., 1939), p. 59.

19 Charles H. Heimsath, *The Genius of Public Worship* (New York: Scribner's Sons, 1947), p. 24.

20 H. S. Coffin, *The Public Worship of God* (Philadelphia: Westminster Press, 1946), p. 47.

21 Wm. R. McNutt, *Worship in The Churches* (Philadelphia: Judson Press, 1941), p. 116.

22 Rev. 22:3.

23 Ps. 33:6.

24 II Pet. 3:70.

25 Jer. 23:29.

26 Isa. 40:6 and I Pet. 1:21.

27 Ps. 147:15.

28 Isa. 9:8.

29 Jer. 1:9, 10.

30 Isa. 55:11.

31 John 1:14.

32 Matt. 4:4.

33 Luke 24:27.

34 Ezek. 3:1.

35 Roland DeVaux, *Ancient Israel* (London: Darton, Longman, & Todd, 1961), p. 68.

36 John 1:1-8; I John 1:1; John 5:24; Rev. 19:13.

37 II Cor. 4:2; John 17:6; Phil. 1:14; I Pet. 2:8; II Thess. 3:1.

38 Num. 22:38.

39 Deut. 8:2, 3.

40 II Kings 19:11.

41 I Sam. 3:1, 11.

42 Jer. 1:12.

43 Ezek. 3:17.

44 Luke 24:19.

45 Luke 7:7.

46 Luke 4:36.

47 John 12:48.

48 Mark 16:20.

49 Luke 10:11.

50 Rev. 12:11.

51 Luke 8:11.

52 Acts 4:31.

53 Col. 1:25-27.

54 II Cor. 4:6.

55 I Cor. 4:20.

56 Rom. 10:6-8.

57 I Pet. 1:23-25.

58 Eph. 5:26.

59 I Thess. 2:13.

60 Heb. 4:12.

61 Robert Mounce, *New Testament Preaching* (Grand Rapids, 1960), p. 157.

62 John 8:43.

63 Jas. 1:21.

64 I Pet. 2:1, 2.

65 Gen. 22:5.

66 Isa. 1:11.

67 Mark 12:34.

68 Rom. 12:1, 2.

69 Acts 13:2.

70 Phil. 4:8.

71 Isa. 6:8.

72 Heb. 13:16.

73 I Cor. 16:1; Gal. 6:10; Phil. 3:18; I Thess. 5:14; and I Tim. 6:18.

74 Robert L. Williamson, *Effective Public Prayer* (Nashville: Broadman Press, 1960), p. 101.

75 Heb. 10:19-22.

76 Eph. 2:18.

77 Andrew Blackwood, *The Fine Art of Public Worship* (New York: Abingdon-Cokesbury, 1939), p. 146.

78 For a discussion of the Mennonite view of the Lord's Supper, see Appendix 5.

79 Dom Gregory Dix, *The Shape of the Liturgy* (Westminster: Dacre Press, 1954), p. 50.

80 Oesterly, Leitzmann, Brillioth, Srawley, MacDonald, Kay, Devon, Hedley, Gavin, Macgregor, and others all favor the view that Christ's Chaburoth group and meals together formed the background of the Lord's Supper and early Christian love feasts.

81 A. B. MacDonald, *op cit.,* p. 212.

82 Heb. 6:5.

83 Dom Gregory Dix, *op. cit.,* p. 4.

84 For a discussion of "Form and Structure versus Freedom and Spontaneity in Worship," turn to Appendix 4.

CHAPTER V

1 J. M. Gustafsen, *Treasure in Earthen Vessels,* (New York: Harper & Bros., 1961), p. 22.

2 Illion T. Jones, *The Pastor, the Man and His Ministry* (Philadelphia: Westminster Press, 1961), p. 30.

3 Joseph McCabe, *The Power of God in a Parish Program* (Philadelphia: Westminster Press, 1959), p. 119.

4 J. O. Nelson, ed., *Work and Vocation* (New York: Harper's, 1954), p. 169.

5 Guy F. Hershberger, *The Way of the Cross in Human Relations* (Scottdale: Herald Press, 1958), p. 112.

6 Deut. 15:9.

7 Ex. 22:25.

8 Lev. 19:9.

9 Matt. 19:21.

10 Matt. 19:27.

11 Luke 12:33.

12 Acts 6:2.

13 Jas. 2:16.

14 Eph. 4:28.

15 I Cor. 16:2.

16 Gal. 2:10.

17 Acts 4:32.

18 Gal. 6:10.

19 Samuel Southard, *Religion in Nursing* (Nashville: Broadman Press, 1959), p. 107.

20 The Celso Press, Burnsville, North Carolina, 1962.

21 Jessica Mitford, *The American Way of Death* (New York: Simon & Schuster, 1963), p. 163.

22 *Manual of Simple Burial,* p. 51.

23 Acts 10:39.

24 James A. Peterson, *Toward a Successful Marriage* (New York: Charles Scribners' Sons, 1960), p. 164.

25 Gen. 4:26.

26 See Appendix 7 for a sample of a dedication for parents' ceremony.

27 See Appendix 6 for a sample wedding ceremony which is also a service of Christian worship.

28 Samuel Southard, *Pastoral Evangelism* (Nashville: Broadman Press, 1962), p. 28.

29 Russell Krabill, *Beginning the Christian Life* (Scottdale: Mennonite Publishing House, 1958), p. 4.

30 Acts 16:15.

31 Acts 2:37-41.

32 N. van der Zijpp, "Catechism," *Mennonite Encyclopedia,* Vol. I, (Scottdale: Mennonite Publishing House, 1955), p. 527.

33 Wesner Fallaw, *Church Education for Tomorrow* (Philadelphia: Westminster Press, 1960), p. 36.

Appendixes

APPENDIX 1

The Significance of the Laying on of Hands in Christian Ordination

Daube begins his detailed treatment of the subject of "laying on of hands" in the Biblical records with the statement: "There is widespread confusion regarding this matter." Likely the early Christians brought with them from Judaism and the synagogue its patterns of setting apart elders. The service in the synagogues was very simple and the ceremony was not usually intended to actually convey grace or power to the recipient. In contrast with this, there were always some who held the view that the laying on of hands actully conveyed something. Thus the sins of Israel were actually conferred to the head of the scapegoat,[1] and the responsibilities of the firstborn were transferred to the Levite.[2] Jacob made Joseph's sons his own by laying his hands upon the second-born one so as to give to him the firstborn's blessing.[3] Moses seemed to confer a charge and also a part of his spirit and wisdom upon Joshua by laying his hands upon Joshua's head.[4] Moses' service of commissioning, charging, assigning of leadership, and investing of Joshua with responsibility has served as a pattern for all later ordinations.

Some among the Jews sought to perpetuate the sacramental concept of ordination. They taught that when a teacher pressed his hands down upon his pupil some of his own wisdom and spirit was poured into his pupil. But most rabbinic ordinations, called *Semikha*, merely marked graduation from studies and gave authority to teach, to act as judge in matters of dispute, and to answer questions about the interpretation of the law.[5]

The New Testament stresses rather the free movement of the Holy Spirit in equipping and calling leaders and gives no indication that the more sacramental assumptions of the *Semikha* tradition practiced among some of the Jews was borrowed by early Christians.[6] Whenever such ideas can be found in early Christian apocryphal literature, they represent an alien or later intrusion and the exception rather than the rule.

The New Testament pictures the laying on of hands as the recognition of a gift already given to faith. Certainly Christ did not elevate the laying on of hands to sacramental power. He healed some persons without touching their bodies at all. Furthermore, some Christians received the Holy Spirit simultaneously with the laying on of hands but many others did not. Luke was careful to mention that the seven "ministers of mutual aid" described in Acts 6:1-6 already were filled with the Holy Spirit and with wisdom before hands were laid upon them. Paul reminded Timothy of the time hands were laid upon him and offered this as an added reason why Timothy should kindle or develop to the full his God-given gift,[7] but said that the gift was given by "prophetic utterance." Paul did not say that the laying on of hands actually conferred the gift. Rather, it is implied that some brethren with prophetic insight discerned the gifts Timothy had which qualified him for leadership. Then Paul laid hands upon him as a public recognition of his gift and gave to him an official charge to use it to serve the church. There is no indication that Paul expected a part of his own spirit and power to flow into Timothy by the ritual. Paul certainly does not regard the laying on of hands, which he experienced, as his ordination. Nothing is said about hands having been laid upon Titus. The writer of Hebrews cites laying on of hands as a doctrine which is elementary and beyond which believers need to go on to perfection.[8]

On the basis of the New Testament example it is safe to conclude that the "laying on of hands" meant the same in ordination as it meant in baptism, prayers for healing, and benediction. It was simply a symbol of definiteness, bringing the whole matter to a point in time, and indicating the focusing of the prayers and charge of an entire congregation upon the head of one person. The symbolic act gave to the recipient a sense of a "before" and an "after." It brought what might have been only a gradual awareness to one sharply focused crisis event. The laying on of hands in ordination was akin to Christ's touching the children in blessing, touching the tongue of the dumb man, and touching the injured ear of the high priest's servant. The epistles contain not one reference to laying on of hands. Christ never commissioned a disciple by the laying on of hands. In fact, Daube suggests that the laying of hands upon the seven servants in Acts 6 was done by the entire brotherhood rather than merely by the apostles.[9]

Furthermore, it is noticeable in the New Testament narratives that the laying on of hands was at times associated with the undertaking of a specific missionary task. It is possible that the prayer for blessing and the laying on of hands were repeated with each new assignment, just as the synagogue sent a *salaih* messenger to do a job. It might have been regarded as a renewal of the baptismal vows which accompanied a previously experienced imposition of hands. The laying on of hands is thus primarily a token of fellowship and group solidarity; it is only secondarily an effective symbol of the gift of the Spirit; it becomes such a symbol only when given and received in faith in the midst of the church of the Spirit. The Christian church very wisely made prayer the central and most important part of ordination, and so laying on of hands received less attention.

It is likely that the pressure of Christian influence helped to purge the sacramental notion from even the synagogue ordination ceremonies by the second century. By that time rabbis merely prayed for healing of the sick and no longer laid hands upon them as a part of their ministry to the sick.[10] It is likely that the sacramental conception of ordination only became prominent in the Christian church at the same time that sacramentalism gained ascendance with regards to baptism and the Lord's Supper. Clear records of ordination do not appear in the church fathers until the third century.[11] By that time notions of sacramentalism and hierarchial rank had invaded the thinking of the church fathers so that every area of church life was affected.

As a result of the importation of many ideas throughout church history the Christian church has become sadly divided in its understanding and practice of the meaning of ordination and laying on of hands. At one extreme stands the Roman Catholic Church which regards ordination as a sacrament, administered by one successor of the Apostle Peter to another. The sacrament of Catholic ordination is intended to convey grace and the enablement to perform the priestly task and rites, and is supposed to leave an indelible imprint upon the soul of the one who receives it. This Catholic conception of ordination as a sacrament can be traced through a Byzantine liturgy to a fourth-century patriarch of Antioch. The Byzantine formula of ordination includes the words: "Divine grace, which ever gives strength to weakness and supplies what is lacking, chooses (Brother so and so) as bishop."

The Catholic writers are consistent also in spelling out a definition of a layman as "one who is not in the clerical orders and, therefore, not capable of clerical functions." Most dictionaries of Catholic theology go on to spell out an elaborate recognition of lay status in such words as lay sisters and lay confession.[12]

Those who argue for a sacramental view of ordination say

that just as baptism brings the person from the world into a state of grace, so the imposition of hands in ordination qualifies him with special gifts so that he can serve Christ in the world. "The former ministers to him the divine charis (grace), and the latter the manifold charismata" (ability to serve).[13] Christian groups which refuse sacramental regeneration, and insist upon a salvation which comes by faith's response and by a conscious act of the will, should also refuse sacramental ordination.

It is urgent that believer's baptism be regarded as the real ordination into the priesthood of every believer. The specialized ministry to which ordination calls a brother is not to be a sacerdotal priestly office, either to repeat what Christ has done (Roman Catholic idea), or to finish what Christ left undone (Anglican idea). The only "priestly" aspects of the ordained minister's task are to lead the congregation in their responses to what Christ has done, and to lift up the heart cries of the entire worshiping people in the corporate pastoral prayer.

1 Lev. 16:21.

2 Num. 8:5-20.

3 Gen. 48:19.

4 Num. 27:18-23.

5 Cornelius Dyck, "Some Theses Concerning Ordination," unpublished MSS, dated April 30, 1962, in the files of the author, Elkhart, Indiana.

6 Heber F. Peacock, "Ordination in the New Testament," *Review and Expositor,* Vol. XV, N. 3, July, 1958, p. 268.

7 II Tim. 1:6.

8 Heb. 6:2.

9 David Daube, *The New Testament and Rabbinic Judaism* (London: Athlone Press, 1956), p. 237.

10 *Ibid.,* p. 234.

11 Heber Peacock, *op. cit.,* p. 265.

12 *Catholic Encyclopedic Dictionary* (N.Y.: Gilmary Society, 1941), p. 549.

13 R. F. Weidner, *The Doctrine of the Ministry* (N.Y.: Fleming H. Revell, 1907), p. 60.

APPENDIX 2

The Historic Episcopate or Apostolic Succession Theory of the Ministry

The apostolic succession theory of the Roman Catholic Church asserts that, whereas the other eleven apostles did not ordain successors who continued their authority down through history, Simon Peter alone did so. They claim that Peter's successor then passed on the keys of Peter to the successor whom he ordained, and so an unbroken line of key-holding popes have ruled the church as vicars of Christ, with infallible wisdom and final authority in faith. Roman scholars insist that this is proved by "monumental evidence," but when they set forth this evidence it turns out to be inference, things "admitted by common consent," and arguments drawn from noncanonical sources. They declare that Anglicans did not merely "wash their faces" at the time of the Reformation, but actually "washed off their heads" and have been a truncated church ever since.[1]

The historic episcopate or episcopal succession theory of the Anglicans declares that all of the apostles ordained successors, and that the succession resides not in one bishop, the pope, but in all bishops duly ordained by successors of the twelve apostles. Anglicans do not declare so absolutely that the line of succession has remained unbroken, nor that the ministry of someone not in the succession could not possibly be a channel of grace. But Kirk points out that just as the God-ordained Bible was several centuries in assuming final form, so the episcopate (essential ministry) required several centuries to mature into its final God-ordained pattern.[2] The church threw up three defenses against Gnosticism—the creed, the Scriptures, and the apostolic or episcopal succession. Scholars who defend the historic episcopate feel that believers now should accept all three with equal seriousness.

Both of the above-mentioned theories of the ministry rest upon a sacramental theory of ordination. They presuppose that ordination confers supernatural charismata, or enablement, upon the recipient. They affirm this just as they believe that baptism conveys divine life which causes the person to become a "believer," and the Lord's Supper renews the divine life in the believer. They insist that the incarnation is itself a sacrament, wherein God used sensible and material channels to convey supernatural grace. They add that the church herself is a human channel for divine grace, and so it is to be expected that her leaders should be sacramentally equipped persons whose central task is to administer the other sacraments.

Many Anglican leaders have avoided scholarly examination of the Biblical evidence and theological assumptions underlying their dogma of episcopal succession. They have retreated behind their plea that the episcopate is a sacred office, a "mysterium." Like all ultimates and mysteries of the faith, it can neither be explained nor defined. Some Episcopal scholars frankly admit that the theory cannot be proved from the Bible. Montefiore notes the fact that their pleading attempts have not won general acceptance. He says that "the evidence from the New Testament is too scattered, inconclusive, and even inconsistent." He concludes this section of his monograph by saying: "There can therefore be no support from the Bible for the belief that the apostolic succession through the laying on of hands guarantees the church."[3]

Vanstrone further admits that "the term *episcopos* did not denote for New Testament writers an office distinct from and superior to the presbyterate. . . ."[4] Others, such as Gregory Dix, seek support in "the living tradition" of the church fathers where traces of episcopacy do emerge after the close of the first century, and then plead that "one may infer" or "we may regard it as probable" that episcopacy obtained in the first-century church.[5]

Those who dogmatically carry episcopal succession to its logical conclusion declare that the episcopate guarantees the existence of the church, carrying it forward in time and keeping it in contact with God's power and guidance. By the hierarchy which sacramental ordination creates, the church fulfills Christ's kingly ministry: through sacerdotalism, His priestly ministry; and through teaching, His prophetic ministry. Other ordinations would, therefore, be invalid, and bodies like the Methodists would be only "proselytes at the gate," being "outside the covenant," belonging to the "soul of the church, but not to the body," and able to minister some grace, but only "uncovenanted grace." These advocates of episcopal succession believe that if the succession of ordained ministers were cut off, the church would disappear from the face of the earth.[6]

The Roman Catholic authorities declare that Anglican ordination is invalid because at the time of the Reformation the words, "receive power to offer sacrifice to God and to celebrate masses as well for the living as for the dead," were omitted from the ceremony of ordination. The Anglican ordination rite for a bishop, while it thus avoids the odious sacerdotalism of the Roman Catholic Church, includes other emphases just as foreign to the New Testament. For example: "The bishop stands as a father-in-God praying for his sons in the Gospel, for the subsidiary ceremonies—vesting, anointing, and this final laying on of hands—he sits after the manner of a magistrate conferring insignia of office on his subordinates. . . ."

Any thoughtful student of church history can see why the Anglican Church should love her bishops. Bishops took the lead in the theological reform which England knew at the time of the Reformation, and saved the church from Rome and from collapse. But in a great many of the Anglican pleas for episcopal succession inference is mistaken for evidence. Anglican theologians usually "prove" their theory of episcopal succession by dogmatic, abstract reasoning. Starting from their assumption that sacraments are the absolute center of the life of the church, the way in which God visits and redeems His people, they then argue backward from the necessity to have an unbroken succession of such men, going back to the apostles. Thus they guarantee the unity of the contemporary church with the apostolic band and with Christ Himself.

Dom Gregory Dix begins his study of "The Ministry in the Early Church," not with the New Testament epistles, as one would expect, but with the writings of St. Hippolytus of Rome, admittedly as late as A.D. 215. After finding plenty of episcopal ideas here, enough to retread the whole Anglican system, Dix begins the labored attempt to prove that all of this was "intended by the apostles." He notes condescendingly that "the origins of Christianity lie over the borders of that world in the alien barbarian tradition of Semitic Judaism . . . any institutions which can fairly claim to be aboriginal in the Christian religion will prove to be Jewish rather than Hellenistic in their affiliations." . . . "Jewish institutions formed the original basis or model for the earliest Judaeo-Christian polity."[7]

It is a source of constant embarrassment that the Jewish models of polity and ministry show so few parallels with the present episcopal system.

The theory of "episcopal succession" is untenable for the following reasons: (1) The assumption that only bishops (and not presbyters) ordained successors cannot be proved from the New Testament evidence.[8] (2) Arguments from the Hebrew *shalaich* (sent one) as the precedent of an apostle sending his bishop successor (such as Titus) will not bear all the weight which pleading scholars assign to it.[9] (3) It is doubtful whether the "genius of the Gospel" really molded the episcopal system as it developed in the second century, but whether it was not rather a decadent church, borrowing too uncritically from her surrounding society certain patterns which were alien to her essential Gospel of priesthood of all believers. (4) The New Testament writers never suggested when founding churches that the pattern of the Old Testament priesthood might make a good pattern for polity. It lay ready to hand, but they carefully avoided it.[10] (5) The argument that Judaizing Christians at Jerusalem preserved the Old Testament priestly and hierarchial system and launched it as the polity of the church is not supported by evidence. Furthermore, judging from Paul's rejection of their influence as pictured in the Book of Galatians, it is inconceivable that he would adopt their program in regards to polity.[11]   (6) Some argue that, since episcopal polity crystallized about the same time as the canonical Scriptures were assembled, both deserve the same reverence as equal instances of God's working through His church. Rather, it is the faith of Protestantism that the written Scriptures judge the oral tradition as well as polity forms of the church. In the case of episcopal polity, the Scriptures find it wanting.   (7) Anglican scholars remain completely obscure as to just what the mysterious "it" is that is transmitted in sacramental ordination. They talk vaguely about "grace," or "gift," or power, but never quite say what they mean.[12] (8) Because Scriptural evidence is so meager as to be almost nonexistent in defense of episcopal succession, Thornton resorts to "mystical exegesis" and typology to draw in every conceivable parallel from Old and New Testament to bolster his foregone conclusions. Stephen Neill complains also that Thornton's exegesis seems to assume the verbal inspiration of the Septuagint.[13]   (9) The assumption that God would preserve an unbroken line or succession of bishops as His way of preserving His people runs exactly contrary to God's declared way of working. God rather calls a people that were "not my people" to become the people of His hand. He will raise up children unto Abraham from the stones, rather than to grant to a vested-interest group an inalienable right to retain their office and their guarantee to God's favor.[14]   (10) The apostolic writings, reverently searched by an obedient church, are the center of apostolic authority upon earth now. The succession is not in one person, mysteriously qualified by a sacramental ordination. The faithful church, returning under the guidance of the Holy Spirit to the apostolic writings, has the power to bind and to loose. The true church is found, not where the bishop is present necessarily, but where a congregation of believers are living in the same faith, obedience, and Holy Spirit power which characterized the apostolic church.

1 J. Wilhelm, *"Apostolic Succession," Catholic Encyclopedia* (New York: Encyclopedia Press, Inc., 1913), p. 642.

2 K. E. Kirk, ed., *The Apostolic Ministry* (London: Hodder and Stoughton, 1946), p. 8.

3 H. W. Montefiore in *The Historic Episcopate,* K. M. Cary, ed. (London: Dacre Press, 1954), p. 110.

4 W. H. Vantrone in *The Historic Episcopate,* p. 25.

5 Stephen Neill, *The Ministry of the Church* (London: Canterbury Press, 1947), p. 15.

6 H. W. Montefiore, *op. cit.,* p. 105.

7 Dom Gregory Dix, "Ministry in the Early Church" in Kirk's, *The Apostolic Ministry*, pp. 227-236.

8 Stephen Neill, *op. cit.*, p. 16.

9 Armond Erherdt, *The Apostolic Succession* (London: Lutterworth, 1953), p. 16.

10 F. W. Dillistone, *The Ministry of the Church*, p. 69.

11 Richard E. Higginson, "Apostolic Succession," *Baker's Dictionary of Theology*, Everett F. Harrison, ed. (Grand Rapids: Baker Book House, 1960), p. 60.

12 Paul Clifford, *The Pastoral Calling* (New York: Channel Press, 1961), p. 15.

13 Stephen Neill, *op. cit.*, p. 9. See also L. S. Thornton, "The Body of Christ," in *The Apostolic Ministry*, p. 63.

14 N. van der Zijpp, *Mennonite Encyclopedia*, "Apostolic Succession," 1955, Vol. I, p. 141.

APPENDIX 3

The Word-Centered Service in the History Of Christian Worship

As His favorite medium to communicate His life and presence to His people during worship God has ever pressed toward the use of a rational, quotable, and even printable word. The seer, with his half-conscious dreams and occult ways to probe to the meaning of life's phenomena, dropped out of the life of God's people quite early. The seer in Israel operated too near to the ways of the dervishes among the Canaanites.[1]

God guided His prophets to begin to write their messages into a book. Elisha and Elijah, of the great prophets, did not do so, but other chroniclers collected and wrote down some of their words. God guided His people in the gathering and use of the Deuteronomic Code, and this helped spell the doom of irrational speech. The reluctant "yes and no" of the *Urim* and *Thummim* were not regarded as a "Word."[2] After the word of the prophet was committed to writing, people could come back again and again to ponder God's Word through the prophet. The supreme test which divided a false prophet from a true one was whether his predictions came to pass.

The phenomena of daily life, such as the boiling of a caldron or the budding of an almond tree, continued to evoke a "Word" from God to the heart of the pensive prophet as he brooded with God over His people and world. But the Word thus evoked dared not remain in mere mutterings like those of some medium of Endor. The prophet always felt the urge: "What thou seest write in a book." In fact, Jeremiah insisted that his message be written down the second time, after Zedekiah had the original autograph destroyed.

God was abundantly able to reveal Himself through the noumenous, but He led His people beyond this to a communion by and through the Word. The "fear of the Lord" was always more than a mere "awareness of world stress." It was more than the "feeling of creaturehood and dependence" before a power "inherently other." It was more than an "eerie feeling," being daunted and fascinated before a purpose and power uncomprehended.[3] God's self-disclosure did cause a "holy dread," a noumenous awareness that "God is in this place." But God came through to His people also in words which were rational, quotable, and printable. These words could be passed on to the rising generation and could induce the immediacy of God-encounter for them.

God directed the priests of the Old Testament worship away from their other duties and toward the ministry of teaching the sacred writings. The priestly system, likely encouraged by Jethro, priest of Midian, and father-in-law of Moses, included at first many elements very much like the priest worship of Egypt. The priest was at times a keeper of the fires, burner of incense, judge, soothsayer, custodian of the sacred lot, and butcher. But God intended the priest to stand alongside of the prophet and to supplement his ministry. As the prophet gave God's particular message to the specific situation of the moment, the priest sought to interpret the Torah and sacred writings. Thus the abiding, transculturally relevant Word of God from the inspired writings was set alongside of the prophetic insight of the hour.[4]

The priest as teacher was to aid worshipers in grasping the meaning of life in a God-centered world, to guide men in finding, facing, and fulfilling the divine will. Priests were to take the common fund of facts which worshipers had and to deepen, broaden, and enrich them. Teaching the rich meaning of the cherished faith of God's people was extremely important. God wanted His people to love Him with all their mind. Their faith was not to rest upon magic, pure mystery, emotionalism, or pressure devices.[5]

Further evidence that God intended word (and not sacramentalism and mystery) to be the central bearer of reality in worship may be seen in the fact that the patterns of temple worship faded out so completely from the worship of God's people. If God had wanted His people to continue in a sacramentally centered worship, the temple pattern, so honored by the later prophets of the Old Testament, lay ready at hand for a mold.

But Duchesne himself, defender of sacramental worship, admits that "the temple worship did not in any way influence Christian worship."[6]

Christ Himself taught in the temple but largely ignored its sacramental worship. The inspired writers of the Gospels merely use the temple for background for their narratives and then with overtones of disparagement. Matthew's narrative lists 27 activities done in the temple and the Synoptic writers 18 activities, but they consistently ignore the sacramental center of the temple system. The liturgical sequence and the details of the sacrifices are never cited.[7] Rather, Jesus ignored the sacrificial system, but showed His intention that the word should be supreme in worship by repeatedly teaching, even in the temple.

The writers of the Gospels also reveal their desire and intention that worship should be word-centered by the way they treat the synagogue worship. They systematically ignore seven or eight aspects of synagogue worship, even some of which the Jews were most proud, and concentrate upon the teaching, admonition, and Scripture reading parts of the worship. The verbal symbol was obviously honored above the material, dramatic, or sensory symbol. MacDonald says that "worship poured from them (early Christians) like the full-throated song of a bird."[8]

The actual experiences of worship services as pictured in the New Testament do not at all suggest that the central reality was Christ's presence in wafer and wine, or even in the dramatic action of the breaking and partaking of sacramental emblems. In the John 13 account the sacrament is omitted and the dramatic action of footwashing stresses service rather than sacrament. In the John 20 glimpse of worship the disciples are told not to rely upon touch and sensory aids, but that they are more blessed when they believe without touch. In the worship experience of Acts 2 the sacrament is not central, but inspired speech is. In Acts 3 worshipers go to the temple for prayer and engage in healing and testimony in words.

Again in Acts 5 believers are together in the place of worship (Solomon's Porch) but not for a sacramental-type worship. When a worshiping group meet in the house of Cornelius, the word is central. When believers are together again in the house of Mary the prayer experience is central. The worship experience pictured in Acts 13 is called "ministering to the Lord" and again the sacrament, either as transubstantiated wafer or dramatic action, is conspicuous by its absence. In the worship gathering in Philippi the emphasis again falls upon speaking and prayer. In the Acts 17 and 18 accounts "reasoning out of the Scriptures" is central. In Acts 19 baptism and receiving the Holy Spirit is central, but Paul feels no urgency to make certain that the Ephesian believers are observing the Lord's Supper correctly.

Even in the classic passage in Acts 20 wherein the worship service at Troas is described the emphasis is not upon the sacrament. The believers broke bread, but this was likely the *agape* love feast so common among early believers. The emphasis is again, as always, upon the preached Word. In fact, Paul preached so long that one dozer fell out of a window and was picked up dead. Paul sought to curb the drunken love feast and the glossolalia or ecstatic cries in the worship at Corinth, and insisted upon words that edify.

The gaze of the worshiper was upon what God had done in history and in Christ, as this was revealed through the inspired writings, and upon what God was doing here and now by His Spirit. There is absolutely no evidence that worshipers gazed toward an altar as the center of Christ's mysterious presence in the room. The living Christ was so real in their newly empowered lives that their words spoken in the meetings were very closely joined to daily life experiences: "Whatever ye do in word and deed."[9] They did not come from a secularized week to have Christ become real again in the sacrament. Rather, they came from a week of hourly obedience in which Christ was made Lord at any cost, and met together to have their Lord guide them further by His Word in the path of faithfulness and service.

The whole idea that the material, dramatic, and sensory symbols should be the primary mediator of God's grace and presence to His people (rather than word and indwelt personality) only invaded the church in the second century. The sacramental notion owes much more to borrowings from the mystery religions than to either Old Testament temple, New Testament worship experiences, or New Testament writings. In Clement, the Didache, and Pliny's letter to Trajan sacramentalism has not yet made serious inroads. But in Ignatius, Justin Martyr, and Irenaeus the shift has begun.

As sacramentalism came to dominate Christian worship, a host of subtle changes came along with it. Now Christ's presence was no longer sought in the midst of the two or three, but was sought in the transmuted bread and wine. God's presence on the altar became the "theophany" and the "eschaton inbreak." The joy of early Christian worship gave way to awe and mystery. The Holy Spirit's presence was no longer invoked upon persons, but upon things (the wafer and wine). The *agape* love feast and the oracle of the word faded out. Worship became a spectacle, and the miracle of the Mass replaced the miracles which early Christians expected in their common life. Elaborate buildings, ceremonies, vestments, and vessels came into use.

An understanding of the message of the Bible was lessened. Scriptures were "scissors-and-pasted" into a liturgy with a scheme which showed more mastery of the concordance than of the Bible message. The laity became silent and passive. A foreign liturgical language became acceptable. The sense of fellowship faded out of worship. The apostasy from worship as pictured in the Book of Acts was almost complete.

All the explosive power of the Protestant Reformation was required to bring the Word back into centrality in worship. A "faith through the Word" mysticism replaced the "substance mysticism" of Catholic sacerdotalism. Scripture reading and preaching in the vernacular again became characteristic of worship. The didactic element flourished in worship as magic and superstition faded, or rather as the teaching aspect caused magic to fade out. The Reformation at least partially succeeded in restoring the word, fellowship, and testimony-centered worship of the New Testament congregations.

The centrality of the Word in worship was threatened again as a result of the liturgical revival. Led first by Newman, Kebel, and Pusey at Oxford in 1833, the movement sought a revival of seriousness, reverence, and reality in worship. Leaders felt that the Reformation movement had become iconoclastic and had destroyed and abandoned many rich treasures in Christian worship. In America some leaders felt that the barren worship of the frontier had turned out to be only a baptized pragmatism.[10] Changes which the Reformation and Puritanism had brought into worship were referred to as "unfortunate departures," "indefensible innovations," or "lamentable impoverishments."

Many of the leaders of the liturgical revival were really devout men, seeking for a revival within the Anglican Church which would be carried by a richer worship, and a renewed response to the holy, and a reassertion of God's sovereignty through the sacrament. They sought to return to the richness and beauty of the third- and fourth-century worship. They asserted that the soul of man has an irresistible need for devotion, adoration, mystery, and beauty in worship.[11] They lamented that the barren intellectualism of Puritanism and the sheer subjectivity of Pietism had robbed worship of its mystery and power like the sun dissipates mist. Economic prosperity coupled with increased aesthetic sensitivity now enabled leaders to develop worship as an "art."

215

A flurry of tracts and later on of books helped to launch the movement. Writers like W. Sperry, Von Ogden Vogt, Schultz, and Fiske advocated it. Liturgical societies arose within the denominations and altar guilds in local congregations. Hymnbooks and liturgies were revised and the movement touched most of Christendom.

Changes brought into worship by the liturgical revival included an increased use of medieval music, music in the Latin language, and musical responses. "Framing" appeared in worship services, along with vestments and an increased use of creeds. Orders of service grew more complicated, and the church year received more attention. Glass, sculpture, paintings, and textiles were used for artistic purposes. Altars became fixed to the rear wall of the church and some leaders of worship began to genuflex before them. Chancels were divided, the pulpit pushed to one side, and the priestly tended to replace the prophetic and didactic note in worship.

After a little more than 100 years the liturgical revival movement is still going strong. While there is much in the movement which has been good and ennobling, the loss of the centrality of the Word in worship is a cause for grave alarm. Without a strong preaching ministry at the center of worship the increased use of symbol and sacrament will almost certainly lead back toward Catholicism and magic.[12] It is to be devoutly hoped that the renewal of Biblical theology will bring a revival of power and depth in Christian preaching so that Word-centered worship, so important in New Testament worship and so dearly regained by the Protestant Reformation, may not be lost.

1 Joseph C. Badgett, *Conflict Between Prophet and Priest in the Old Testament*, Th.D. dissertation, 1946, Southern Baptist Theological Seminary, p. 36.

2 James Wm. Cox, *The Doctrine of the Word of God in the Old Testament*, Th.D. dissertation, Southern Baptist Theological Seminary, 1953, p. 78.

3 Rudolph Otto, *The Idea of the Holy* (New York: Oxford University Press, 1923), p. 36.

4 Roland DeVoux, *Ancient Israel* (London: Darton, Longman, & Todd, 1961), p. 354.

5 Howard H. Charles, *The Charismatic Life of the Apostolic Church* (unpublished doctor's thesis, University of Edinburgh, 1958), p. 222.

6 L. Duchesne, *Christian Worship* (London: S.P.C.K., 1937), p. 46.

7 Sylvan D. Schwartzmann, *"The Jewish Institution of the Synagogue and Temple in the Synoptic Gospels"* (unpublished doctor's thesis, Vanderbilt University, Nashville, Tennessee, 1952), p. 272.

8 A. B. MacDonald, *Christian Worship in the Primitive Church* (Edinburgh: T. and T. Clark, 1934), p. 2.

9 Col. 3:16.

10 Yngve Brillioth, *Eucharistic Faith and Practice* (London: S.P.C.K.), p. 219.

11 Horton Davies, *Christian Worship,* p. 52.

12 Yngve Brillioth, *op. cit.,* p. 218.

APPENDIX 4

Form and Structure Versus Spontaneity
And Freedom in Worship

The Biblical patterns of worship are largely of the ordered, structured type. The temple pattern which God prescribed for His people was highly structured, formal, and almost liturgical. It included ritual, dramatic action, and made much use of the nonverbal symbols. Importance was attached to the building and to special hours of worship. Leaders wore robes, and the primary focus of the worship was an objective one. The prophets attacked the insincerity of Israel's worship, but never denounced order and form as such.

Although the synagogue of the inter-testamental period was less liturgical, it was by no means an unstructured worship. Symbols were verbal rather than sensory, and leaders could be laymen rather than a religious hierarchy. But the sense of history was strong in the meeting. A creed was said in unison (the *Shema*), confessions and prayers were recited, psalms were sung, and Scripture readings were prominent. It was still ordered and structured worship, but with some elements of freedom and spontaneity. Any layman could read Scripture and give his word of admonition based upon it. Even the creation narrative of Genesis 1 appears litanized in the earliest manuscript, thus indicating its repeated use as material for ordered worship.[1]

Jesus did not criticize the formalism and structures of temple worship. The Qumran community found fault with the wrong calendar used in the temple and such like issues. But Jesus was not a peevish iconoclast. Jesus warned against elaboration in prayer and against the parading of piety, but never rebuked structured worship as such. He gave instruction about the proper spirit in which to give alms, pray, fast, but never insinuated that an ordered worship would curb the spirit which He advocated. In Christ's most agonized prayers He still quoted portions of synagogue prayer which He had memorized in childhood. Christ taught His disciples a form of prayer and did not rebuke John the Baptist for having done the same.

Early Christian church worship had many elements of order, form, and structure. The many portions of the New Testament which appear rhymed in the Aramaic or early Greek manuscripts indicate that believers recited these portions in worship. Many doxologies appear which, even in modern translations, bear traces of liturgical use.[2] The narrative of the Lord's Supper is in rhythmic prose in the Matthew account, suggesting liturgical use.[3] When the writer of the Book of Revelation pictures worship, he thinks of something ordered, majestic, and with form and holy dignity about it. There was much reading of the apostles' memoirs and letters, since believers had to rely upon worship meetings to refresh their knowledge of their faith. They had no Bibles in their hands.[4]

Malachi warns that God's people are becoming apostate when they grumble against the complex duties of worship.[5] The church after Pentecost felt no need to rebel against formal hours of prayer but continued to observe them.[6] Delling says that they consciously sought to copy heaven's worship rather than either temple or synagogue. They faced toward the New Jerusalem rather than toward the one in Palestine.[7] There were fixed forms of triadic formulas (Father, Son, and Holy Spirit) (faith, hope, and love) and fixed patterns of eulogy. "Worthy is the Lamb" was probably repeated often. "Abba" and "Maranatha" were frequently used, as well as "Amen." "Jesus is Lord" was a shortened form of a creed. Even the spiritual songs which burst forth, such as the "Magnificat" and the song of Zechariah, were reverently conceived and soon became formally repeated. Some scholars go so far as to see the whole Gospel of Mark as a compilation of materials which made up a worship lectionary.[8] Garrett insists that the earliest New Testament churches followed a worship which combined liturgical order with charismatic freedom.[9] When in the carnal Corinthian congregation worship became too free so that confusion threatened, Paul wrote to correct the situation.

A worship service which has order, form, and continuity has distinct advantages for the thoughtful worshiper who is trying to love his God with his mind as well as with his emotions. Minds can join at a deeper level if not caught off guard by unexpected novelty. When all have prayed "Our Father which art in heaven" —then all know the next movement is adoration. Individual worshipers can cry "hallowed be" with more depth of meaning if they can prepare to say and try to mean the words they are about to say.

The welter of individual experiences which worshipers have can be brought together into a sequence and orderly movement toward a climax, if worshipers will humbly try to follow an agreed-upon order together. Each worshiper should not try to force his own private preferences upon his brethren, but all should agree upon a form.[10]

A fixed worship saves the congregation from man-centeredness, and the temptation to regard the minister as a prima donna or a performer. The congregation can rise above the moods and whims of a given worship leader at a given hour.[11] Few preachers can toss off on the impulse of the moment prayers which are as unselfish in content, comprehensive in scope, and so apt in expression as are some of the prayers which have stood the test of years of use. The story goes the rounds of the old lady who said of her new pastor. "He asks God for things which our former pastor didn't even know God had."

It is the passive audiences in supposedly "free" church worship services which actually say and do the least during an hour of worship. Ordered, liturgical worship calls for much more response and active participation.[12] Deadness and unreality overtake the worship services in which everything is "homemade," just as frequently as in the services which follow a prearranged order.

A fixed liturgy can help conserve doctrine. Many perils lie in unpremeditated speech and worship. The path of a congregation's worship life may be strewn with the ideas which their preacher held for a month or so. It is safer if prayers come out of the church of history rather than merely out of the heart of one preacher in a given moment of spontaneous creation. The lofty psalm sentiments can kindle deeper emotions than most prayers which men can create off the cuff.[13]

There is a strong sense of being joined with the church triumphant in worship when the ancient psalms and hymns are used. Familiarity need not breed contempt, if the materials are sublime and grand in their reach and concepts. People do not tire of sunsets or great sonatas, and will not tire of great Scriptures, psalms, and hymns.

However, the church should not borrow and use prayers and other materials from decadent periods of church history and life. This is one of the weaknesses of the Catholic Mass. Error as well as truth can be entrenched in a liturgy. Materials which do not really express the full New Testament faith should not be used, merely to fill up time. Some psalms are hardly suitable for repetition in worship.[14]

Furthermore, although the morning worship may concentrate upon Scripture readings, hymns, exposition of Scripture, and carefully premeditated prayers, the church should hold other worship services in which the Spirit may "blow where it listeth." Spontaneous testimonies and experience-centered songs can contribute to a type of worship service which has great power and appeal to a wide segment of people. In these worship services free prayers can recognize and focus upon the need of the hour. Worshipers should sometimes cry to God "out of the depths" of a pressing anxiety, even as the psalmist did long ago. Fellowship is greatly increased in worship when people seek together for Christ's mind about a problem in Christian obedience, or when they witness to one another about the current work of God's grace in their experience. There is a unique type of blessing which comes through the objective Thou-centered worship service. There is also a unique blessing in the more subjective experience-centered service. The Christian church impoverishes her own life if she is satisfied with only one type and never learns to experience and enjoy the other type. The two types should be kept somewhat distinct, and not be homogenized. The genius of both the Episcopal and the Nazarene worship services are lessened if they are mixed through one another.

The worship leader must embody in his own spirit the best of both the prophetic and the priestly traditions of worship. While he leads the "community of commemoration," recounting again the acts of God as told in the inspired documents, he should help the worshiping congregation to really feel and express hope and expectancy. While he uses the revered forms of the past, he should humbly expect the "livingness" of God to break in also in transforming power. He should be alert for the time when God's Spirit may desire to work so newly and creatively that no old wineskins can quite hold the new wine.

The worship leader should try to lead a rationally consistent service so that worshipers can love the Lord their God with their minds, but he should be open to the mysterious, the transcendent, and the suprarational in faith and worship. He should use the ordinance (the material and dramatic symbols), but should expect God's Spirit to come upon persons rather than upon things. While premeditating his prayers, he should keep open to the right of the Holy Spirit to come upon him or another worshiper in such a way as to drive to utterance.[15] He should use familiar forms and ceremonies but expect God sometimes to collide with the status quo and do a new work.

He should talk much about the God who has come to His people in the past but should stand in quivering expectancy of a visitation of God who is now redeeming His people. He should honor beauty, the aesthetic experience, and the art form as aids to worship, but he should honor Spirit-inspired speech as the first sacrament of worship. He should stress the "family gathering" aspect of worship, as a Father seeks and children respond, but he should always remember the "inconceivable otherness" of God and be crying from the depths of his own soul, "Holy, holy, holy."

1 Claus Westerman, *A Thousand Years and a Day* (London: S.C.M. Press, 1962), p. 6.

2 Dom Gregory Dix, *The Shape of the Liturgy* (London: Dacre Press, 1960), p. 29.

3 H. H. Hislop, *Our Heritage in Public Worship,* (Edinburgh: T. and T. Clark, 1936), p. 67.

4 W. O. E. Desterly, *The Jewish Background of the Christian Liturgy,* (Oxford: Clarendon Press, 1929), p. 121.

5 Mal. 1:6-13.

6 Acts 3:1.

7 D. Herbard Delling, *Worship in The New Testament* (London: Darton, Longman, and Todd, 1962), p. 45.

8 D. H. Delling, *ibid.,* p. 98.

9 T. S. Garrett, *Christian Worship* (London: Oxford University Press, 1961), p. 37.

10 Massey H. Shepherd. *The Worship of the Church* (Greenwich, Conn.: Seabury Press, 1956), p. 49.

11 Collin Dunlap, *Anglican Public Worship* (London: S.C.M. Press, 1943), p. 35.

12 J. O. Dobson, *Christian Worship* (London; S.C.M. Press, 1941), p. 146.

13 Raymond Abba, *Principles of Christian Worship* (New York: Oxford University Press, 1957), p. 61.

14 Collin Dunlap, *op. cit.,* p. 106.

15 Walter Eichrodt, *Old Testament Theology* (Philadelphia: Westminster, 1961), p. 344.

APPENDIX 5

The Lord's Supper as Viewed by Representative Mennonite Writers

Mennonite writers cited specific reasons why believers should observe the Lord's Supper or communion. These were: (1) it has been made the memorial of God's redemption, replacing the Old Testament Passover; (2) it was instituted by Christ; and (3) it was commanded by the apostles. Believers who were enjoying the peace with God which Christ purchased by His death should share in the Lord's Supper as a memorial of that death.[1] Believers whose pure lives already pictured something of the glory of Christ's coming should observe the Lord's Supper "till he come." Believers should let their minds go back in sympathetic sadness to Christ's sufferings, go out to the surrounding opportunities to do His will, and go ahead in fond anticipation of His coming again to receive His own.[2]

The Lord's Supper should symbolize the broken body of Christ and the believer's faith in Christ, the new vows and covenant of discipleship with Christ into which the believer has been called, and the one fellowship of the body of believers who feed together upon the life of Christ.[3]

Mennonite writers refuted vigorously both transubstantiation and consubstantiation as serious errors. One writer argued that since Christ's literal body was in plain sight when He said, "This [bread] is my body," therefore He could only have meant these words and have been understood in a typical sense. Mennonite leaders were not willing to admit that partaking of the Lord's Supper was a means of grace, and no official source even listed it among the aids or basic steps needed to live a successful and victorious Christian life. It was not at all regarded as a "theophany" to make Christ's presence real. Mennonite theologians believed strongly that Christians do partake of two worlds at once, but did not regard the Lord's Supper as a way by which the divine invades the human world.

On the contrary, Mennonite leaders made the Lord's Supper one of the primary occasions for church discipline. There was no assurance that worthy partaking was a means of grace, but there were stern warnings that unworthy eating meant "eating and drinking damnation." Furthermore, the persons to be excluded from the Lord's Supper included not only unbelievers with whom the believer should not have fellowship, but "careless, worldly, or unconcerned individuals who profess membership in the church of Christ . . . those who wanted to regard church membership and partaking of communion as a ticket to heaven" and "those openly polluted with sin."[4]

The reasons given to justify excluding even the sincere and admittedly spiritual Christians of other denominations from the table of the Lord were: "The Bible does cite requirements for continuing as members of a church" (the incestuous member of Corinth was noted); some denominations do not strictly insist upon Biblical standards of life for their members; Mennonites cannot lower their standards to a level of lukewarmness. For these reasons it becomes regrettably necessary for the Mennonite Church to exclude all Christians of all other denominations from her table of the Lord, lest some sinful member whom another denomination allowed into its membership, might commune at the Mennonite observance of the Lord's Supper.

As a preparation for partaking of the table of the Lord, Mennonite writers urged self-examination, but insisted that church discipline would be meaningless if only the individual himself were the judge as to whether he enjoyed full fellowship in the congregation. The congregation must judge and examine its members and "point unworthy ones back." This act would enable the church "to keep the Lord's table in order." This action by the congregation was intended to keep Christian obedience from becoming a matter of private pietistic decision, and to involve the entire brotherhood in church discipline.

Mennonite leaders, by their decision to use the Lord's table as a tool of discipline, set up a kind of second-rate membership in the congregation. Unworthy members were not readily expelled from membership, but they were refused the right to commune. One official source declared that "no one should be excluded from the church who earnestly desires to live the Christian life, no matter how weak and failing he may be"; but another source urged "pointing unworthy ones back from communion." The plight of these second-rate members who lived under church censure, being refused access to the communion table, was never examined. The implicit assumption was that their condition was to be only a temporary one.

The practice of excluding unworthy ones from communion, which has been based upon the necessity of avoiding fellowship with devils, served as a heavy hand of social pressure to induce conformity to church standards. The "demon" with whom the obedient one dared not commune too readily included all Christians (as well as any Mennonites) who did not copy the detailed cultural patterns then prevalent and officially approved. One writer urged that all members should be very much alike, just as the flour from individual grains of wheat was so inseparably mixed together that it was impossible to tell the flour from the several grains apart. However, the alikeness which guaranteed access to the table of the Lord was not just a common sharing in the life of Christ; often it was an identity of cultural forms.[5]

Mennonite writers assumed that exclusion from the table of the Lord was the only method available for a congregation to define its membership and maintain standards of discipline. One leader said, "Only the wide-open churches who admit all classes of people regardless of their faith and practice can consistently advocate open communion." Another asked whether "the church which has a high standard for membership and communion shall lower these standards?"[6]

The possibility that a church might define her membership and exercise discipline over members at some other point than the communion table, and might observe a worship-type communion open to all believers who testified that they had engaged in serious self-examination, was never admitted or discussed by any official source of Mennonite theology. All writers who dealt with the problem moved upon the same unexamined assumption, namely, that to have no close communion meant to have no discipline. Apparently all assumed that Paul's warning against eating with unbelievers could be extended to include almost any cultural application which the church elected to cherish and preserve.

There was no discussion among Mennonite leaders of the effect which a discipline-oriented Lord's Supper might have upon the slumbering guilt of a group of worshipers. Obviously, Mennonite leaders had taken an ordinance (regarded by most of the Christian church as a means of grace) and had shifted its emphasis until it had become primarily a discipline threat by which to maintain constantly changing cultural applications of nonconformity (a guilt-creating rather than a guilt-relieving instrument).

Mennonite writers did not appear to take notice of the many meanings being assigned to the Lord's Supper by other brotherhoods. There was no recognition of the insistence of Fox that the meal should remain a "love feast,"[7] no mention of the emphasis of Brillioth that it should be a Eucharist or thanksgiving,[8] no notice of Dunlap's view that the Supper should be self-sacrifice, an offering of the worshiper to God in Christ's eternal offering of Himself.[9] Luther's doctrine of the real presence in the sacraments was discussed and rejected; but Mennonite writers took no notice of Wedel's idea that the Supper should be an *anamnesis,* a remembering and a dramatization of the event of the crucifixion;[10] or no notice of Dodd's theory that in the Supper believers re-entered history at its crucial moment.[11] Neither the massive arguments of Dix regarding the shape of the liturgy,[12] nor the suggestions of other scholars that the vitalization of the natural order favors a sacramental concept of the Supper, received any attention whatsoever. Mennonite leaders made the Lord's Supper an important and meaningful occasion in the life of the church, but did not enter conversation with other households of faith in deciding what that meaning should be. The Mennonite Church borrowed little from any other household of faith in formulating its own doctrine regarding the Lord's Supper.

However much the Mennonite leaders may have missed some of the fullest and richest meanings of the Lord's Supper, they did discern and insist upon a concern too often ignored by many brotherhoods. Mennonite leaders believed that God will not force any of His means of grace upon the careless or the undisciplined believer. A "Preparatory Service" or "Council Meeting" was held so that each worshiper might examine his own readiness to partake of the Lord's Supper. Each one who desired to commune was required to declare that he "had peace with God, with his fellow man, and with the church."[13] There was a determined intention to take the Lord's Supper seriously.

Furthermore, Mennonite leaders expected the congregation to be a functioning reality in discipline. The members felt their responsibility in preserving the faith and the purity of the church. In many instances the vote of the congregation was required before the leaders could proceed with the Lord's Supper. In other instances, members were invited to admonish their leaders regarding their "housekeeping in the church," or their methods in leading a disciplined congregation.[14] The church was not called into being by the sacrament, turned on like a lightning bug flashes its light, but was a living organism between observances of the Lord's Supper.

1 "Christian Fundamentals," adopted at Garden City, Missouri, printed in *Mennonite Polity* (Scottdale, Mennonite Publishing House, 1944), p. 72.

2 Daniel Kauffman, *Doctrines of the Bible* (Scottdale, Mennonite Publishing House, 1929), p. 397.

3 John C. Wenger, *Introduction to Theology* (Scottdale, Herald Press, 1954), p. 242.

4 John C. Wenger, *Separated unto God*, (Scottdale, Mennonite Publishing House, 1954), p. 213.

5 Daniel Kauffman, *op. cit.*, pp. 396-400.

6 John C. Wenger, *op cit.*, p. 242.

7 Norman Fox, *Christ in the Daily Meal* (New York: Fords, Howard, & Hulburt, 1898), p. 14.

8 Yngve Brillioth, *Eucharistic Faith and Practice* (London: S.C.P.K.), p. 26.

9 Collin Dunlap, *Anglican Public Worship* (London: S.C.M. Press, 1953), p. 99.

10 Remarks by Wedel at the Workshop of Professors of Theology in the Practical Fields, held at Richmond, Virginia, June 12-16, 1960.

11 C. H. Dodd, *The Bible Today* (New York: Macmillan Co., 1947), p. 122.

12 Dom Gregory Dix, *The Shape of the Liturgy* (Glasgow: Dacre Press, 1945), p. 48.

13 Harold S. Bender, "Council Meeting," *Mennonite Encyclopedia, Volume I* (Scottdale: Mennonite Publishing House, 1955), p. 723.

14 Cornelius Krahn, "Communion," *Mennonite Encyclopedia, Volume I* (Scottdale: Mennonite Publishing House, 1955), p. 653.

*The New English Bible, © the Delegates of the Oxford University Press and the Syndics of the Cambridge University Press, 1961.

APPENDIX 6

A Suggested Worship Service for A Christian Wedding

PREPARED BY PAUL M. MILLER

PRELUDE

PROCESSIONAL

Fathers enter when humming begins—O Father All Creating
Bridal party enters
When humming ends:
>"Will the congregation please stand for the call to worship."

CALL TO WORSHIP (octet sings)—Jesus Stand Among Us

INVOCATION PRAYER

"Almighty and everlasting God, before whose face the generations rise and pass away. In Thee we live and move and have our being. Unto Thee all hearts are open, all desires known, and from Thee no secrets are hidden.

"Have mercy upon us, O God, according to Thy loving-kindness, and according to Thy tender mercies blot out our transgressions. Thou hast taught us that in returning and rest we shall be saved, and that in quietness and confidence shall be our strength. Now, by the might of Thy Holy Spirit lift us, we pray Thee, to Thy very presence—where we may be still and know that Thou art God.

"O Thou all-loving God our heavenly Father, in whose heart and mind the plan for a godly marriage was first formed; help us by Thy grace to reach and to realize Thy holy intention in this marriage. O Thou living Christ, who didst grace the wedding in Cana of Galilee by Thy presence, make Thy presence to be real, and personal, and powerful in this wedding service. O Thou Holy Spirit who hast moved with the Father in creating man and woman one in Eden, brood and hover with Thy power and blessing over these dear ones in whose honor we are met today, and make them to become one in holy reality.

"Not of our worthiness, but because of Thy tender mercy, hear our prayer, for the sake of Jesus Christ Thy Son, our Lord. Amen.

"Let us sing together hymn number 14, 'Now Thank We All Our God,' as the octet leads us."

CONGREGATIONAL HYMN

RESPONSIVE READING—I Corinthians 13

CHORAL RESPONSE—Beloved, Let Us Love

MEDITATION

"Love Even as Christ"   Ephesians 5:21-33
Christ's love will bring a deeper mutuality.
Christ's love will bring a new tenderness to headship.
Christ's love will bring exciting wedding anniversaries.
Christ's love will bring a spiritual oneness in your marriage.
(After meditation) . . . "And so, _____ and _____,
we are gathered here in the sight of God to witness and to hear the covenant and vows you wish to make with one another. No other ties are more tender, no other vows more sacred than those you now assume. We counsel you to enter this covenant in the fear of God.

MARRIAGE COVENANT

To Groom: "_____, do you take _____ to be your lawful wedded wife? And do you solemnly promise, before God and these witnesses, that you will love, honor, and cherish her; and that forsaking all others, you will keep yourself for her alone, until God, by death, shall separate you?"

(Groom—"I do.")

To Bride: "_____, do you take _____ to be your lawful wedded husband? And do you solemnly promise, before God and these witnesses, that you will love, honor, and cherish him; and that forsaking all others, you will keep yourself for him alone, until God, by death, shall separate you?"

(Bride—"I do.")

To Both: "Since it is your desire to take each other as husband and wife, please indicate this desire by joining your right hands, and by repeating to each other in this presence your marriage vow."

_____ to _____: "I take you, _____, to be my wedded wife; and I promise before God and these witnesses to be your loving and faithful husband, in plenty and in

227

want, in joy and in sorrow, in sickness and in health, as long as we both shall live, according to God's holy ordinance."

_____ to _____: "I take you, _____, to be my wedded husband; and I promise before God and these witnesses to be your loving and faithful wife, in plenty and in want, in joy and in sorrow, in sickness and in health, as long as we both shall live, according to God's holy ordinance."

To Couple: "Inasmuch then as you, _____, and you, _____, have consented together in holy wedlock and have declared the same before God and these witnesses, I now by the authority vested in me as a minister of the church of Jesus Christ do pronounce and declare you to be husband and wife by the ordinance of God—in the name of the Father, and of the Son, and of the Holy Ghost, and what God hath joined together, let not man put asunder." (Pause. . . .)

To Congregation: "Let us pray, as the couple kneels."

PRAYERS:

"Almighty and merciful God, Thou hast first taught us the meaning of covenant by inviting us into a covenant of love with Thyself. Hear the covenant which these two followers of Thine now are making with one another before Thy face. Grant to them Thy grace and Thy strength to ever fulfill this covenant of love which they this day are making and sealing with one another. Grant that the home they found and in which this covenant of love is to be translated into relationships may be truly Christian in every thought and word and deed. May the commonest relationship of their daily walk together be lived under Thy lordship. Enable them by Thy Spirit's power to always live Thy limitless love with one another. Perfect Thy strength through their weakness, glorify Thy grace in the victory they experience in their daily lives, and may they dwell together in Thy peace. Through Jesus Christ our Lord. . . ." (Octet sings Choral Response.)

CHORAL RESPONSE—O Lord, We Pray Thee

(Couple stands up again.)

To Congregation: "Let us sing together hymn number 594, 'O Perfect Love,' as the octet leads us."

CONGREGATIONAL HYMN—O Perfect Love
Church Hymnal No. 594

VOW OF DEDICATION:

"As you now recall your personal commitment to Christ and your consecration to Him and His service, do you now renew your pledge, and endeavor by the grace of God to establish a home in which Christ shall be the Head, in which His love shall be practiced, His Word shall be read, and His church shall be honored and upheld? If you are willing to assume this responsibility, then answer with one heart and one mind, we do."

(Couple responds—"We do.")

SCRIPTURE:

"Let us hear then the admonition from the Word of God for the lives of His people."

(Read Romans 12.)

"Therefore, my brothers, I implore you by God's mercy to offer your very selves to him; a living sacrifice, dedicated and fit for his acceptance, the worship offered by mind and heart. Adapt yourselves no longer to the pattern of this present world, but let your minds be remade and your whole nature thus transformed. Then you will be able to discern the will of God, and to know what is good, acceptable, and perfect.

"In virtue of the gift that God in his grace has given me I say to everyone among you: do not be conceited or think too highly of yourself; but think your way to a sober estimate based on the measure of faith that God has dealt to each of you. For just as in a single human body there are many limbs and organs, all with different functions, so all of us, united with Christ, form one body, serving individually as limbs and organs to one another.

"The gifts we possess differ as they are allotted to us by God's grace, and must be exercised accordingly: the gift of inspired utterance, for example, in proportion to a man's faith; or the gift of administration, in administration. A teacher should employ his gift in teaching, and one who has the gift of stirring speech should use it to stir his hearers. If you give to charity, give with all your heart; if you are a leader, exert yourself to lead; if you are helping others in distress, do it cheerfully.

"Love in all sincerity, loathing evil and clinging to the good.

Let love for our brotherhood breed warmth of mutual affection. Give pride of place to one another in esteem.

"With unflagging energy, in ardour of spirit, serve the Lord. Let hope keep you joyful; in trouble stand firm; persist in prayer. Contribute to the needs of God's people, and practise hospitality. Call down blessings on your persecutors—blessings, not curses. With the joyful, be joyful, and mourn with the mourners. Have equal regard for one another. Do not be haughty, but go about with humble folk. Do not keep thinking how wise you are.

"Never pay back evil for evil. Let your aims be such as all men count honorable. If possible, so far as it lies with you, live at peace with all men. My dear friends, do not seek revenge, but leave a place for divine retribution; for there is a text which reads, 'Justice is mine, says the Lord, I will repay.' But there is another text: 'If your enemy is hungry, feed him; if he is thirsty, give him a drink; by doing this you will heap live coals on his head.' Do not let evil conquer you, but use good to defeat evil."*

LORD'S PRAYER: "Let us stand and pray in unison the prayer our Lord taught us."

(Pray.)

CHORAL BENEDICTION (octet)—The Lord Bless Thee "Will the congregation please be seated."

RECESSIONAL: O Father, Lead Us.

APPENDIX 7

Dedication for Parents of Children

(Also a service of dedication for the pastor and congregation, as the family of God, who assist the parents in their sacred task)

PREPARED BY PAUL M. MILLER

1. Do you recognize that this ceremony does *not* save the soul of your child, but that your child is safe while yet in innocence because of the universal atonement wrought by Jesus Christ?

2. Do you humbly accept this immortal soul as a *gift from the hands of the creating God,* recognizing that the deathless life

230

and divine image your child possesses have been given by an act of the sovereign God?

3. Do you here solemnly promise, before God and these witnesses, that you will *dedicate your life* to the sacred task of bringing up this child in the nurture and admonition of the Lord to the end that he (or she) will freely accept Christ as Saviour and Lord upon reaching the age of accountability?

4. Do you promise to surrender and *gladly to help send* this child anywhere on the earth, when God *calls your child* in Christian service? (The congregation, as the family of God, is invited to declare their readiness to share in the above vows, by rising to their feet for the prayer of dedication.)

Bibliography

CHAPTER I

Bender, Harold S. *These Are My People*. Scottdale, Pa., Herald Press, 1960.

Charles, Howard H. *The Charismatic Life in the Apostolic Church*. Unpublished thesis.

Charles, Howard H. "The New Testament Pattern of Church Organization," *Church Organization and Administration*. Study conference, March 25-27, 1955.

Clifford, Paul, *The Pastoral Calling*. New York, Channel Press, 1961.

Daube, David. *The New Testament and Rabbinic Judaism*. London, Athlone Press, 1956.

Fast, Victor. "A Study of Ordination." Unpublished mss. (in files of author).

Goerner, Henry C. *Thus It Is Written*. Nashville, Broadman Press, 1944.

Henry, Carl F. H. "The Minister in the Mirror," *Christianity Today*. April, 1960.

Hiltner, Seward. *The Christian Shepherd*. New York, Abingdon Press, 1959.

Homrighausen, Elmer G. *Let the Church Be the Church*. New York, Abingdon-Cokesbury, 1940.

Hoppin, James M. *The Office and Work of the Christian Ministry*. New York, Sheldon and Co., 1949.

Howe, Reuel. *Man's Need and God's Action*. Greenwich, Conn., Seabury Press, 1953.

Hudson, Winthrop. *Conference on Motivation for the Ministry*. Louisville, Southern Baptist Theological Seminary, 1959.

Jones, Illion T. *The Pastor, the Man and His Ministry*. Philadelphia, Westminster, 1961.

Kauffman, Daniel. *Doctrines of the Bible*. Scottdale, Pa., Mennonite Publishing House, 1929.

Kemp, Charles F. *Physicians of the Soul*. New York, Macmillan Co., 1947.

Kirk, K. E., Ed. *The Apostolic Ministry*. London, Hodder and Stoughton, 1946.

Kling, Frederick R. *Motivation for Entering the Ministry*. Educational Testing Service, Princeton, New Jersey, report of February, 1959.

Kramer, Hendrick. *A Theology of the Laity*. Philadelphia, Westminster, 1958.

Lauterbock. "Ordination," *The Jewish Encyclopedia*. New York, Funk and Wagnalls. Edited by Esadore Singer, Vol. IX, 1912.

Lightfoot, J. B. *The Christian Ministry*. New York, Thos. Whittaker, *n.d.*

Manson, T. W. *Ministry and Priesthood, Christ's and Ours*. Richmond, Va., John Knox, 1957.

McGuire, John P. *The Mass Presented to Non-Catholics*. Milwaukee, Bruce Publishing Co., 1958.

McNeill, John T. *A History of the Cure of Souls*. New York, Harpers, 1951.

Miller, Donald. *Fire in Thy Mouth*. New York, Abingdon, 1954.

Miller, Haskell. *Compassion and Community*. New York, Association Press, 1961.

Miller, Paul M. *How God Heals*. Scottdale, Pa., Herald Press, 1960.

Minier, Paul S. *Horizons of Christian Community*. Missouri, Bethany Press, 1959.

Minier, Paul S. *The Images of the Church in the New Testament*. Philadelphia, Westminster, 1960.

Newbigin, Lesslie. *The Household of God*. New York, Friendship Press, 1960.

Niles, D. T. *The Preacher's Calling to Be Servant*. London, Lutterworth Press, 1959.

Oates, Wayne E. *Protestant Pastoral Counseling*. Philadelphia, Westminster, 1962.

Olofsson, L. E. *The Conception of the Inner Light in Robert Barclay's Theology*. CWK Gleerup, Lund, 1954.

Peacock, Heber F. "Ordination in the New Testament," *Review and Expositor* Vol. XV, No. 3, July, 1958. Louisville, Southern Baptist Theological Seminary.

Pearson, Ray, *The Ministry of Preaching.* New York, Harpers, 1959.

Rowley, H. H. *The Biblical Doctrine of Election.* Lutterworth Press, 1950.

Segler, Franklin M. *A Theology of Church and Ministry*, Broadman Press, 1960.

Smart, James. *The Rebirth of Ministry.* Philadelphia, Westminster, 1960.

Thurneysen, E. *A Theology of Pastoral Care*, Richmond, John Knox Press, 1962.

Trueblood, Elton. *The Paradox of the Quaker Ministry.* The 1960 Quaker Lecture of Indiana Yearly Meeting, *n.p., n.d.*

Webber, George W. *God's Colony in Man's World.* New York, Abingdon, 1960.

Williams, Daniel D. *Ministry in Historical Perspectives.* Harper and Brothers, New York, 1956.

Wright, George Ernest. *The God Who Acts.* Chicago, Allenson, 1952.

CHAPTER II

Cairns, David. *A Gospel Without Myth.* London, S.C.M. Press, 1960.

Garrison, Webb B. *The Preacher and His Audience.* New York, Revell, 1954.

Glen, J. Stanley. *Recovery of the Teaching Ministry.* Philadelphia, Westminster, 1960.

Grant, Frederick C. in Howard A. Johnson. *Preaching the Christian Year.* New York, Scribner's Sons, 1957.

Jackson, Edgar N. *A Psychology for Preaching.* Channel Press, New York, 1961.

Jones, I. T. *Principles and Practice of Preaching.* New York, Abingdon Press, 1956.

Knox, John. *The Integrity of Preaching.* New York, Abingdon Press, 1957.

Moreau, J. D. *Language and Religious Language.* Philadelphia, Westminster Press, 1961.

Mounce, Robert H. *The Essential Nature of New Testament Preaching.* Grand Rapids, Eerdmans, 1960.

Olofsson, L. E. *The Conception of the Inner Light in Robert Barclay's Theology.* CWK Gleerup, Lund, 1954.

Patton, Carl S. *The Use of the Bible in Preaching.* New York, Harpers, 1936.

Smart, James. *The Interpretation of Scripture.* Philadelphia, Westminster Press, 1961.

Tillich (Paul) in Hans Hoffman. *Making the Ministry Relevant.* New York, Scribner's Sons, 1960.

Weatherspoon, J. B. *Sent Forth to Preach.* New York, Harpers, 1954.

CHAPTER III

Bonhoeffer, Dietrich. *Life Together.* London, S.C.M. Press, 1956.

Hiltner, Seward and L. G. Colston. *The Context of Pastoral Counseling.* New York, Abingdon Press, 1961.

Hulme, William. *Counseling and Theology.* Philadelphia, Muhlenberg Press, 1956.

Jackson, Edgar N. *A Psychology for Preaching.* Great Neck, Channel Press, 1961.

Kean, Charles D. *Christian Faith and Pastoral Care.* Greenwich, Conn., Seabury Press, 1961.

Menninger, Karl. *Theory of Psychoanalytic Technique.* New York, Basic Books, Inc., 1958.

Mowrer, O. Hobart. *The Crisis in Psychiatry and Religion.* New York, D. Van Nostrand Company, 1961.

Narramore, Clyde. *The Psychology of Counseling.* Grand Rapids, Zondervan.

Oates, Wayne E. *Protestant Pastoral Counseling.* Philadelphia, Westminster, 1962.

Oates, Wayne E. *Where to Go for Help.* Philadelphia, Westminster, 1957.

Price, John M. *An Introduction to Pastoral Counseling.* Wayne E. Oates, Editor, Nashville, Broadman Press, 1959.

Thurian, Max. *Confession.* London, S.C.M. Press, Ltd., 1958.

Thurneysen, Edward. *A Theology of Pastoral Care.* Richmond, John Knox Press, 1962.

Tournier, Paul. *Guilt and Grace.* New York, Harpers, 1962.

Ungersma, A. J. *The Search for Meaning.* Philadelphia, Westminster Press, 1961.

Williams, Daniel Day. *The Minister and the Cure of Souls.* New York, Harpers, 1961.

CHAPTER IV

Abba, Raymond. *Principles of Christian Worship.* New York, Oxford University Press, 1957.

Benson, Lewis. *Prophetic Quakerism.* Philadelphia, Friends Book Store, 1944.

Benson, Louis F. *The Hymnody of the Christian Church.* New York, George H. Doran Company, 1927.

Blackwood, Andrew. *The Fine Art of Public Worship.* New York, Abingdon-Cokesbury, 1939.

Brenner, S. F. *The Art of Worship.* New York, Macmillan Company, 1961.

Coffin, H. S. *The Public Worship of God.* Philadelphia, Westminster Press, 1946.

Cox, James W. *The Doctrines of the Word of God in the Old Testament.* Unpublished doctoral dissertation, Southern Baptist Theological Seminary.

Cullmann, Oscar. *Early Christian Worship.* London, S.C.M. Press, 1953.

Delling, Gerhard. *Worship in the New Testament.* London, D. T. Todd, 1962.

DeVaux, Roland. *Ancient Israel.* London, Darton, Longman, & Todd, 1961.

Dix, Dom Gregory. *The Shape of the Liturgy.* Philadelphia, Westminster, Dacre Press, 1954.

Dobson, J. A. *Worship.* London, Student Christian Movement Press, 1941.

Eichrodt, Walter. *Theology of the Old Testament.* Philadelphia, Westminster Press, 1961.

Garrett, T. S. *Christian Worship.* London, Oxford University Press, 1961.

Heimsath, C. N. *The Genius of Public Worship.* New York, Scribner's Sons, 1947.

Knox, John. *The Integrity of Preaching.* New York, Abingdon Press, 1957.

McDonald, A. B. *Christian Worship in the Primitive Church.* Edinburgh, T. & T. Clark, 1934.

McLeod, Donald. *Preaching and Worship.* New Jersey, Prentice-Hall, 1960.

McLeod, Donald. *Word and Sacrament.* New Jersey, Prentice-Hall, 1960.

McNutt, William R. *Worship in the Churches.* Philadelphia, Judson Press, 1941.

Micklem, D. R. *Our Approach to God.* London, Hodder and Stoughton Press, 1961.

Mounce, Robert. *New Testament Preaching.* Grand Rapids, 1960.

Mowinckel, Sigmund. *The Old Testament as Word of God.* New York, Abingdon Press, 1959.

Palmer, Albert. *The Art of Conducting Public Worship.* New York, Macmillan Company, 1939.

Powell, M. S. *Guiding the Experience of Worship.* New York, Methodist Book Concern, 1935.

Thurian, Max. *Confession.* London, S.C.M. Press, 1958.

Thurneysen, Edward. *A Theology of Pastoral Care.* Richmond, John Knox Press, 1962.

Williamson, Robert L. *Effective Public Prayer.* Nashville, Broadman Press, 1960.

Wingren, Gustaf. *The Living Word.* Philadelphia, Muhlenberg Press, 1958.

CHAPTER V

Fallaw, Wesner. *Church Education for Tomorrow.* Philadelphia, Westminster Press, 1960.

Feifel, Herman. *The Meaning of Death.* New York, McGraw-Hill Book Company, 1959.

Hershberger, Guy. *The Way of the Cross in Human Relations.* Scottdale, Pa., Herald Press, 1958.

Jones, I. T. *The Pastor, the Man and His Ministry.* Philadelphia, Westminster Press, 1961.

Krabill, Russell. *Beginning the Christian Life.* Scottdale, Pa., Mennonite Publishing House, 1958.

McCabe, Joseph. *The Power of God in a Parish Program.* Philadelphia, Westminster Press, 1959.

Peterson, James A. *Toward a Successful Marriage.* New York, Scribner's Sons, 1960.

Rinehart, Bruce. *The Institutional Nature of Adult Christian Education.* Philadelphia, Westminster Press, 1962.

Southard, Samuel. *Pastoral Evangelism.* Nashville, Broadman Press, 1962.